1959

WILLIAM COWPER

HUMANITARIAN

*The University of North Carolina Press, Chapel Hill, N. C.;
The Baker and Taylor Company, New York; Oxford University
Press, London; Maruzen-Kabushiki-Kaisha, Tokyo; Edward
Evans & Sons, Ltd., Shanghai; D. B. Centen's Wetenschap-
pelijke Boekhandel, Amsterdam.*

WILLIAM COWPER

HUMANITARIAN

By

LODWICK C. HARTLEY

In Faith and Hope the world will disagree,
But all mankind's concern is Charity:
All must be false that thwart this one great end,
And all of God that bless mankind or mend.
Pope, *Essay on Man*

Chapel Hill

THE UNIVERSITY OF NORTH CAROLINA PRESS

1938

TO THE MEMORY OF

MY FATHER

PREFACE

WILLIAM COWPER has not been a neglected poet. In recent years Mr. Hugh Fausset, Lord David Cecil, and Mr. Gilbert Thomas have written competently, and even brilliantly, about him. However, their studies of Cowper's life and literary genius have tended to emphasize the poet's isolation. To a considerable degree their books have reflected the perennial controversy over the relation of the poet's religion to his insanity. Unfortunately, this very real enigma remains unsolved. Certain aspects of Cowper's verse have received very satisfactory treatment. Much has been said about his nature poetry—his observing eye and its influence on the new school of literature developing at the end of the eighteenth century. Critics as widely separated as Marian Harland (whom one associates with cook books) and the great Charles Augustin Sainte-Beuve have written about his *poésie domestique.* One would attempt to say nothing new in this field.

Much, then, has been said of Cowper as a recluse of Olney and little of him as a citizen of the world. Obviously, he was not admired by Charles James Fox, Thomas Clarkson, and William Wilberforce because he had attacks of insanity, kept pet hares, and wrote charmingly of drinking tea. Nor for any of these reasons did the *Critical Review* praise his "originality of thought, strength of argument, and poignance of satire." One should not forget that his poetry bore the imprint of Joseph Johnson, that courageous publisher of such "radicals" as Priestley, Tooke, Holcroft, and Mary Wollstonecraft.

This study attempts to demonstrate the vitality of Cowper's thought by presenting his poetry against the rich and dramatic background of eighteenth-century humanitarian activity. Because it questions Mr. Fausset's statement that "Cowper's life offers more of an adventure of understanding than his poetry," it seeks to minimize the importance of the sad biographical facts to an appreciation of the poet's thought. As far as possible, it allows Cowper to speak for himself, in the way in which he probably spoke to his contemporaries, on a wide variety of humanitarian subjects ranging from the abolition of slavery to the humane treatment of animals. In short, it presents the most popular English poet between 1780 and 1800 as a spokesman of a movement that made great contributions to modern civilization.

Bibliographical notes cannot acknowledge with complete adequacy my debt to a large mass of antecedent scholarship. Sir Leslie Stephen and the Reverend Stopford Brooke were very valuable trail blazers. More recent scholars have contributed to the social, historical, and literary background. My indebtedness to individuals has also been great. The stimulation and guidance of Dean R. K. Root have been invaluable. I can best acknowledge simply what I can in no wise repay. Dr. Louise Lanham, a highly competent student of Cowper and of the Evangelical Movement, has made important suggestions at various stages of the work. Professor Richmond P. Bond and Dr. N. C. Hannay have kindly given bibliographical assistance. My colleagues, Professor Roger P. Marshall and Mr. Frank H. Lyell, have given generously of their time and counsel. Not the least of my indebtedness is to the staff of the Princeton University library and to the staffs of the libraries at the Chapel Hill and Raleigh units of the University of North Carolina. For the shortcomings of the book I alone assume responsibility.

LODWICK C. HARTLEY

Raleigh, North Carolina
March 1, 1938

CONTENTS

[ix]

WILLIAM COWPER

HUMANITARIAN

Chapter I

THE SOCIAL PASSIONS WORK

Thought fond man
Of these, and all the thousand nameless ills
That one incessant struggle render life,
One scene of toil, of suffering, and of fate,
Vice in his high career would stand appalled,
And heedless rambling impulse learn to think;
The conscious heart of charity would warm,
And her wide wish benevolence dilate;
The social tear would rise, the social sigh;
And into clear perfection, gradual bliss,
Refining still, the social passions work.
—Thomson, *Winter*

§ 1

THE EIGHTEENTH century was one of great change—not sudden and cataclysmic, but slow and steady, and so sweeping as to make the entire fabric of life and thought at the end of the century of a remarkably different pattern from that of the first. The change is clearly reflected in literature. There is an easily apparent revolution, if you please, between Pope's *Essay on Man* and Burns's "Is There for Honest Poverty"— the one an analysis of universal man in brilliant couplets, the other an assertion of the dignity of the common man in passionately rugged verse. To say that the Age of Reason had given way to the Age of Feeling is to rely upon dangerous labels. No one could be made to believe that people in the early part of the century were not capable of feeling very deeply. In fact, it seems a good deal safer to look upon the

[1]

early eighteenth century as "the cradle of sensibility" rather than an age of rigid classicism. But the early part of the century *was* a period in which most people who set down their thoughts kept them more definitely under the control of the intellect than people did later in the century. What brought about the change might be made the subject of extended analysis. The Industrial Revolution and the steady rise of the middle class as dictators of taste and manners were important factors. All over Europe the individual was beginning to emerge as superior to exterior labels. The phenomenon seemed a part of the natural and inevitable law of change. In France it brought about a bourgeois revolution, full of bloodshed and violence. In England it brought about the social and political changes that led to the Reform Bill of 1832 and that, much earlier, gave a new note to literature.

Except perhaps in the instance of the slave trade, cruelty to men and animals was not a great deal more flagrant in Cowper's day than it was in Pope's. Nor is it true, of course, that men in Pope's day were callous to inhumanity. Yet it seems that at the end of the century there came a relatively sudden and notably widespread consciousness of conditions that men had not noticed before. It is not until the last quarter of the century that the really great humanitarians begin to emerge. The efforts of Oglethorpe, Berkeley, and Hanway—important though they were—are hardly comparable with those of John Howard and William Wilberforce. Nor can the scattered philanthropic projects of the opening of the century be compared with the concerted action that makes the end of the century one of the most significant periods in humanitarian history. Though neither Thomson nor Pope went untouched, as poets as well as men, by the humanitarian activities of their own day, their response to these activities is in no way comparable to that of William Cowper, who in the last quarter of the century became the laureate and seer of the great humanitarian movement.

Although in the eighteenth century the word *humane* was used in its present sense, *humanitarian* was used entirely in its theological sense; that is, in relation to the doctrine that Christ was man and not god, and that the human race is capable of perfection without superhuman aid. In the following century the word acquired both ethical and social connotations. In its ethical sense it is most generally taken to mean "the deliberate and systematic study of humane principles, the attempt to show that humaneness is an integral part, if not the actual basis of morals."[1] So defined it applies directly to a great body of ethical thought in the eighteenth century. In its social sense the term has frequently been used as one of opprobrium or contempt, the relation being to fanatical zeal for reform, or oversensitivity to human or animal suffering. It is also frequently used broadly to refer to the whole process of the struggle for freedom of the individual. Consequently, there is a wide application of the term to things as remotely separated as antivivisectionism and socialism.

There is, of course, no fundamental difference between humaneness and humanitarianism. As Sir Henry Salt observes, humanitarianism is "nothing more than conscious and organized humaneness."[2] Professor Crane Brinton further clarifies the problem:

A humanitarian seeks to lessen suffering and increase enjoyment among all forms of sentient life. . . . Humanitarian movements have been chiefly directed toward preventing recognizable physical cruelty to men or animals or both. Where humanitarian efforts seek a positive addition to the happiness of sentient beings, it is to make the unhappy happy rather than the happy happier.[3]

Since the humanitarian impulses of the century are constantly regarded as a phase of its *sentimentalism,* some dis-

tinction between sentimentalism and humanitarianism is
pertinent. Sentimentalism is most often used to refer to
emotional license particularly in the direction of luxuriating
in grief. We find "Estimate" Brown writing in 1758:

Effeminacy begets Cowardice, and a Dread of enduring and
suffering of every Kind. Minds thus constituted are easily moved
by apparent Sufferings of others: Hence where the opposite Passions prevail not, Pity is generally strong in Women: and hence
Pity, or Humanity, is the natural Growth of an effeminate Nation: That is, of a Nation which resembles woman.[4]

To apply sentimentalism of this sort to much of the practical
humanitarian effort of the century is manifestly to be unfair.
This Brown himself seems to realize, for he continues by
saying that "so far as Humanity, ariseth from Courage tempered by pure Religion, it will be regular, extensive, and
consistent." But sentimentalism may also be used to mean
"the sympathy of the good Samaritan for the sick and
wounded in the struggle."[5] In this sense, its application to
the humanitarian efforts of the century is manifestly appropriate.

We can hardly consider as humanitarian the sentimental
effusions in which the novelists of the mid-century and later
indulged. Supercilious Mr. Horace Walpole probably did
violence to the actual facts when he sneered that Sterne
wept over a dead ass and let his mother die in jail, but the
statement is delightfully illustrative of the distance between
the sentimentalists and the real current of humanitarian
effort in the century. Sterne, Richardson, Goldsmith, and
their followers might here and there reflect the injustice and
corruption of their age with a deprecating touch, but they
are not reformers or revolutionists. They rarely, if ever, get
beyond "the social tear" or "the social sigh." Unlike Rousseau, as Sir Leslie Stephen has observed, they did not in-

dulge their emotions with the conscious aim of bringing about social change.

In this study, therefore, *humanitarianism* will essentially have reference to humaneness intelligently directed and focussed. As far as possible, it will refer to the practical efforts of the age to alleviate suffering or to promote happiness among sentient beings. Nevertheless, it may be necessary at times to employ the word in its limited ethical sense, and even in its broad social connotation. In spite of this fact, there seems to be no need for real confusion.

§ 2

In eighteenth-century ethical thought the subject of benevolence was an extremely vital one, for on it almost the whole moral problem was made to turn. The widespread philosophical discussion of the subject in England is largely traceable to a reaction to the philosophy of Hobbes, who in the *Leviathan* contended that all man's natural tendencies are self-regarding and that the *jus naturale* is "the liberty each man hath to use his own power as he will himself for the preservation of his own nature."

To such an unflattering picture of human nature as Hobbes gave, one of the foremost to make reply was the third Lord Shaftesbury, whose *Characteristics of Men, Manners, Opinions, Times, etc.* (1711) was destined to be one of the most popular philosophical works of the century. Shaftesbury's philosophical system is as optimistic as Hobbes's is pessimistic, and conceives of man as nobly as Hobbes's conceives ignobly. In a marvelous universe of fixed laws and profound harmonies such as Newton had revealed, man, far from being a depraved creature, is essentially virtuous and possesses a "moral sense" capable of determining his action if he will only be natural—that is, follow his instinct.[6] Shaftesbury makes a threefold division of human passions: the natural affections, leading to public good; the "self-affections," leading to the good of self; and the injurious or "unnatural affections." Virtue consists of eliminating the last and achieving a proper balance or harmony between the first two. In the *Inquiry concerning Virtue and Merit* Shaftesbury observes further that Hobbes's conception of the natural man would be true only if one considered man as an isolated individual. But man must be considered in relation to a larger system of which he is a part, and he is "good" only when his actions tend toward the good of the whole. Shaftesbury, therefore, places much emphasis on the social affections, although he can admit that they may be injurious when excessive.

In contrast to the evaluation of virtue by the Church on a system of rewards and punishments, Shaftesbury insists that virtue is its own reward, to be sought for its intrinsic beauty and the satisfaction it can produce. Taken out of the profit and loss column, virtue is transferred to the field of aesthetics in the "virtuoso" identification of the Good and Beautiful. Naturally, Shaftesbury exalts the beauties of benevolence.

The ramifications of the philosophy of benevolence after Shaftesbury are many. In his *Inquiry into the Original of our Ideas of Beauty and Virtue,* Francis Hutcheson, the Scotch philosopher and economist who began as a disciple of Shaftesbury, makes a further vindication of the reality of benevolence, resolving all virtue into it. Bishop Butler, with no respect for the deism of Shaftesbury, argues for the disinterested character of benevolence and regards it as the "sum of virtue." Moralists like Clarke and his school, concerned with working out a system of morality in which intellect would have ascendency over feeling, succeeded in reducing the Golden Rule to a mathematical equation.[7] Mention should also be made of Hartley's theory of "association" and the "disinterested charity" at which the philosopher arrived through his theory, the "sympathetic" benevolence of Adam Smith, and Hume's demonstration of the reality of the altruistic sentiments. Utilitarianism concluded that the pleasures of benevolence were high and lasting.

Not all philosophers, of course, were on the side of Shaftesbury's optimism. Mandeville's coarse *The Fable of the Bees* (1723)—in which the author, like Hobbes, resolved all benevolence into selfishness—is an attack on Shaftesbury's position. Although Bolingbroke considered benevolence to be the supreme law of nature and the one possibility of happiness, he could not accept Shaftesbury's idea that benevolence is instinctive. He scorned the "inward light" that made natural religion as ridiculous as revealed.[8] Instead of assigning to man two sets of affections, Bolingbroke gives him only self-love, insisting that virtue and benevolence are to be attained through reason.

Thus philanthropy is kept within the rationalistic system of philosophers and divines "either by making a recognition of the duty of benevolence . . . part of the intellectual equipment implanted in men's minds by God, or by assuming . . . that reason would naturally lead men to benevolence as one of the primary laws of nature."[9]

It is undoubtedly erroneous to give Shaftesbury the entire credit for displacing the established attitude of the Church toward philanthropy with a disinterested benevolence extending through the whole range of sentient beings, or to attribute entirely to him the credit for the belief in natural goodness. Much of what seemed to be Shaftesbury's influence in the century has in recent years been shown to be directly traceable to Newton and the school of divines who popularized the metaphysical implications of Newton's work. It may be shown that what Shaftesbury said about the "natural" sociability of man, the pleasures of doing good, and the harmony of self-love and benevolence did not represent a new departure in ethics, but was very firmly rooted in what divines and philosophers had been saying from the pulpit and in print in the last part of the seventeenth century. Nevertheless, the *Characteristics* was a convenient and attractive repository of these ideas, and its influence and popularity were large.

James Thomson is one of the first poets to embody the popular ethical ideals of the age in his verse. Moreover, he is the first poet of the century to reflect extensively the practical philanthropic efforts of the age. He expresses interest in the founding of Georgia, in prison reforms, in the establishment of the Foundling Hospital, in the improvement of education, and in the purging of fraudulent and oppressive justice. He depicts luridly the horrors of the slave trade, and he can visualize vaguely a sort of Utopia, "a beauteous order," where the "social labourer" can lift his "unguarded head," and where men shall not "yield to government in vain." But his passion for social reform is not very deep. He makes no attempt to probe the social sores, and he has no indictment to make of society. His critics have not failed to see that he leans toward the philornithic rather than the philanthropic, especially in *The Seasons*. Nevertheless, his pioneering is of importance.

The *Essay on Man* and the *Epistles* give Pope an important place among the benevolists. Since he seems to draw from both Bolingbroke and Shaftesbury (although the influence of the latter is unacknowledged), there are inconsistencies in his theory of benevolence.[10] However, he follows the fashion, already popular, of insisting that benevolence is man's greatest virtue, as his greatest bliss is the hope of a happy eternity:

At once his own bright prospect to be blest,
And strongest motive to assist the rest.
[*Essay on Man,* IV, ll. 351-52.]

Henry Needler, Mark Akenside, John Gilbert Cooper, James Harris, Henry Brooke, David Mallet, and Soame Jenyns were among the lesser poets who expressed the idea that cruelty and suffering are out of place in a universe so neatly ordered as that of Newton. Among the orthodox was such a benevolist as Edward Young, part of the purpose of whose *Night Thoughts* is to argue that benevolence has always prevailed among true believers. However, although *benevolence* and *charity* became firmly rooted in poetic diction, the practical aspects of philanthropy were somewhat beneath the notice of most of the benevolists, who were chiefly concerned with harmonizing the soul "to a responsive regularity and sympathetic order" (as Cooper puts it in the "Design" prefixed to *The Power of Harmony*) with the perfect and beautiful in nature.

§ 3

Not all the benevolence of the early eighteenth century was in philosophical disquisitions or in poetry. In fact, the close of the seventeenth and the beginning of the eighteenth century mark the beginning of a new departure in charities —the formation of "societies" for carrying on religious and philanthropic work—and an awakening of general interest in practical benevolence is easily apparent. One of the first portents of the great humanitarian destiny of the century was the foundation of such organizations as the Society for Propagation of Christian Knowledge (1698) and the Society for Propagation of the Gospel in Foreign Parts (1701). Other evidences of religious and humanitarian activity include the first scheme on an extensive scale to provide education for the poor in charity schools and an effort to relieve the poverty of ministers.

Defoe wrote in 1725:

The innumerable Alms-Houses, which are to be seen in almost every Part of London, make it certain that there is no City in the World can show the like Number of Charities from private Hands, there being not less than 20,000 People maintained of Charity, besides the Collections at the annual Feasts of several Kinds.[11]

The report is undoubtedly somewhat overcomplacent, but charities from private hands *were* increasing. The century's commercial and industrial expansion was developing merchant and banker princes, the new bourgeoisie, who with the gradual assurance of their social and political position opened their purses to the less fortunate. Of these Henry Hoare and the Quaker David Barclay[12] were well known as philanthropists. It will also be remembered that such a public benefactor as Jonas Hanway was a merchant. Even the South Sea speculation had its effect on philanthropy. In 1724 Thomas Guy, who bought and sold South Sea stock at the right time, founded Guy's Hospital.[13]

After the first two decades of the century movements to aid the sick and helpless steadily gained impetus. Between 1719 and 1746 Westminster, St. George's, London, and Middlesex hospitals were all founded by public subscription. In 1739 the first foundling hospital was established through the exertions of Captain Coram. Three maternity hospitals were founded between 1749 and 1752, and St. Luke's for lunatics was founded in 1751. There were also asylums for young delinquents and for deserted girls, as well as a society founded by Jonas Hanway for collecting street waifs and training them as sailors. In 1772 a society was formed to aid people in prison for small debts; and The Royal Humane Society, founded in 1775 for resuscitating the drowned, received wide support. Moreover, there were large collections for the aid of victims of catastrophes in foreign lands. In compliment to the quickness of philanthropic response, Dr. Johnson wrote in *Idler* No. 4 for May 6, 1758: "No sooner is a new species of misery brought to view and the design of relieving it proposed than every hand is open to contribute something, every tongue is busied in solicitation, and every art of pleasure is employed in the interest of virtue." Yet, in historical perspective, we know that Dr. Johnson, like Defoe, was guilty of some overstatement. Only a beginning had been made in philanthropic effort.

A most interesting evidence of the way that humanitarianism was married to the commercial aspirations of the middle class is to be found in the poetry of the "Whig panegyrists."[14] Addison and Defoe sang the praises of commerce in prose. Since England's maritime commerce had brought great wealth to the nation, it was only natural that many versifiers should chant the praise of England's commercial glory. For our consideration, the interesting thing about this poetry is the way in which the panegyrists professed to see in the commercial policy the humanitarian design of improving the condition of the lower classes. Defoe had argued early in the century the insufficiency of charity to cope with the real problem of pauperism and had urged the adoption of some national policy that would make the poor self-supporting. The concentration of laborers in industrial centers, a change that began in the eighteenth century, naturally made the problem of poverty depend more directly than it had done on the nation's commercial success. The importance of maintaining British commercial supremacy was patent. The Whigs were thus inclined to defend all measures protecting commerce and manufacture as policies essential to the preservation of the poor. The part of the poets in the program of "benevolent commercialism" is noteworthy. Young in *Imperium Pelagi* saw possibilities of employing the poor in the manning of ships. Savage in *Of Public Works* saw an outlet for the surplus population of England in commercial and territorial expansion. Thomson in *Britannia* felt the close correlation between the well-being of the laborer and the success of foreign trade. In the event of the decay of trade, he pictures a desolate England in which "the cheerful voice of labour" will be heard no more.

The great woolen industry seems to have received special attention because of its size and because of serious danger of inroads into its prosperity by French fabrics. Professor Moore has characterized *The Fleece* (1757) of John Dyer as "a verse pamphlet of the various departments of the woolen industry in its relation to other forms of philanthropy." Dyer's idea is that poverty may be averted and national prosperity secured by setting the poor to work and by opening a world-wide market for their product.[15] Although Dyer has sympathy for the poor, he takes the position of Defoe in asserting that charity administered through ordinary channels will have no permanent effect. He is a thoroughgoing Whig in taking the view that commerce is the greatest civilizing force known to man.

§ 4

It is not possible to say just what proportion of the philanthropic activities of the first half of the century should be directly traced to the popular rationalistic theories of benevolence. It would certainly be unwise to trace all the benevolent activities of the end of the century to the revival of a religion in which feeling came again into its own. Religion has no monopoly on benevolent sentiments. Lecky wisely makes no attempt to distinguish between feeling of religious and non-religious origin in his explanation of the great humanitarian movement.[16] Indeed, at the end of the century we may observe Evangelicals, Benthamite free-thinkers, Whig and Tory humanitarians, all working toward the same benevolent end. Nevertheless, it is hardly a matter of argument that the Evangelical movement was the most important single humanitarian force in the century.

In the first half of the century the activity of the Church in humanitarian endeavor leaves much to be desired. The religious apathy that seemed to begin with the accession of George I, the political turmoil, and the fights between the orthodox and the deists manifestly weakened the Church and its benevolent activities. The religious collapse seems to be explained by the dread of the Church's falling either "into the Scylla of Romanism on the one hand or the Charybdis of Puritanism on the other."[17] To avoid the danger, ministers were noncommittal. For the most part they preached a comfortable morality of which true altruism was really no part.[18]

It would naturally be erroneous to suppose that nobody in this period of rationalism in religion was subjective and emotional. An important exception is William Law, tutor of Gibbon, author of *On Christian Perfection* (1726) and *A Serious Call* (1728), and a thinker to whom John Wesley owed much. *On Christian Perfection* condemns attempts to evade Christ's commands on the matter of benevolence; and *A Serious Call* sharply satirizes hypocritical charity. Furthermore, Law practiced what he preached in his own philanthropic efforts, not all of which were wise.

The Evangelical movement, which began just before the middle of the century and swept into greatness before the century closed, was patently a moral and philanthropic movement rather than a theological one. The Evangelicals in their benevolent efforts did not deny the existence of charity outside their fold, but they felt that it existed on the wrong basis and constantly questioned the sincerity of its motives. Miss Hannah More wrote in 1788:

There is scarcely a newspaper but records some meeting of men of fortune for the most salutary purposes. The noble and numberless structures for the relief of distress, which are the ornament and glory of our metropolis, proclaim a species of munificence unknown to former ages. Subscriptions, not only to hospitals, but to various other valuable institutions, are obtained almost as soon as solicited.

Although Miss More acknowledges with "liveliest joy . . . the delightful truth," she has cause to wonder "whether it be not the fashion rather as a substitute for Christianity than as an evidence of it." She sees as one of the salient errors of the "age of benevolence" the fact that all religion has been "reduced to benevolence and all benevolence to almsgiving."[19] But Miss More's insistence that the religion needed as a basis of true charity is a "turning of the whole mind to God" should not mislead one into thinking that Evangelicalism placed emphasis on the future life to the exclusion of the present. Evangelical or Wesleyan philanthropy was in effect highly practical.

The humanitarian aims of the Wesleyan movement are, in fact, closely tied up with its economic ideals.[20] Wesley seemed to have little impulse to condemn material gain as unworthy. The making of money appeared justifiable on the grounds that much good might be done with it and that the process encouraged economic virtues. "It is the will of God," Wesley wrote, "that every man should labour to eat his own bread."[21] He did what amounted to reviving the Puritan ethic of work in insisting that industriousness was not only a condition of happiness but a mark of moral character. Such a theory had its basis in the fact that poverty was the most irritating of social evils and that idleness manifestly brought profligacy. Working as he did among laboring people, he quickly saw the expediency of inculcating diligence, frugality, and cleanliness. Money-making is, of course, not held up as an end in itself. Money, says Wesley, "is unspeakably precious, if we are wise and faithful stewards of it."[22] It is good in so far as it has social usefulness and so long as it is not an obstacle to the spiritual life of the possessor. Therefore, whereas it is not wrong to have money, it is dangerous to have that which might lead, if not properly used, to self-indulgence and pride.

The sermon on "The Good Steward" furnishes Wesley's most complete comment on the subject of property in general. In his thinking, ownership of property is nothing more, as Mr. Warner has observed, than "a convenient fiction representing the nature of a relationship between man and the moral purpose of God,"[23] for everything belongs to God—"our souls, our bodies, our goods and whatever other talents we have received"—and man as a steward merely holds property for God, the master. The Christian has the right of "supplying thy reasonable wants, together with those of thy family." Further property rights he has none, for God has commanded that he restore

. . . the remainder to me, through the poor whom I had appointed to receive it; looking upon thyself as only one of that number of poor, whose wants were to be supplied out of that part of my substance which I had placed in thy hands for this purpose; leaving thee the right of being supplied first, and the blessedness of giving rather than receiving.

Such a philosophy would naturally imply an attack on extravagance and luxury. On this point Wesley speaks very plainly. "No Christian," he insists, "can afford to waste any part of the substance which God has entrusted him with."

At least one critic[24] has observed that Wesleyanism agrees with Rousseau's sentimentalism in denouncing the luxury and corruptions of existing society. However, whereas Rousseau explains the diseased state of society by pointing to its departure from the natural state, Wesley points to the corruption of the human heart.

In the eighteenth century there were three popular theories of the causes of poverty. First, economic necessity. In this view poverty was inescapable; therefore, to those who assented, the only recourse left open to the indigent was to accept their poverty and be conditioned to it. Second, the debauchery and sloth of the poor themselves. This theory was often held not only by those who were callous to philanthropic effort but by many who took a sympathetic attitude toward the problem. Third, a theory that combined the first two, with an additional cause discovered in the will of Providence. To no one of these three as such did Wesleyanism subscribe. Rather, "economic distress was ascribed to human failure which defeated divine purpose."[25]

It is not difficult to see how Evangelical trust in Providence might be applied to wealth, and how class distinctions might be justified on this basis. To such a conclusion came many Evangelicals, especially those of marked Calvinistic leanings. But Wesley seems to have tried to keep the mood of Methodist societies equalitarian. He plainly disliked the idea of inheritance and he championed the communism of primitive Christian communities. Nevertheless, unlike Rousseau, he could take the side of the poor without feeling the need of breaking in pieces a rigid system of class privilege.[26] The failure was not in one class of society: the root of the evil was not a mere matter of the tyranny of the upper classes over the lower. It resided rather in the failure of both classes to fulfill their reciprocal responsibilities. According to Wesley's theory of stewardship, the rich and privileged were immoral when they did not give to the needy what they found above their reasonable wants. Hence, there arose an inequitable distribution of the products of industry, allowing luxuries to the few and denying necessities to the many. On the other hand, there was an undeniable lack of industrial virtues among all classes. Luxury had sloth as a concomitant. But the apparent sloth of the poor was not so much due to their innate corruption as to the paralyzing effects of injustice.[27]

The solution offered by Wesley is as simple as it is obvious. If everyone works, avoids luxuries, and provides employment for all, the problem of poverty will vanish.

To return more specifically to the matter of benevolence, it must be remembered that in the thought of the leaders in the Evangelical revival philanthropy must be not merely a *social* but a *Christian* virtue. To leave it merely in the plane of social virtues was not to go beyond the rationalist philanthropy of the age, and to give "good works" anything like the dignity of "grace" or faith was not to go beyond the papists. The Evangelical suspicion of philanthropy not grounded on the "true faith" we have already seen in Miss More. Wesley had been her predecessor in insisting that the mere matter of good works is not enough. True benevolence must be an habitual social affection grounded firmly in Christian faith. "You . . . believe this love of human kind cannot spring but from the love of God," Wesley wrote in an open letter to Methodists. "You think there can be no instance of one whose tender affection embraces every child of man (though not endeared to him either by ties of blood, or by any natural or civil relation), unless that affection flow from a grateful, filial love to the common Father of all."[28] But if Evangelicals insisted that faith should be placed above works, they could do so without minimizing the value of works.

Since the giving of one's goods to the needy was nothing more than the execution of a divine command, such an act could reflect no glory on the giver. Hence, one must not expect credit for one's benevolence. One of the most important laws of Evangelical philanthropy was that it should be conducted in "as secret a manner as possible."

In general, the Evangelical movement made religion a personal concern and gave man a new sense of responsibility. If the movement had produced only William Wilberforce, it would have to be accounted as a very great humanitarian impulse. It, however, produced scores of others who worked untiringly for the good of humanity. The impossibility of calculating the real extent of philanthropic effort motivated by the great religious revival is due to the widely accepted idea that charity should be kept secret.

§ 5

Even before considering the humanitarian projects of the last quarter of the century, one may see that benevolence had not been a neglected subject in English thought. Early in the century its origin had provided a battle ground for the philosophers and its beauties had supplied inspiration for the poets. Moreover, practical philanthropic effort had got an early and an auspicious start. A great religious revival with a theory of benevolence in militant opposition to that of the rationalist philosophers had injected new zeal into the century's humanitarian efforts and had widened their objectives.

Within and without the great religious movement, the last quarter of the century was vibrant with humanitarian activity. Adam Smith was fostering an increased interest in the poor, and inquiring into the relations of capital and labor, landowners and tenants. The oratory of humanitarian Edmund Burke was ringing in the House of Commons. Clarkson, Wilberforce, Henry Thornton, and hundreds of others were in ardent activity for the abolition of the slave trade. John Howard was pursuing earnest research in the problem of jails and bridewells. Robert Raikes was attempting to end the neglect of children by the Church. By the end of the century the currents of humanitarianism were running in so many channels that they are often followed with difficulty. The chief objectives, however, were wiser poor relief, prison reform, better government for India, the improvement of education, the improvement of hospital facilities, Catholic emancipation, the abolition of slavery, and the founding of missionary societies. Added to these was a growing interest in the rights of animals.

It is against such a background that the poetry of William Cowper will be studied.

Chapter II

TH' INDUSTRIOUS POOR

§ 1

NONE OF THE four most important poets writing in the last decades of the eighteenth century went untouched by the humanitarian spirit of the century. The passion for liberty glowed in Burns, Blake, Crabbe, and Cowper. Zeal for the common man has never burned more brightly than it did in Burns, limited though he was by his nationalism. Rarely has the vision of mankind been more apocalyptic than it was in Blake. Few poets have had a more penetrating insight into social ills than Crabbe. Yet neither Burns, Blake, nor Crabbe reflects so well as Cowper the practical humanitarian impulses of the century, especially as they were reshaped and reinterpreted by that most important humanitarian force, the Evangelical revival.

Unfortunately, it has always been easier to pity Cowper than to appraise his genius or thought. "Cowper is charming," wrote Jane Welsh to Carlyle in 1822, "but draws so largely on my pity that I cannot spare him much of my admiration." The Brontës admired him chiefly because they pitied him, and his sad story moved Mrs. Browning to sentimental verse. Mr. Oliver Elton made the revelatory remark that "Mrs. Browning's verses on his grave show less self-control than any of Cowper's own."[1] Far and wide "Poor Cowper!" has been an Open Sesame for the floodgates of sentimentality, and it has been impossible for many people to visualize him save as a charmingly pathetic creature engaged, while not under the cloud of insanity, in amusing himself with his pets, drinking tea, walking in his garden, or playing Hercules to Mrs. Unwin's Omphale.

"There is an effeminacy about him," wrote Hazlitt, "which shrinks from and repels sympathy." The unfairness of such a judgment is evident, for it interprets Cowper entirely in terms of his outer life and obscures the many masculine qualities of his thought. As a matter of fact, effeminacy was anathema to the poet, and nothing provoked his satire more quickly than

> Fops at all corners, lady-like in mien,
> Civeted fellows, smelt ere they are seen.
> [*Tirocinium*, ll. 829-30.]

In one of his nineteenth-century editors Cowper's masculinity found a very staunch defender. Mr. H. T. Griffith wrote, ". . . there are few of our poets so thoroughly masculine as he, both in the matter and manner of his writings."[2] In spite of the apparent exaggeration, the statement is worth observing. Cowper's hatred of insincerity and affectation, his fearlessness in seeking the truth, and his belief in the integrity of his own judgment are masculine enough. That he had a feminine tenderness and a refined and delicate taste no one can deny; but one must agree with Mr. Griffith that in most instances "what is feminine is not contradictory of what is masculine, but is complementary of it."

In the introduction to his edition of Cowper's poetry, even such a well-wisher as Mr. J. C. Bailey throws a deterrent in the way of one who would consider Cowper's thought worthy of treatment. "He lived in a dull and obscure country village," writes Bailey, "among old maids and dissenting clergymen, and knew nothing of the commanding minds of his day."[3] Fortunately, the editor later finds cause to modify the strain somewhat. As the statement stands, it contains some truth. Its inaccuracies, however, are patent. Neither Mrs. Unwin, Lady Austen, nor Lady Hesketh was an old maid; nor was Newton or Scott a dissenting clergyman, although William Bull was. It is more important to point out that the statement needlessly exaggerates the provinciality of Cowper's life. The two titled ladies and such men as Newton and Scott were far from provincial. Certainly Cowper did not have widely extended personal contacts with the great of his day; but a man who is influenced directly or indirectly by such widely divergent thinkers as Wesley, Rousseau, and Burke could hardly be said to know nothing of the "commanding minds" of his day. That Cowper was touched by a surprising number of currents of eighteenth-century thought it will be part of the purpose of this study to show. If we demand of the "isolated" poet of Olney "What's the world to you?" we shall find from Cowper himself a very satisfactory answer:

> Much. I was born of woman, and drew milk,
> As sweet as charity, from human breasts.
> I think, articulate, I laugh and weep,
> And exercise all functions of a man.
>
> [*Task*, III, ll. 196-99.]

Thus the poet, apart from the center of greatest action, justly assumes authority for his fearless criticism of life.[4]

No one could put forward extravagant claims for Cowper as a thinker. But in spite of his mental infirmity, the tone of his recorded thought is remarkably healthful and the soundness of his judgment is often amazing. It is true that his originality is not great and that he is not always consistent. But he is often able to think clearly and vigorously, and to give poetic expression to thoughts that before his time were barely beginning to be regarded as material for poetry. The very fact that *The Task* was the most popular poem of the end of the century argues that the humanitarian and religious ideas in it were sown abroad over a wide area. Cowper's poetry was read by many who never read a line of directly Evangelical literature, and in this way he was able to exert over public opinion an influence that one more definitely marked with the stigma of Methodism could not have done.[5] Even the worldly Charles James Fox could be so moved by the Olney poet as to quote from *The Task* in the House of Commons and to call Cowper "one of the first of our modern poets."[6]

The efficacy of Cowper's humanitarian thought is attested by the contemporary writer of a series of articles in the *Flapper*,[7] a Dublin periodical of the *Spectator* type that has the distinction of presenting the first comprehensive appraisal of the poet's genius. According to the critic, although Cowper lacks the sublimity of Milton, Shakespeare, Dryden, and Pope, he ranks above them in "that his muse is but the minister of his benevolence—that under his culture, Parnassus itself teems with a new growth, since on every stem he has engrafted the scions of charity." The critic of the *Edinburgh Review* of April, 1803, is offended at Cowper's "coarseness or lowness" of expression and the "enthusiastic intolerance" of his devotional passages; yet he is ready to commend "the sterling weight and sense of his observations."[8] The testimony of Thomas Clarkson, the great abolitionist, is important. Of Cowper's part in the abolition movement he wrote, ". . . a great coadjutor he was when we consider what value was put upon his sentiments, and the extraordinary circulation of his works."[9]

I have already deprecated overemphasis on Cowper's removal from the world. It is too easy to forget that the poet was over thirty when he left London, the city in which the formative years of his youth were spent; that his family connections enabled him to move in excellent social circles there; and that he was connected in London with a vigorous, if not profound, group of young men whose interests in the affairs of the world and of society were undoubtedly of a broad scope. It is unfortunate that we do not know more about these London years. Such knowledge would undoubtedly give a better-balanced picture of the poet's life than we now have. From the time of his serious mental derangement in 1763 until the recovery in 1774 from his attack of the previous year, Cowper was almost completely removed from interest in national affairs.[10] In 1768 he wrote, "Whether the nation is worshipping Mr. Wilkes or any other idol, is of little moment to one who hopes and believes he shall shortly stand in the presence of the great and blessed God."[11] But after 1774 the letters show a continually broadening interest. Newton's removal from Olney to London in 1780 is not infrequently pointed out as the beginning of Cowper's freedom from some of his cramping religious inhibitions. It is much more important that Newton's being in London gave the poet, through letters, a valuable means of contact with the metropolis and hence with the world. Periods of depression, such as Cowper's fight in 1782 to ward off the decennial attack of his mental malady, caused interest in outside affairs to wane. But in general, between 1780 and 1786, the poet's period of greatest creative activity, Cowper's interest in the affairs of the world seems unusually keen. From the fourth mental attack in 1787 to the beginning of the period of final darkness in 1794 the poet's response to national affairs is at best spasmodic. His reluctance in entering upon such an undertaking as the anti-slavery poems in 1788 will be discussed elsewhere.

Cowper was more of an occasional poet than his strictly occasional poetry would suggest. The didactic poems and *The Task* offer many evidences of his quick response to current events. It should be remembered that Cowper wrote in a period in which the newspaper was becoming a powerful political and social force, and in which modern editorial practices were being developed. In the retirement of Olney the newspaper was to Cowper an important means of access to the outside world. Since the unfortunate experience of his serious mental derangement in London, he had hated the city. The newspaper, however, provided him with an excellent means of enjoying contacts with the city without encountering any of the disadvantages of urban life. Cowper literally dramatized the life that was brought to him between the folds of the *General Evening Post* and the *Morning Chronicle*. The famous scene at the beginning of "The Winter Evening" is convincing evidence of the thoroughgoing way in which he was able to enter the world of news. "The folio of four pages, happy work!" naturally provided him with a means of escape from his devastating introspection, but it also did vastly more. The completeness with which Cowper was able vicariously to absorb experience must be considered one of the basic reasons for his ability to touch so many of the interests of his century.

Even between 1780 and 1786 Cowper at times renounced his interest in the world, but these renunciations are not to be taken too seriously. For example, on December 4, 1781, he wrote to Newton that he was done with "politics" because his "present to the Queen of France" and the "piece addressed to Sir Joshua Reynolds" had contained predictions concerning the American Revolution that had been falsified by the defeat of Cornwallis. He also wrote to Newton in February, 1783: "You will suppose me a politician, but in reality I am nothing less. These are the thoughts that occur to me when I read the newspaper, and when I have laid it down I feel more interested in the success of my early cucumbers than in any part of the great and important subject. If I see them droop a little I forget we have been many years at war; that we have made an humiliating peace; that we are deeply in debt, and unable to pay." But Cowper's

discerning analysis of the "humiliating peace" that England
has just made shows with what a serious eye he had been
following events. The letter should therefore not be ad-
duced as evidence that Cowper was merely an amused
spectator of the world's passing show.[12] Again, it is also
true that Cowper has said in verse—

> 'Tis pleasant through the loopholes of retreat
> To peep at such a world; to see the stir
> Of the great Babel, and not feel the crowd.
>
> [*Task*, IV, ll. 88-90.]

But, as Sainte-Beuve has observed,

. . . il avait trop de sensibilité, de patriotisme, de mouvements
humains et chrétiens pour en rester à cet état de spectateur amusé,
et il s'échappait à tout instant en elancements et en effusions dou-
loureuses qui peuvent sembler aujourd'hui toucher à la declamation, mais qui, à les bien prendre et à les saisir dans leur jet,
étaient surtout des àpropos eloquents.[13]

§ 2

In 1753 Samuel Richardson published his last novel. It
was the year of Cowper's recovery from his first mental derangement and the year of his religious experience at South-
ampton. The appeal that Richardson's paragon of male
Christian virtue made to the youth of twenty-two is apparent in "An Ode on Reading Mr. Richardson's History of Sir
Charles Grandison." The poem is important not only as an
evidence of the poet's early religious preoccupation but also
as an evidence of his first approach to the formulation of a
humanitarian philosophy in direct opposition to that of the
rationalistic benevolists of his age. The opening stanza
launches into an attack on the "apostate and profane
wretches" who unblushingly disclaim allegiance to God and
who foolishly cherish virtue for its own sake. The real
virtues—those that distinguish from the crowd "the great

and good, the guardians of mankind"—are the humanitarian virtues:

> To rescue from the tyrant's sword
> Th' oppress'd; unseen, and unimplor'd,
> To cheer the face of woe;
> From lawless insult to defend
> An orphan's right, a fallen friend,
> And a forgiven foe.

Such virtues, the young poet asserts, have no earthly source but must be derived from heaven alone. Cowper had, indeed, arrived through his own emotional experience at several fundamental concepts of Evangelical philanthropy some ten years before he had his first real contact with Evangelical teaching at St. Albans.

There is a notable gap in what we have of Cowper's verse between 1753 and 1762. In 1762 Mrs. Greville, the former Miss Macartney, published in the *Annual Register* a poem called "The Prayer for Indifference" in which she, unlike most of her contemporary poets of sensibility, prayed for immunity to both pleasure and pain. Cowper replied in lines "Addressed to Miss Macartney on Reading the Prayer for Indifference," a poem that perhaps excels in sentimentality anything else that he wrote. To Cowper it was inconceivable that there should be a female heart smothering "at once both bliss and woe." "All the true delights of man," he asserts, "should spring from *Sympathy*," and "grief itself has comforts dear the sordid never knew." The luxury of sentimentalism reaches its height in the twenty-second stanza:

> Still may my melting bosom cleave
> To suff'rings not my own;
> And still the sigh responsive heave,
> Where'er is heard a groan.

Fortunately, Cowper did not persist in this strain. If he had done so, he would have been a palpable incarnation of

Mackenzie's "man of feeling" and would have completely warranted Hazlitt's judgment. Naturally, there is hardly a shred of originality in the whole poem. Almost every phrase had had some currency. But there must be recognized in it a fundamental sincerity resting in the poet's feeling of acute need for the extension of his sympathies. The sentiments of the poem, modified by much common sense and restraint, are later to be restated several times as the basis of Cowper's humanitarianism. Sir Henry Salt has observed that humanitarianism and altruism are not altogether synonymous. Altruism, strictly speaking, is due regard for the interests of others. The humanitarian acts to satisfy his own needs and instincts involved in those of the sufferer—"it is self-fulfilment rather than self-sacrifice that he desires."[14] Here, certainly, is one key to the humanitarianism of Cowper, for perhaps no one ever needed more peculiarly than he the extension of his feelings.

These poems are but flags in the wind. To discover any real development of Cowper's humanitarian thought one must vault over a period of twenty years—a period of much pain and suffering—to the didactic poems of the 1782 volume.

Although all eight of the poems were written between December, 1780, and October, 1781, they are not all instinct with the same mood of didactic severity. From first to last, however, Cowper is consciously striving for a "monitor's" rather than a "poet's praise." Especially may one see in the last two an increase in the flecks of gold that are undoubtedly scattered through even those didactic poems nearest the Evangelical somberness of Newton's teachings. Saintsbury's wish that Newton had been consigned to the sharks following his slave ship for prey is reflected in the treatment that the reformed slaver and leading Evangelical divine has received at the hands of many of Cowper's critics and biographers.[15] Indeed, Newton has been unduly maligned. Yet no one can doubt the salutary effect on Cowper of Newton's leaving Olney in June, 1780—an event which made possible for the poet a new self-dependence and the healthful secularization of his activities.[16]

Truth, the second of the didactic poems in date of composition, is a typical Evangelical sermon on "grace" as opposed to "works," involving, of course, humility and pride. Cowper here reflects the Evangelical tendency to hold suspect the charitable efforts of the age that were outside the true Christian fold. To him it was futile to attempt to win a future life without first an appeal to "grace." But the narrowness of the Evangelical view did not spare the attempt to win heaven through "works" by giving it the mere label of futility. The judgment was vastly more severe. In *Truth* Cowper frames an attack upon three principal kinds of benevolence: first, that of the deists who based their system on a "golden chain" including all sentient beings and who urged charity for its own sake; second, that of the Catholics who believed that works were worth as much as faith; and, third, that of the religiously apathetic church member whose giving was nothing more than a matter of form. If a man has not accepted grace, his "exact morals" can be only an evidence of pride. To Cowper the plea of works is "arrogant and vain," and gifts may be "but a sordid bargain for the skies." In the hermit's solitary contemplation and the Brahmin's self-inflicted torture the poet sees a further extension of man's pride in the thought that he can bargain for a future life. He borrows Miss Bridget from double immortality in Hogarth's "Morning" and Fielding's *Tom Jones* to pose for the hypocritical churchgoer who, having given

> half an angel in her own account,
> Doubts not hereafter with the saints to mount.
>
> [*Truth,* ll. 149-50.]

For the deistic "universal system" and "chain of being" Cowper substitutes "the golden one of love." Pope, it is true, had also spoken of a golden chain of love in the third epistle of the *Essay on Man*. But Cowper was able to recognize that Pope's use of *love* in that particular instance indicated little more than the recognition of the inter-dependence of all things and was far removed from the Evangelical notion of the essence flowing from the throne of God. Man's infinite obligations to his fellow man, Cowper will admit, are a part of the deist's conception; but again he insists that "heaven" approves as "honest and sincere" only "the work of gen'rous love, and filial fear." He, therefore, must arrive at the conclusion that virtue "unless of Christian growth" is "mere fallacy, or foolishness, or both."

In *Charity* Cowper returns to an attack on the benev-olence of the deists. Here one finds what appears to be a direct attempt at a refutation of the *Essay on Man*. Pope ends his philosophical poem with "All our knowledge, is OURSELVES TO KNOW." In Pope's system the benev-olence of man is not to be traced, in contradistinction to the idea of Shaftesbury, to any natural goodness within himself but arises out of the rational and universal law of coherence or order. To know oneself is then really to be thoroughly cognizant of one's relation to the universe, society, and man. This recognition can bring about in man only benevolent action. Cowper bases his refutation on the grounds of St. Paul's pronouncement in II Corinthians 1: 9-10: "But we had the sentence of death in ourselves, that we should not trust in ourselves, but in God which raiseth the dead: Who delivered us from so great a death, and doth deliver: in whom we trust that he will yet deliver us." He asserts that man, "still the progeny and heir of sin," cannot find sufficient guidance in reason:

> Blind was he born, and, his misguided eyes
> Grown dim in trifling studies, blind he dies.
>
> [Ll. 357-58.]

To expect self-knowledge through the instrumentality of
reason is foolish; but there is another kind of self-knowledge:

> Self-knowledge, truly learn'd, of course implies
> The rich possession of a nobler prize;
> For self to self, and God to man, reveal'd,
> (Two themes to nature's eye forever seal'd)
> Are taught by rays that fly with equal pace
> From the same centre of enlight'ning grace.
>
> [Ll. 359-64.]

The "ties of nature" of which Pope has made very much
"do but feebly bind."—And then comes the pronouncement
of the insufficiency of philosophy as a basis of benevolence:

> Philosophy, without his heav'nly guide,
> May blow up self-conceit and nourish pride;
> But, while his province is the reas'ning part,
> Has still a veil of midnight on his heart;
> 'Tis truth divine, exhibited on earth,
> Gives Charity her being and her birth.   [Ll. 373-78.]

Having established Grace as the source of "th' o'erflow-
ing well of Charity," the poet gives the subject a personal
turn. Several times in the didactic poems Cowper shows
that the emotional basis of his benevolence lies in his own
suffering. To the soul "that ever felt the sting of sorrow,"
he writes in *Retirement,* "sorrow is a sacred thing." In
Charity he asserts that true charity comes only through the
soul's recognition of its weakness and its need for reliance
on divine power. But the full explanation of the personal
basis of his humanitarianism has to wait for a beautiful passage in the fourth book of *The Task.* In this passage the
two-edged nature of his benevolence is apparent—it enables

the poet both to bear his own ills and to sympathize with
the ills of others:

> In such a world; so thorny, and where none
> Finds happiness unblighted; or, if found,
> Without some thistly sorrow at its side;
> It seems the part of wisdom, and no sin
> Against the law of love, to measure lots
> With less distinguish'd than ourselves; that thus
> We may with patience bear our mod'rate ills,
> And sympathize with others, suff'ring more.
>
> [Ll. 333-40.]

In *Charity* Cowper naturally finds it necessary to separate
false benevolence from the real. He arrives at a distinction
between alms and charity that might have come from
Wesley himself. That which is given to ease a "queasy conscience," he insists, is alms. Charity is that which intends
only another's good.

As we have already seen in the caricature of Miss Bridget,
Cowper makes use of satirical portraits as *exempla* in his
"sermons." The injection of such portraits into verse satire
is, of course, well grounded in tradition. Pope's Atticus and
Sporus are among the century's most brilliant examples of
the use of charactery for devastating personal satire, and
imitations are plentiful. However, Cowper seems to have
learned most about the introduction of charactery for a
moral purpose from William Law's *A Serious Call to Holy
and Devout Living* (1728). As a practitioner of false charity,
Cowper's Flavia is a condensed version of Law's character
of the same name, with an obvious Popean echo:

> Flavia, most tender of her own good name,
> Is rather careless of her sister's fame:
> Her superfluity the poor supplies,
> But, if she touch a character, it dies.
> The seeming virtue weighed against the vice,

> She deems all safe, for she has paid the price:
> No charity but alms aught values she,
> Except in porcelain on her mantle tree.
>
> [*Charity*, ll. 453-60.]

Continuing, Cowper vigorously propounds Wesley's thesis that philanthropy for show is sheer mockery. He subjects to severe criticism the popular eighteenth-century practice of raising subscriptions for the distressed. Every calamity, he argues, produces its share of those who relieve suffering merely for self-advertisement. An interesting parallel to this argument in *Charity* (ll. 461 ff.) is a letter to William Unwin dated November 4, 1782:

It is a pity that men of fortune should be determined to acts of beneficence sometimes by popular whim or prejudice, and sometimes by motives still more unworthy. The liberal subscription raised in behalf of the widows of the seamen lost in the Royal George was an instance of the former. At least a plain, short, and sensible letter in the newspaper convinced me at the time, that it was an unnecessary and injudicious collection: and the difficulty you found in effectuating your benevolent intentions on this occasion, constrains me to think that had it been an affair of more notoriety than merely to furnish a few poor fellows with a little fuel to preserve their extremities from the frost, you would have succeeded better. Men really pious delight in doing good by stealth: but nothing less than an ostentatious display of bounty will satisfy mankind in general.[17]

In *Charity* Cowper draws one of his best satirical portraits— that of the Squire who, called upon in church to contribute to the destitute, fumbles through his large gold pieces only to give a small one; but who lets it be known that he has given gold. We are not surprised that Cowper's Evangelical point of view would not allow him to accept the figures of contributions to the destitute from a calamity as an index to the real benevolence of the nation. A large contribution, he contends, might be merely an evidence of colossal national pride.

As Cowper questions extra-Christian charity, he also questions any attempt at reform not firmly grounded in love. Even satire itself is not justifiable if it is not motivated by love. Cowper has little patience with the satire of Swift and Pope. Swift "too often rails to gratify his spleen" and Pope's satire is the wrong kind both in material and method. Cowper continues with the theory that no works of any kind can find acceptance with God unless they have their origin in love. Self must be annihilated:

> If self employ us, whatsoe'er is wrought,
> We glorify that self, not him we ought.
>
> [*Charity,* ll. 569-70.]

This should effectually dispose of any attempt to erect philanthropy on a rational basis. The true conception of charity and universal love can come only from a contemplation of Christ and his triumph through suffering.

§ 3

The largest part of Cowper's theorizing on benevolence in opposition to the rationalists is in the didactic poems. Although he never got very far away from the Evangelical point of view on charity, he was able in *The Task* to break away from much of the heavy didacticism of the 1782 volume and to substitute for ethical and theological considerations of philanthropy the consideration of practical problems of charity in society.

But whereas in the 1782 volume Cowper seemed largely concerned with theories of benevolence and was more often interested in the problem of the giver than in that of the receiver, the poems are not without traces of the practical treatment of charity that the poet was to develop in *The*

Task. The Progress of Error presents for the first time an important article in Cowper's social creed:

> Have you no touch of pity, that the poor
> Stand starv'd at your inhospitable door?
> Or, if yourself, too scantily supplied,
> Need help, let honest industry provide.
> *Earn if you want; if you abound, impart.*
>
> [Ll. 249-53.][18]

No single line could sum up Wesley's view on the matter more neatly than the last. The passage follows an attack on luxury and false pleasure. Whereas the wealthy are obligated to give, the poet argues, the indigent have no right to allow themselves passively to be pauperized.

"If you abound, impart" is a statement of the positive duty of the rich to the poor. Cowper's sympathy with the Wesleyan stewardship idea is even better shown in *Charity*. "God makes some rich," he writes apropos of John Thornton, the great philanthropist, "for the supply of all." In the same poem the negative side of the relationship of rich and poor also receives statement: "To smite the poor is treason against God." But, although Cowper may attack the extravagance and waste of the upper classes, like Wesley he does not visualize an oppressive caste upon whom to charge the miseries of the poor. Cowper nowhere shares the feeling of Henry Brooke, who makes the sentimental hero of *The Fool of Quality* say: "I look upon the money amassed by the wealthy, to have been already extracted from the earnings of the poor; the poor farmer, the poor craftsman, the hard-handed peasant, and the day labourer. . . ."[19] Nor does he feel that wealth must necessarily bear the taint of sin. In his remarks jotted down on the philosophy of the Marquis de Caraccioli may be seen the common sense of Wesleyan economics:

It is vain to tell mankind that gold and dirt are equal, so long as their experience convinces them of the contrary. It is necessary therefore to distinguish between the thing itself and the abuse of it. Wealth is in fact a blessing when honestly acquired and conscientiously employed: and when otherwise, the man is to be blamed and not his treasure.[20]

Throughout his poetry, Cowper handles the matter of poverty with remarkable level-headedness, refusing to over-sentimentalize the poor. The vices of poor and rich he saw alike, as well as their virtues. While sentimental novelists were portraying heroes like Harley, Mr. Fenton, and Harry Sandford who view every spectacle of poverty with tearful compassion, Cowper voiced through the "sage" of *Hope* what was often his own feeling:

> The poor, inur'd to drudg'ry and distress,
> Act without aim, think little, and feel less.   [Ll. 7-8.]

The doctrine of work stated in *The Progress of Error* is developed in some detail in *The Task*. In Book I the poet summons those "that press your beds of down and sleep not" to see the thresher—

> see him sweating o'er his bread
> Before he eats it.—'Tis the primal curse,
> But soften'd into mercy; made the pledge
> Of cheerful days, and nights without a groan.
> [Ll. 363-66.]

Pope had written, "But all subsists by elemental strife." Cowper uses the same lesson from nature to show that work is essential to a healthy life, writing in almost the very words of Pope: "By ceaseless action all that is subsists." Through being buffeted by the winds, the oak strengthens its roots. If man desires hours of ease, he must have hours of toil.

The doctrine of work is further developed in the poet's contemptuous picture of gypsy life—a subject that had not yet become romanticized. Cowper's attitude toward the "vagabond and useless tribe" is typical of his attitude toward all who seem not to wish to work:

> Strange! that a creature rational, and cast
> In human mould, should brutalize by choice
> His nature; and, though capable of arts
> By which the world might profit, and himself,
> Self-banish'd from society, prefer
> Such squalid sloth to honourable toil!
>
> [*Task,* I, ll. 574-79.]

Of such a doctrine of work Cowper's theory of poverty is a natural consequence. The poet rejects the argument of economic necessity as a cause for poverty. Although man's wants are many, he asserts, supply is within easy reach "of temp'rate wishes and industrious hands." Cowper has not arrived at Wesley's highly enlightened theory of the neglect of reciprocal duties in all classes of society. Poverty, he asserts, is in most cases "self-inflicted woe"—"th'effect of laziness or sottish waste." (*Task,* IV, l. 431.) The poor persist in stealing and in getting drunk!

Herein Cowper's view is plainly limited by the restricted scope of his observation and is perhaps more definitely colored by his purely personal reaction than he himself suspected. In "The Winter Evening" there is a charmingly indignant description of a thief who plunders the garden, the wood pile, and the henroost (ll. 445-51). As several of his critics have suggested, the description is so vivid and the note of indignation is so clear that one is tempted to suspect that Cowper is thinking of the way in which his own garden and hencoop have suffered from marauders. At any rate, he refuses to find any extenuating circumstances for thieving. It would be possible, he asserts, to excuse the thief if he stole to provide for his hungry family; but this Cowper is sure cannot be a defense. The thief steals because of the "quenchless thirst of ruinous inebriety," and his family starves the while. Such a man is indeed a brute, fit only for the most convenient noose.

The public house, that den of vice and snare to the poor, is attacked with vehemence:

> There sit, involv'd and lost in curling clouds
> Of Indian fume, and guzzling deep, the boor,
> The lackey, and the groom: the craftsman there
> Takes a Lethean leave of all his toil;
> Smith, cobbler, joiner, he that plies the shears,
> And he that kneads the dough; all loud alike,
> All learned, and all drunk!   [*Task*, IV, ll. 472-78.]

Throughout England, living conditions in the eighteenth century were extremely poor. In the factory towns a working day of fourteen hours was not unusual, and where there were double shifts, factory hands sometimes had to work both shifts. The rapid rise of industrial centers gave rise to hopelessly overcrowded conditions. Water supply, sewage disposal, and drainage were all in a most primitive condition. Although Olney was not an industrial center, it is very probable that housing conditions among the poor there were not much better; for there was a great deal of overcrowding even in rural districts, on account of the demolition of cottages by landed proprietors in order to keep down the poor rates.[21]

In an environment unhealthful for both mind and body, the laborer must have had an extremely dull existence. In his ignorance of reading and writing he was cut off from mental nourishment, and no wholesome means of recreation were at his disposal. We do not wonder, even though Cowper does, that laborers should develop into rough boors and that they should seek "Lethean leave" in the public house.

In a sense, it is a little ironical that Cowper, who had a gentleman's highly developed instincts for leisure and comfort, should insist very rigidly on a gospel of work and should condemn sternly those who deviated from it. To say that if he had been healthy his life might have been a more strenuous one hardly meets the issue. If he had been perfectly normal, his gentlemanly instincts would probably have been very nearly the same. However revolutionary Cowper's social passion may seem to be, it is always well to remember that in his way of thinking class distinctions were an indispensable part of the social order and were not indiscriminately to be broken down. To this feeling his Calvinistic trust in Providence gave sanction. Here and there in his poetry and letters crop out expressions of Cowper's feeling that those of the lower classes should know and keep their places. For example, he holds in contempt "th'unwashed artificer" who dares

> T'indulge his genius after long fatigue,
> By diving into cabinet intrigue.
>   [*Table Talk*, ll. 153-54.]

"Poor people," he wrote to Newton under provocation of gossip, "are never well employed even when they judge one another; but when they undertake to scan the motives and estimate the behavior of those whom Providence has exalted a little above them, they are utterly out of their province and depth."[22] To Lady Hesketh he wrote in 1790 when the French Revolution was tearing away all class distinctions: "Differences of rank and subordination are, I believe, of God's appointment, and consequently essential to the wellbeing of society." Work, then, is essential for those who should work, and a gospel of work is the only feasible plan for the correction of the poverty that Cowper sees around him.

But to emphasize the poet's belief in class distinctions is to neglect something more obvious—his very real sympathy for the hardships and suffering of the deserving poor. Unlike such a contemporary painter as Morland, he is not given to idyllic pictures of rural life in which are shown colorful and neat low cottages with thatched roofs and small windows, as well as the ruddy smiling faces of the cottagers themselves. To the poet the "peasant's nest" is charming on account of its beautiful site and its remoteness from the tumult of town or city, but he realizes that the tranquillity of the place is overbalanced by its miseries. Instead of drinking water from a "crystal well," the wretched cottager

> dips his bowl into the weedy ditch,
> And, heavy-laden, brings his bev'rage home,
> Far-fetch'd and little worth; nor seldom waits
> Dependant on the baker's punctual call,
> To hear his creaking panniers at the door,
> Angry and sad, and his last crust consum'd.
>
> [*Task,* I, ll. 241-46.]

Crabbe himself has not given a more realistic or touching picture of the miseries of peasant life than Cowper gives in "The Winter Evening." The details are dramatic:

> The frugal housewife trembles when she lights
> Her scanty stock of brushwood, blazing clear,
> But dying soon like all terrestrial joy.
>
> . . . .
>
>   the brown loaf
> Lodg'd on the shelf, half eaten, without sauce
> Of sav'ry cheese, or butter, costlier still.
>
> . . . .
>
>   All the care
> Ingenious parsimony takes but just
> Saves the small inventory, bed, and stool,
> Skillet, and old carv'd chest, from public sale.
>
> [Ll. 380 ff.]

But it must be noticed that the poor of the household deserve compassion because they are "yet industrious, modest, quiet, neat" and because

> They live, and live without extorted alms
> From grudging hands.   [Ll. 403-4.]

The scene gives Cowper a chance to attack the administration of the Poor Law. Since their institution in the Elizabethan period the poor laws had developed many problems, the main one concerning the treatment of able-bodied men who declared themselves willing to work but unable to get employment. It was, of course, a common agreement that the aged and infirm should be maintained and that some form of punishment should be meted out to the able-bodied who refused to work. But the problem of finding suitable employment for the able-bodied presented great difficulties. It was also difficult to find a means of distinguishing between the worthy poor and "sturdy rogues and vagabonds."[23] The solution that was offered in the seventeenth century was the workhouse, or "house of industry." But this system was by no means a great success. The assumption that such institutions could carry on manufacturing at a profit soon proved to be a fallacy; nor did the system test very effectively the applicant's willingness to work. Attempts were made in the later eighteenth century to strengthen the work-house test, imposed in 1722, by improved administrative measures. Although some of the experiments worked for a while, they sooner or later seemed to revert to inefficiency. If poor rates were at first reduced, they soon began to rise again. Rather than persist in refusal of outdoor relief, overseers found it feasible to give applicants small doles in aid of wages.[24]

At the time of Cowper's writing, the administration of the Poor Law was in a period of extreme laxity. In many instances the work-house test was entirely disregarded, and there was the same sort of leniency in the matter of outdoor relief that the relief agencies of our own government have had to contend with in recent years. "Gilbert's Acts" of 1782 provided for the combination of better poor-house facilities. Although the intentions of the promoters were excellent, the results were far from satisfactory. To the poor-houses only the helpless poor were to be sent, but there was a provision that the guardians were to find work for the able-bodied. The provision called for the guardian's maintenance of the laborer, who was to reimburse the guardian out of his earnings and keep the surplus. In practice, of course, there was never a surplus.

In words that clearly show that Cowper can harden his verse when he is pleading a cause, the poet praises the poor who endure their poverty,

> choosing rather far
> A dry but independent crust, hard earn'd
> And eaten with a sigh, than to endure,
> The rugged frowns and insolent rebuffs
> Of knaves in office, partial in the work
> Of distribution; lib'ral of their aid
> To clam'rous importunity in rags,
> But oft-times deaf to suppliants, who would blush
> To wear a tatter'd garb however coarse,
> Whom famine cannot reconcile to filth.
>
> [*Task*, IV, ll. 408-17.]

Naturally, the criticism that the industrious, clean, and honest poor are neglected while the ragged and slothful are helped is made of almost every attempt to administer philanthropy; but the particular timeliness of Cowper's utterance makes it of significance. Unfortunately, the subsequent history of the Poor Law in the century does not present a more cheerful picture. The interest in reforms that had begun about 1760 both on account of a growing scientific interest in pauperism and the general humanitarian bent of the century seems to have been dissipated in the last decade of the century, when, as Sir Charles Grant Robertson puts it, England "built walls and more walls to prevent a drop from the toxic tides surging without, poisoning the paradise within. And those who protested that it was no paradise were Levellers, the enemies of God and home."[25]

In lieu of unsatisfactory poor relief, Cowper very generously offers to the industrious poor his own aid and that of a man who prefers to be nameless. The nameless benefactor is Robert Smith, a rich banker of Nottingham, who afterward became Lord Carrington.[26] Solicited by William Unwin, Mr. Smith contributed forty pounds to the Olney poor in 1782 and continued his charity for several years afterward. This is, of course, typical of the kind of charity produced by the Evangelical revival.

Another and a more important philanthropist whose friendship Cowper claimed was John Thornton. The two Thorntons, John the father and Henry the son, were wealthy merchants. Henry became a member of the famous "Clapham Sect," of which Wilberforce was the brilliant light. Than these two philanthropists few were closer to Wesley's idea of stewardship. The elder Thornton met and became a close friend of John Newton, mainly because Newton's life story had thrilled him. On a visit to Olney, Thornton offered Newton two hundred pounds a year, and more if necessary, for charitable distribution in the town. Newton declared that during his incumbency at Olney he distributed some three thousand pounds of Thornton's money. Thornton also proved his friendship by taking one thousand copies of the *Olney Hymns* and by sending a copy of Cowper's 1782 volume to his friend, Benjamin Franklin. The extent of his charities is described in Newton's *Memoirs:*

... he purchased Advowsons and Presentations, with a view to place in parishes the most enlightened, active, and useful ministers. He employed the extensive commerce in which he was engaged, as a powerful instrument for conveying immense quantities of Bibles, Prayer-books, and the most useful publications, to every place visited by our trade. He printed ... large editions of the latter for that purpose, and it may be safely affirmed, that there is scarcely a part of the known world, where such books could be introduced, which did not feel the salutary influence of this single individual.[27]

Henry Thornton became an even more important humanitarian force than his father.

To Thornton Cowper twice pays tribute in his poetry. In *Charity* there is high praise for the philanthropist's "stream of lib'ral and heroic deeds." On his death in 1790 Cowper wrote a fine eulogy in which it is plain that Thornton represented the fulfilment of many of the poet's philanthropic ideals. First, he had "an energy for doing good" as restless as that of him "who toils and sweats for food." Second, his liberality was discreet and sensible. (Cowper rigidly insisted upon discrimination in philanthropy; charity must not encourage the slothful.) Third, Thornton's charity was anonymous—an unalterable rule of Evangelical philanthropy—and finally, it was a matter of well-organized, not of sporadic, giving.

If Cowper had a keen eye for the vices of the poor and if he constantly insisted upon discriminating philanthropy, he could also feel that "almost all the real virtue that is in the world is to be found living and dying in a state of neglected obscurity." In *Truth* he wrote:

> O, bless'd effect of penury and want,
> The seed sown there, how vig'rous is the plant!
> No soil like poverty for growth divine,
> As leanest land supplies the richest wine. [Ll. 361-64.]

The point is made apropos of Voltaire's atheism and Cowper's own thesis that wit and learning may be snares to entrap the soul. The cottager in her simplicity, ignorance, and humility is destined, the poet affirms, for a happier fate than the great French thinker in his learning and pride. "So far as Cowper attacked the self-conceit of a narrow rationalism, or exalted the integrity of the poor and simple above the affectation and license of the rich," observes Mr. Hugh Fausset, "he was of course vindicating the truth which Wordsworth was later more profoundly to affirm."[28] But it is important to remember, Mr. Fausset continues, that Cowper can accord the state of poverty only the advantage of allowing the poor to escape the temptations and affectations of the rich.

Cowper's contribution to the elevation of humble life to a position of dignity and worth as poetic material is considerable. Though Thomson had depicted the farm house and the laborer and Joseph Warton, the woodman and the milk-maid, and though Gray's contribution to the literature of humble life in the "Elegy" is too well known to need more than bare mention, no one before Cowper had done anything comparable with the "Crazy Kate" episode in *The Task*. This episode was widely acclaimed by contemporary critics, and must be accorded an important place in the development of the literature glorifying the simple life, of which Wordsworth produced both the best and the worst examples. The portraits of the cottager who knew "her Bible true," the thresher, the waggoner in the snow storm, the woodman and his dog, all attest Cowper's delineative power and his sympathies.

§ 4

Cowper was by no means merely a "closet philanthropist." Except when the cloud of his mental disease was hanging over him, he was often busy relieving the suffering of the Olney poor. He had been initiated in philanthropic work by his friend John Newton, who had dispensed the bounty of Mr. Thornton. With Newton's leaving in 1780, Cowper seems to have felt that the duty of acting as guardian angel to the indigent and oppressed of Olney had fallen directly upon him.

In the sixteenth century Protestant refugees from Mechlin, escaping from the Inquisition, had settled in Buckinghamshire and had brought their lace-making industry with them.[29] In Cowper's day lace-making was still the most important industry of his own little Buckinghamshire town. The story of the exploitation of lace-makers is a long one, extending almost up to the present day. Fluctuation in lace prices could be astonishing and bewildering. Whereas at times lace-makers might make a pound a week, at others they would make only three or four shillings. In 1780 the misery of the lace-makers in Olney seems to have been extreme. Cowper wrote to Joseph Hill in July: ". . . there are very near one thousand two hundred lace-makers in this beggarly town."[30] All of them, he continued, looked upon "every loaf they bought as the last they should be ever able to earn." Two years later he wrote to William Unwin: "We make none but the cheapest laces and the price of them is fallen almost to nothing. . . . Olney is a populous place, inhabited by the half-starved and the ragged of the earth."[31]

The lace-makers of Olney had to face in 1780 not only low prices for their product but increased tax levies of a nation that needed funds to pursue her wars.[32] In June, 1780, Cowper wrote of a petition that had been sent to Lord Dartmouth, beseeching him to aid the lace-makers. A few weeks later the poet wrote to one of his friends, Joseph Hill: "If you ever take the tip of the Chancellor's ear between your finger and thumb, you can hardly improve the opportunity to better purpose than if you should whisper into it the voice of compassion and lenity to the lacemakers."[33] The Chancellor was Thurlow, who had been an intimate friend in Cowper's London days.

By 1782 Cowper had given up hope of getting aid from Parliament and had begun seeking the aid of philanthropists. He turned first to William Unwin, whom he requested to enlist his wealthy friends in an effort to relieve the Olney poor. The response of the future Lord Carrington has already been discussed. Cowper wrote Unwin on November 18, 1782, to thank him and to have him tell Mr. Smith that the name of the benefactor would be kept, as requested, in strict secrecy. Evidently, the philanthropist had requested that the money be distributed to those who were not professing Christians and who were therefore perhaps outside the bounds of church charity. Cowper writes:

We shall exercise our best discretion in the disposal of the money; but in this town, where the Gospel has been preached so many years . . . it is not an easy thing to find those who make no profession of religion at all, and are yet proper objects of charity. The profane are so profane, so drunken, dissolute, and in every respect worthless, that to make them partakers of this bounty would be alone to abuse it. We promise, however, that none shall touch it but such as are miserably poor, yet at the same time industrious and honest. . . .

How tenaciously Cowper clung to the "deserving poor" as the ideal for charity! In a letter to Unwin he tells of giving a rug to an *"industrious poor widow* with four children, whose sister heard her shivering in the night, and with some difficulty brought her to confess the next morning that she was half perished for want of sufficient covering."[34] In another letter to Unwin, containing what is perhaps Cowper's most touching prose picture of human suffering, the same philanthropic ideal is discernible: "There is no one article of this world's comforts, with which, as Falstaff says, they [the poor] are so heinously provided [as with bedding]. When a poor woman, and *an honest one,* whom we know well, carried home two pair of blankets, a pair for herself and husband, and a pair for her six children; as soon as the children saw them, they jumped out of their straw, caught them in their arms, kissed them, blessed them, and danced for joy."[35]

But not all his life did Cowper keep an even balance between his heart and his head. Before Cowper left St. Albans in 1764, he persuaded Dr. Cotton to part with a servant, Sam Roberts, who had served him faithfully and wanted to go with him. Besides Roberts, Cowper took with him to Huntingdon Dick Coleman, a lad of seven or eight, of whom the poet said, "He is the son of a drunken cobbler at St. Albans, who would probably have starved him to death by this time or have poisoned him with gin, if Providence had not thrown him in my way to rescue him." This benevolence Cowper later had many causes to regret. Dick's subsequent history is eloquently told in a postscript to a letter to Joseph Johnson in 1792: "There is one Richard Coleman in the world, whom I have educated from an infant, and who is utterly good for nothing; but he is at present in great trouble, the fruit of his own folly. I send him, by this post, an order upon you for eight guineas." And thus was the drunken cobbler's son saved!

Undeterred by this experiment, Cowper and Mrs. Unwin took in 1781 another protegée, Hannah Wilson, a child of Dick Coleman's wife by a former husband. Although she was taken into the house to be a trained servant, she was treated more like a daughter. Mrs. Unwin even paid for her education in a boarding school. But she, too, proved her unworthiness by her extravagance and negligence during the illness of Mrs. Unwin.

In 1791 Cowper's mental condition was such that he had come to rely pathetically on the absurd schoolmaster of Olney, Teedon, and to consider him an oracle of God. To Teedon in return for his oracular services the poet gave countless meals and a yearly income of thirty pounds. Lady Hesketh, who contributed generously to Cowper's support, seems to have protested, for Cowper writes that his cousin has been misinformed about "a person who lives luxuriously at my cost." In 1793 we find Lady Hesketh writing John Johnson, another cousin and benefactor of the poet, that she had given Cowper "hints of the many *idle people* his un-bounded liberality helped to make such, and of ye *swarms* who lived in his kitchen, but he took no notice of this."[36] Lady Hesketh was doubtless referring to Roberts, his wife Nanny, his mother, and his sister Sukey—all at times recip-ients of Cowper's bounty.[37] We are not surprised that Cow-per found his idea of charity for the worthy easier in theory than in practice. However, in a healthier state of mind he at least might not have been guilty of the Teedon philan-thropy.

§5

Cowper's theoretical position in regard to benevolence is clear. In the didactic poems he is conscious of the need of overthrowing the rationalistic ideas of benevolence that had often been propounded in prose and verse. He attacks the rationalistic position deliberately, annihilates it, and pro-ceeds to set up "Christian"—that is, Evangelical—charity in its stead. In dialectic of this sort the narrowness of his views is likely to become only too evident. But even in the 1782 poems most of this narrowness vanishes when he considers practical philanthropic efforts rather than the academic question of benevolence. As an Evangelical he insists that Grace is the only acceptable basis of philanthropy, which, of course, must be kept secret. When he considers the social implications of philanthropy, he feels that discrimination in charity cannot be overemphasized; for charity should lead to a correction rather than to the perpetuation of the social evil of poverty. His ideal philanthropist is notably far from the type of benevolent gentleman rapidly becoming popular in the sentimental novel—a paragon of virtue who could scatter tears and guineas in equal profusion and with equal lack of discrimination.

Cowper's inability to see the broad social implications of poverty is naturally a serious limitation of his humanitarian thinking, but it by no means invalidates his gospel of work as a practicable principle through which conditions of the poor might be improved, even though a complete cure of poverty could not be effected through it. It is the same sort of gospel that Cowper's staunch admirer, Thomas Carlyle, with his vastly greater understanding of the nation's social and economic structure, preached in *Past and Present*. It agrees with the idea of Malthus that self-dependence should be inculcated in the poor. More important still, it is the kind of doctrine that Methodist and Evangelical leaders took to the rapidly growing industrial centers of England. Here through such teaching really remarkable improvements in living conditions were brought about. Whatever, then, may be the theoretical objections to Cowper's treatment of poverty, it has the distinction of having had its practicability demonstrated.

Chapter III

PITY FOR POOR AFRICANS

§ 1

In 1723 England hailed as a triumph the Assiento Treaty allowing the subjects of Great Britain to import slaves into Spanish colonies; yet in 1815 the denunciation of the trade in the Treaty of Vienna was widely considered the treaty's most valuable article. Such a reversal of opinion makes the anti-slavery movement the most dramatic of all the humanitarian movements of the eighteenth century.

We have already considered the development in England of a benevolent philosophy including all sentient life in its chain of being. The century was one of voyage and discovery, and travel books were very popular. Among the best sellers of the period were the travel books of John Cooke, Dampier, Forster, Clipperton, James Cook, Hawkesworth, Anson, and Byron. If one couples a philosophy insisting upon the natural goodness of man and a large amount of material about primitive peoples brought to light by discovery, one may easily understand the primitivism of the century. Naturally, the glorification of a primitive state of society and of the Noble Savage has important bearing on the question of human slavery.[1]

In the century one may find a wide variety of opinions on the Negro. To some he was little more than a tailless ape; whereas to others he was superior to the white man. But the Negro's rise to recognition as a Noble Savage seems to have been a relatively slow process.[2] For a number of years the ugly Africans went unnoticed, while Europeans, seemingly led by aesthetic considerations, expressed humanitarian sentiments in behalf of the beautiful Indians. At-

[51]

tacks on Spanish cruelty to Indians date from Las Casas' *Brevísima Relación de la Destruyción de las Indias* in 1539, and the theme of Spanish atrocity received dramatic treatment as early as 1658 in Davenant's *Cruelty of the Spaniards.*

But the neglect of the African as an object of sympathy did not rest on anything so unsubstantial as aesthetics. The real thing that blinded the world to the inhumanity of the slave trade was the necessity for slaves in the expansion of Britain's colonial empire and the huge profits that the slave trade brought in. Thousands of slaves were needed for the plantations of the West Indies. Slave trade rose so rapidly in the century that for long periods between 1680 and 1786 more Negroes were brought from Africa than Europeans from Europe.[3] The annual importation after the middle of the century amounted to over one hundred thousand. A mad race was on. European vied with European to capture slaves for the fabulously lucrative plantations. Unnoticed went the horrors of the trade—the capture of slaves and the "middle passage," most dreaded of inhumanities. In the meantime the commercial wealth of England was growing at an enormous rate.

Blindness to the vicious nature of the trade was widespread, extending even to Christian ministers, humanitarian reformers, and philosophers who dilated upon the beauties of benevolence. Although slavery was prohibited in Georgia, one may be reminded that Oglethorpe was Deputy Governor of the Royal African Company, which under the Assiento Treaty contracted to deliver to the Spanish colonies 4,800 slaves annually for a period of twenty years and which did deliver more than that number to the American colonies in the very year in which Oglethorpe made a speech declaring the trade a "horrid crime."[4] Berkeley owned slaves in Rhode Island, whereas Whitefield found biblical justification for slavery and argued that the institution was a necessity in the Southern colonies.[5]

Even Locke, generally a stalwart champion of human rights, could be uncertain in his teachings about slavery. In his *Constitutions of Carolina* (1669) he invested the freeman with absolute authority over the slaves. A more mature work, *Two Treatises on Government* (1690), begins, to be sure, with the statement: ". . . slavery is so vile and so miserable an estate of man, and so directly opposite to the generous temper and courage of our nation that it is hardly to be conceived that an 'Englishman,' much less a 'gentleman,' should plead for it." But the freedom of an Englishman and that of an African turn out to be somewhat different things. Locke finally agrees that, although a man cannot make himself a slave because he cannot give away what he does not possess (i.e., power over his life), slavery can be justified as a continuation of war between the conqueror and the conquered.[6]

The theme of Negro slavery seems to make its first appearance in fiction with Mrs. Behn's *Oroonoko* of 1678, and in the drama with Southerne's dramatization of Mrs. Behn's story in 1696. Mrs. Behn can hardly be considered an early Harriet Beecher Stowe. She was obviously under the spell of the heroic tragedy and was interested in her hero rather because he was noble than because he was a Negro. But there are humanitarian implications in the story. Southerne dramatized the story, adding a comic subplot and making Imoinda white. If he does anything to the humanitarian implications of the plot, he seems to make them less apparent. Yet both Clarkson and Miss Hannah More[7] praise the "celebrated tragedy" for its anti-slavery feeling. It seems evident that the drama in question was not Southerne's original version, but most likely the 1775 version of Dr. John Hawkesworth, who deleted the comic subplot and emphasized the humanitarian elements.

Defoe attacked slavery in *The Reformation of Manners* in 1702, but he later became interested in the commercial possibilities of the trade. In 1719 he drew a picture of a lovable Negro in *Robinson Crusoe;* and, if he did not attack slavery itself, he did recommend better treatment for Negroes in *Colonel Jacque.*

To the Whig poets who sang the glories of England's commerce the matter of slavery offered some difficulty.[8] The dilemma is perhaps best seen in Dyer, who in *The Fleece* admits that the traffic "wounds the gen'rous heart" and feels that slave traders will be punished for their inhumanity, but who makes no real condemnation of the traffic.[9] Young, however, actually defended the slave trade in *Imperium Pelagi* by laying the blame for slavery on the Negroes themselves:

> Afric's black, lascivious, slothful breed,
> To clasp their *ruin,* fly from toil;
> That *meanest* product on their soil,
> Their people *sell:* one half on t'other feed. [Strain V.]

Grainger managed to make Book IV of *The Sugar Cane* a sort of versified manual of instructions on the purchase of slaves. He discusses the age at which Negroes should be purchased and suggests the distinguishing marks of a sound Negro. He tells which tribes produce good tradesmen, which are addicted to suicide, and which are subjected to worms and dropsical disorders. One section is called "How salt-water, or new Negroes should be seasoned." It is true that in the first few hundred lines of the poem Grainger wishes that he could give to man

> Of every colour and of every clime
> Freedom which stamps him image of his God.
> [Ll. 237-38.]

But the wish hardly strikes one as revealing abolitionist passion. It is also true that before the end of Book IV Grainger finally gets around to the humanity with which slaves should be treated; but one is tempted to feel that the humanity is hardly of a higher order than that for which Dyer pleads for sheep in *The Fleece*.

James Thomson was a Whig who spoke his mind on the miserable business. It is he to whom the credit must be given for being the first poet of the century to depict vividly the horrors of the trade. In his memorable lines from *Summer* he writes one of the most amazing bits of anti-slavery verse of the century. He is no propagandist, but as an artist he has mastered the macabre; and the moral of his poetic justice is sufficiently impressive:

> His jaws horrific armed with threefold fate,
> Here dwells the direful shark. Lured by the scent
> Of steaming crowds, of rank disease, and death,
> Behold he rushing cuts the briny flood
> Swift as the gale can bear the ship along,
> And from the partners of that cruel trade
> Which spoils unhappy Guinea of her sons
> Demands his share of prey, demands themselves.
> The stormy fates descend: one death involves
> Tyrant and slaves; when straight their mangled limbs
> Crashing at once, he dyes the purple seas
> With gore, and riots in the vengeful meal.   [Ll. 1014-25.]

Richard Savage finds occasion in "Of Public Spirit in Regard to Public Works" to make a few observations on the slave traffic. "Why must I Afric's sable children see," he asks, "vended for slaves, though born by nature free?" He speaks of the "nameless tortures" invented by cruel minds to keep slaves in subjection and warns that a day of retribution will come.[10] In Elegy XX Shenstone registers an impassioned protest against slavery.[11]

Pope's invocation to "fair peace" in *Windsor Forest* to spread her reign "till Conquest cease, and Slavery be no more," has reference to the slavery of the Indians of Peru and Mexico, as also does the famous "Lo, the poor Indian"

passage in the *Essay on Man*.[12]   Later in the century Charles
Churchill, Cowper's friend, attacked in *Gotham* the enslavement of Indians in terms strikingly similar to those used in
abolitionist poetry of the last decades of the century.   He
shows some bitterness toward the "roving buccaneers" who

> Cut off that Charter they from Nature drew
> And made them Slaves to men they never knew.[13]

Let Spain and France, "in slavery bred," carry on the trade
if they will, he insists—not England:

> An Englishman, in *charter'd* Freedom born,
> Shall spurn the slavish merchandise, shall scorn
> To take from others, thro' base private views,
> What he himself would rather die, than lose.

The search for gold is the root of the evil.   The attempt to
Christianize the Indians does not escape Churchill's satire:
"Europe took their gold and gave them grace."

The few poetic expressions of anti-slavery feeling are no
real index to the growth of the sentiment.   As Clarkson's
History of the Abolition shows, before the middle of the
century there was a slow but steady increase in pamphlets
and sermons dealing with the slave trade.

The first genuine blow against slavery was struck by
Granville Sharp in the famous Somerset case in 1772.[14]   The
decision that the institution of slavery did not exist in England was a great step toward the final abolition in the colonies.   A similar decision in the case of Joseph Knight in
Scotland in 1778 gave added impetus to the anti-slavery
movement.   From this point expressions of abolitionist sympathy were to increase rapidly.   Between 1770 and 1780 the
pages of a popular periodical like the *Gentleman's Magazine*
showed a marked increase in anti-slavery protests.

In 1773 Thomas Day, the author of *Sandford and Merton,* published *The Dying Negro,* an interesting anti-slavery

poem written in conjunction with his friend Bicknell.[15] The
theme, supposedly based on fact, is the suicide of a Negro
slave who is seized in London and put on a ship to be carried away into slavery. The hero takes his own life rather
than be separated from the white woman he loves. (If
this seems somewhat unusual, it will be remembered that
Imoinda in Southerne's version of *Oroonoko* is white.) The
poem attacks the institution of slavery as fostered by European greed and oppression and it shows great enthusiasm
for the nobility of the Negro race. Here the Negro is
definitely a Noble Savage.[16]

Dr. Johnson was a leading opponent of slavery. Although he was ready to support George III in suppressing
the American colonies in their fight for freedom, he could
oppose the government boldly in the matter of slavery.
"How is it," he exclaims in *Taxation No Tyranny,* "that we
hear the loudest *yelps* for liberty among the drivers of the
negroes?" There is the famous story of his astounding toast
at Oxford, "Here's to the next insurrection in the West
Indies!"[17] His distrust of England's imperialism is patent.
"I do not much wish well to discoveries," he said, "for I
am always afraid they will end in conquest and robbery."
Boswell chose to take the opposite side. "No Abolition of
Slavery," which he published in the *Gentleman's Magazine*
in 1771,[18] argued (and not without some justification) that
Negro slaves were happier than English laborers.

Among the religious sects the Quakers seem to have been
the first to urge the abolition of slavery both in England and
in America. Their efforts reach back into the seventeenth
century. During the early years of Methodism, Wesley and
his followers were outside the growing protest.[19] When
they had anything to do with slavery, their concern was for
the Negro's soul rather than for his body. Although Whitefield defended the institution, his attitude might have been
different if he had lived later in the century. Wesley's

attention was focussed on the slave trade by a pamphlet written by Anthony Benezet in 1772. Two years later he wrote his *Thoughts Upon Slavery,* easily one of the most important anti-slavery documents of the century. Wesley quotes Judge Blackstone to annihilate the theory of the three origins of slavery as given by Justinian: (1) the right of slavery arises from captivity, (2) slavery may begin by one man's selling himself to another, (3) men may be born slaves by being the children of slaves. Having demolished the legal argument for slavery, Wesley attacks and renders absurd two popular arguments: first, that the land from which slaves were taken was a dreary, unhealthful, and uncultivated waste; and, second, that the Negroes sold into slavery were in their native state fierce, savage, and cruel, devouring one another. His whole attitude toward slavery is summed up in his insistence that the Negro has "the same natural right as an Englishman" to freedom, because "no human law can deprive him of the right which he derives from the law of nature."

The Methodists were now definitely in the field of abolition. Anti-slavery propaganda was spread abroad through sermons, pamphlets, and the pages of the *Arminian Magazine;* and Methodists gave coöperation to other groups in the effort to stamp out the dreadful evil. In the last decade of the century one of the most important evidences of Methodist zeal for the cause was an organized movement, spread through the agency of preachers, to boycott slave-produced articles. The *Arminian Magazine* in 1790 reminded Methodists "how many backs have sweated for the sweet your cane affords,"[20] and Methodist ministers urged abstention from the use of rum and sugar until the slave trade was abolished.

In the *Wealth of Nations* (1776) Adam Smith argued that slave labor was uneconomic. In the attack upon the economic foundation of slavery he was joined by Jeremy

Bentham. Paley in his *Moral Philosophy* expressed the hope that the world would soon see the end of "this abominable tyranny." Thomas Paine had published his essay on slavery in 1775. Like Dr. Johnson he saw the contradiction in a fight for freedom by a slaveholding nation. He also saw the anomaly in the fact that so-called Christians countenanced slavery.

Two great Frenchmen who began to speak against slavery about the time of the American Revolution were Condorcet and Abbé Raynal. For our purpose Raynal is of special importance on account of the admiration that Cowper had for him. His *Histoire des deux Indes*—a compilation in which he was aided by several members of the *philosophe* coterie and which dealt with the natural resources, climate, and inhabitants of Africa, as well as with slavery and the slave trade—attained great popularity, in spite of its superficiality. Like Wesley, Raynal breaks down the popular defenses of the trade. For those who argued that slaves were taken in war and would have been murdered if the whites had not interfered, the Abbé posed the question, Who instigated the war? To those who argued that slaves were criminals and deserved death, he asked, Are the whites executioners to Africa?[21] He forcefully insisted upon including Negroes in the brotherhood of man: "One common father, an immortal soul, a future state of felicity, such is thy true glory, and such likewise is theirs."[22]

Rousseau was unequivocal in his statements on slavery. In the *Discourse on Inequality* he writes:

... chacun doit voir que les liens de la servitude n'étant formés, que de la dépendance mutuelle des hommes et des besoins réciproques qui les unissent, il est impossible d'asservir un homme sans l'avoir mis auparavant dans le cas de ne pouvoir se passer d'un autre; situation qui, n'existant pas dans l'état de nature, y laisse chacun libre du joug, et rend vaine la loi du plus fort.[23]

He is even more eloquent in *The Social Contract:*

A l'égard du droit de conquête, il n'a d'autre fondement que la loi du plus fort. . . . Ainsi, de quelque sens qu'on envisage les choses, le droit d'esclavage est nul, non seulement parce qu'il est illégitime, mais parce qu'il est absurde et ne signifie rien.[24]

The lull in the slave trade caused by the American Revolution lasted only for the period of the war. The resuming of the trade in full force immediately after the war brought such a revelation of its horrors as the case of the *Zong* in 1783. In order to collect from the underwriters, the master of the vessel threw overboard one hundred and thirty slaves when he was afraid that they would die on board for lack of drinking water. Although civil action was brought by the underwriters, one historian writes, "It seems never to have occurred to the judge . . . or the Court in Banco, to order criminal proceedings against the captain and the crew for their wholesale homicides."[25]

In 1784 a new advocate for the cause of anti-slavery appeared in James Ramsay, who had been a rector in the West Indies and who was one of the first abolitionists to argue from firsthand information. Friendship with Clarkson, Sharp, Sir Charles Middleton, and Wilberforce made it possible for him to use his material effectively.[26] In *An Essay on the Treatment and Conversion of African Slaves in the British Sugar Colonies* (1784) Ramsay supported Adam Smith's contention that the French treated their slaves better than the English did and got more work from them. His picture of slavery was not entirely dark. He could agree with Boswell that the physical condition of the slaves was better than that of the English laborer.

In 1783 the Quakers presented an abolitionist petition to Parliament. A number of books and pamphlets followed. The year 1787 was memorable for two things: Wilberforce's announcement that he would champion abolition in Parliament and the formation in London of the Committee for the Abolition of the Slave Trade with Granville Sharp, already illustrious for his unselfish service to the cause, as president.[27] The parliamentary battle was now on. At first, the movement was for the abolition of the slave trade rather than for the abolition of slavery itself. With Clarkson as the indefatigable field agent, Wilberforce as the parliamentary leader, and Pitt as coadjutor, it is not remarkable that the movement found wide support.

In bringing to light evidence for abolition, Clarkson had a most romantic career, involving all sorts of difficulties and perils. Wilberforce spoke and entertained untiringly for the cause. The supporters of slavery argued that the trade was necessary to further the development of the West Indies, that the plantations could not be cultivated without slaves, that if England abandoned the trade other nations would take it up and profit hugely by it. These arguments Wilberforce answered by showing the horrors of the trade, especially of the "middle passage." His figures were astounding. He showed that $12\frac{1}{2}$ per cent of the slaves perished in passage, $4\frac{1}{2}$ per cent died on shore before the day of sailing, and $33\frac{1}{3}$ per cent more died during the seasoning.[28]

The first parliamentary efforts of the abolitionists were not successful. In 1789 and 1791 the great debaters were unavailing in their eloquence. In 1792 Wilberforce spread his forces and tried to have constituents bring pressure on the House of Commons. Most unfortunately, at this critical moment the French Revolution set the island of Santo Domingo on fire. The perilous position of the whites on the island was used effectively by the powerful West Indian interests to frighten the friends of abolition. The ensuing struggle with France had the effect of postponing most reforms for over a generation.

§ 2

Cowper's treatment of man as a political and religious unit is subject to those contradictions that must arise when a man is a democrat in his politics and an absolutist in his theology. A similar difficulty not infrequently arises in Milton. Man must preserve his dignity in the body politic and his debasement before God. Tyranny may be traced, on the one hand, to the selfishness and vainglory of princes. To tolerate it is to be contemptible. On the other hand, tyranny may be the work of God's hand for the punishment of sin. In that event, one should "kiss the rod." "A slave," said the sainted William Law, "can only live unto God in one particular way, that is, by religious patience and submission in his state of slavery."[29] It is apparent, if the matter is viewed in the light of cold logic, that in Cowper the apparatus for testing the ultimate instrumentality of God is lacking. But Cowper, unlike the rationalists of his age, did not attempt to apply the same unswerving logic to temporal and spiritual affairs. There is for him no contradiction.

The great European ferment of the last half of the eighteenth century—a ferment centering in an interest in Man stripped of all relation to exterior labels—was not without its effect in Olney, where Cowper gave expression to some of the sentiments that culminated in the French Revolution. To attribute to Cowper too much of a revolutionary spirit is to belie the facts. At the same time, it is quite possible to underestimate the importance of his revolutionary ideas, because out of their historical perspective many have become platitudinous. Much that he said about tyrants and liberty may be traced to sources at least as early as Milton's *The Tenure of Kings and Magistrates*. But it is something to the credit of Cowper's courage that he can give expression to a political philosophy in many ways like Rousseau's;[30] and it is indeed to his credit that he can develop an internationalism for the benefit of the Negro and the oppressed, even though he can never quite get away from his national prejudices when he deals with the enemies of England, notably the French. The transition from the "chain of being" to "the brotherhood of man" is not completely realized in Cowper, but an important contribution to the process is made.[31]

Cowper's internationalism is a compound of many simples and is often difficult to analyze. It is easy to see, however, that its basis rests both in his religion and his patriotism. The difficulty arises because his religion and his patriotism can be both motivating and limiting forces in his thought. In attempting to arrive at a concept of human liberty he must begin with the Englishman, his "fav'rite man of all mankind." When he exclaims in the idiom of Rousseau—

> Man made for kings! those optics are but dim
> That tell you so—say, rather, they for him!
>
> [*Table Talk*, ll. 54-55.]

he is thinking in terms of Englishmen. The poet's idealization of the English physique and intellect comes early in *Table Talk*. Of the Englishman he writes:

> His form robust and of elastic tone,
> Proportion'd well, half muscle and half bone,
> Supplies with warm activity and force
> A mind well-lodg'd, and masculine of course.
>
> [Ll. 218-21.]

In explaining both the Briton's physique and his love of liberty, Cowper follows Brown, who states in the *Estimate* that he anticipated Montesquieu in the view that British liberty is a natural growth of the soil.[32] Of "constitutional controul" the Englishman is patient,

> But, if authority grows wanton, woe
> To him that treads upon his free-born toe.
>
> [*Table Talk*, ll. 226-27.]

The poet arrives at a definition of freedom in *Expostulation:*

> True freedom is where no restraint is known
> That scripture, justice, and good sense disown,
> Where only vice and injury are tied,
> And all from shore to shore is free beside.   [Ll. 592-95.]

Whenever Cowper sings the praises of liberty, one may feel reasonably certain that he sings of liberty rather strictly governed by discipline and "preserv'd from wild excess." License has no place in his scheme, and he naturally shrinks from violence. For the mob he has no sympathy. The famous Lord George Gordon riots, "plebeian thousands in a roar," are a horrible example of what will happen if the restraints of liberty are broken.

If true liberty implies restraint, it naturally follows that the chief function of government is to provide control. In *Table Talk* the poet—speaking more or less in the platitudes of his day, especially as they are found in Book I of Churchill's *Gotham*—lists five functions of a king: to keep vice restrained, to nourish the arts, to give religion "unbridled scope," "to keep the matrimonial bar unstain'd," to defend the rights of the country when it is necessary to do so. But a king's rights do not exceed his duties, and he must be regarded purely as a means of preserving liberty. On this point, Cowper later expresses himself in a passage in "The Winter Morning Walk" that reads like a versified excerpt from *The Social Contract:*

> He is our's
> T' administer, to guard, t' adorn the state,
> But not to warp or change it. We are his
> To serve him nobly in the common cause,
> True to the death, but not to be his slaves.
>
> [*Task*, V, ll. 341-45.]

Cowper continues in the same book of *The Task* to express revolutionary zeal. He writes:

> Whose freedom is by suff'rance and at will
> Of a superior, he is never free. [Ll. 363-64.]

But he who allows himself to endure his yoke deserves his slavery. Turning to France, Cowper urges a nation subjected to the yoke of tyrants to strive for liberty, even though the attempt may be defeated. Such an attempt, he believes, is not often unsuccessful, for power usurped, "conscious of wrong," will weaken in the face of opposition and take flight; whereas strength will come to those who seek freedom. An even more spirited passage (ll. 379 ff.) follows in which Cowper directly charges France with opprobrium for permitting the existence of "the house of bondage, worse than that of old . . . the Bastile!" There is not an English heart, says the poet (entirely forgetting his French prejudices in his zeal for liberty), that would not rejoice in the fall of the prison. Here are two very remarkable passages. In them one can almost hear the *Ça ira*. The poet has let himself go, and has achieved an impassioned revolutionary point of view. Surely, he was never closer to the radical thought of his age. Though Cowper becomes somewhat frightened by his own temerity, he does not negate the effect of the passages with his deprecatory footnote: "The author hopes that he shall not be censured for unnecessary warmth upon so interesting a subject. He is aware that it has become fashionable to stigmatise such sentiments as no better than empty declamation; but it is an ill symptom, and peculiar to modern times."

The picture of the prisoner in the Bastile is deservedly well known. Lord Byron, who scorned Cowper but who on several occasions found it convenient to quote him, might have found the passage no mean companion for his "The Prisoner of Chillon."

When Cowper turns to a contemplation of England, he finds with his usual patriotism that, in spite of all her loss of empire and in spite of her recent vicissitudes, his own land is happy among nations because she is free. But within England that freedom is endangered. The poet's feeling on the subject is strong:

> I could endure
> Chains nowhere patiently; and chains at home
> Where I am free by birthright, not at all. [Ll. 477-79.]

Politicians, he finds, are too shrewd and self-seeking, and private virtue is lacking.

From this point Cowper turns to a consideration of what he must finally arrive at as the only true liberty—that which comes through the truth of Christianity. Regardless of his condition of life, anyone who does not possess this freedom is a slave. And, conversely, with this truth even the slave is free. Cowper has not been arguing in a circle. The greater importance of the freedom of the soul has not kept him from giving the greater space in this discussion to the freedom of the body. Many who in the eighteenth century professed to put the freedom of the soul first argued that Negroes had to be enslaved to be saved. Cowper was far from being among that number.

Liberty, then, is to Cowper the gift of God and the noblest right of man, and whoever takes it away is guilty of "treason against God." Cowper builds his protest against Negro slavery both on his religion and his politics. John Wesley argued as much like a barrister (citing Blackstone) as like a clergyman when he argued that the same inalienable rights given to an Englishman should be extended to slave and savage. Cowper blends his view with Abbé Raynal's argument based upon the brotherhood of man.

In *Charity* one finds Cowper's first and most extensive expression of his abolitionist feelings. The poem begins with an enunciation of the idea of man's universal kinship. The chain that unites all mankind is the "social plan" of God, and universal kinship is fixed in all men's common origin in Adam. Differences in language, manners, or in face should have no effect on man's feeling of alliance with all the race. One may well feel that with such a start Cowper may be drawn, if he is not careful, into an optimistic scheme of things like that of Shaftesbury and Pope. That is what almost happens. In spite of the fact that in his theological thought the poet is committed to the doctrine of man's depravity and that in *The Task* he refuses to bow to the Noble Savage cult, at least for the sake of an argument against slavery he is on the side of Shaftesbury and Pope rather than on that of Hobbes. According to Cowper, James Cook, the great and humane explorer, observed that

> Wherever he found man, to nature true,
> The rights of man were sacred in his view.
> [*Charity,* ll. 27-28.]

Nature is likely to be a troublesome word in eighteenth-century usage. Here, however, it is clear that *nature* is synonymous with "God's social plan" and the "various ties" through which men "might feel themselves allied to all the race." A little later in the same poem he speaks of a slave who has been taken away from his native land:

> Yes, to deep sadness sullenly resign'd,
> He feels his body's bondage in his mind;
> Puts off his *gen'rous nature;* and, to suit
> His manners with his fate, puts on the brute.
> [Ll. 151-54.][33]

Nature in this instance is merely disposition. Both statements are far from the conclusion at which Cowper arrives in *The Task:* "War and chase engross the savage whole" (I, l. 608). Here the position is identical with that of Hobbes. In *Charity,* however, Cowper conceives very highly

of the savage nature. It should be remembered that in
Truth (ll. 515 ff.) the poet refused to let his Calvinism influence him to feel that the heathen were damned "for
ignorance of what they could not know." In the same poem
Cowper insisted that God is the source of all virtue, whether
it be found among Christians or heathens. Of those denied
the light of Christian truth he asserts, "Their judge was *conscience,* and her rule their law" (l. 535). Then, to follow
out the logical consequences, the savage in his natural state
is not to be conceived of as a brute, but as a creature en-
dowed by a benevolent God with a sure guide capable of
leading him to good—a good that is independent of Evangelical theology! This is not Shaftesbury, it is true; but it
is not far from the *Essay on Man.* In this way of thinking
the Negro plainly becomes a Noble Savage.

Cowper was certainly not consciously following the reasoning of the *Essay on Man.* We have already seen how he
attacked the ethics of the poem. The immediate reason for
his following such a course of reasoning was the necessity
for meeting the argument of the anti-abolitionists that in
their natural state Negroes are fierce and bloodthirsty, devouring each other. He intended to use essentially the same
argument as that of Wesley and Raynal for the mildness
and tractability of the Negro.

Cook, whose voyages Cowper read with great interest,
is held up as the ideal humanitarian explorer:

> He sooth'd with gifts, and greeted with a smile,
> The simple natives of the new found isle;
>
> .   .   .   .
>
> Nor would endure that any should controul
> His free-born brethren of the southern pole.
>
> [*Charity,* ll. 29 ff.]

In contrast is, of course, Cortez,[34] long a stock villain,
"odious for a world enslaved." The inhumanity of Spain's

explorers is to be explained by Spain's mad thirst for gold. But Spain's payment for her folly was inevitable. God, the defender of the oppressed, "stood not, though he seem'd to stand, aloof." "Art thou too fall'n, Iberia?" the poet exclaims. If the ancient Incas could rise again, they might well taunt once-proud Spain:

> Thy pomp is in the grave, thy glory laid
> Low in the pits thine avarice has made!
> We come with joy from our eternal rest,
> To see th' oppressor in his turn oppress'd. [Ll. 71-74.]

The moral application is simple. Gold gained from the exploitation of the weak can but become "canker'd spoil" to corrode the state and bring its downfall. Thus God works his vengeance. The great wealth that the slave trade has brought to England, the poet is saying by implication, is definitely a menace to the nation.

Next, Cowper proceeds to a revision of the Whig glorification of commerce. "Estimate" Brown wrote:

If we see Commerce in it's first stages, we shall see that it supplies mutual Necessities, prevents mutual Wants, extends mutual Knowledge, eradicates mutual Prejudice, and spreads mutual Humanity. If we view it in it's middle and more advanced period, we shall see it provides Conveniences, increaseth Numbers, coins Money, gives Birth to Arts and Sciences, creates equal Laws, diffuses general Plenty and general Happiness. If we view it in it's third and highest Stage, we shall see it change it's Nature and Effects. It brings in Superfluity and vast Wealth; begets Avarice, gross Luxury, or effeminate Refinement among the higher Ranks, together with general Loss of Principle.[35]

Cowper follows the essential ideas of Brown rather closely, adding a Christian note. Commerce, says the poet, proceeding as all good things from God, was designed "t' associate all the branches of mankind." Since "each climate needs what other climes produce," through trade, "the golden girdle of the globe," each can become complementary to every other one. The result should be "genial intercourse, and mutual aid." This is Brown's first stage. Then comes "ingenious Art" who

> Steps forth to fashion and refine the race;
> Not only fills necessity's demand,
> But overcharges her capacious hand.
>
> [*Charity*, ll. 98-100.]

Furthermore,

> art thrives most
> Where commerce has enrich'd the busy coast;
> He catches all improvements in his flight,
> Spreads foreign wonders in his country's sight,
> Imports what others have invented well,
> And stirs his own to match them, or excel. [Ll. 113-18.]

Through this reciprocation "alternately the nations learn and teach." Commerce, therefore, may bring about a universal brotherhood of man, and a feeling by everyone of "an union with the vast terraqueous whole." This corresponds to Brown's second stage. The third stage Cowper had already treated in the passage dealing with Spain's avarice and luxury, bred by a vast ill-gotten wealth.

Cowper admits the broad humanitarian possibilities of England's commerce, although unlike the Whig panegyrists he does not make application of the benefits of commerce to anything so specific as the woolen industry. He is more concerned with the possibilities of knitting "th' unsocial climates into one," of carrying succor to "wasted regions," of replacing "the smile of opulence in sorrow's face," and of carrying the light of Christian truth to the heathen. However, this idealistic view has been built up very carefully to give emphasis to his attack upon the very dark blot on England's commerce—that "most degrading of all ills," slavery:

But, ah! what wish can prosper, or what pray'r,
For merchants, rich in cargoes of despair,
Who drive a loathsome traffic, gage, and span,
And buy, the muscles and the bones of man? [Ll. 137-40.]

The poet sees "the sable warrior" forced from his native shore and "frantic with regret of her he loves." Here, of course, is the same sort of theatricality that Mrs. Behn, Southerne, Shenstone, and Thomas Day had used for similar situations. Cowper can no more bring himself to accept the idea that submission in regard to slavery is "more than half a cure for sorrow" than he can when he contemplates the horrors of the Bastile. Slavery, which "virtue dreads . . . as her grave," he cannot regard as a visitation of Providence, for

Nature imprints upon whate'er we see
That has a heart and life in it—Be free! [Ll. 169-70.]

This observation from nature applies to both animal and human life. The poet, therefore, comes to the conclusion that a slave not only has a *right* to revolt against his masters but that he *should* revolt: "Patience itself is meanness in a slave." For the expression of this inflammatory sentiment, Cowper has no deprecatory footnote. Few had dared to speak out more boldly.

Locke and others had justified slavery on a basis of expediency; not so with Cowper—

Canst thou, and honour'd with a Christian name,
Buy what is woman-born, and feel no shame?
Trade in the blood of innocence, and plead
Expedience as a warrant for the deed? [Ll. 180-83.]

If so, by the same token you must justify the marauding wolf who lays waste your sheepfold, and the ruffian who, finding it "inconvenient to be poor," helps himself to your household goods. There is certainly no logical soundness,

Cowper argues, in the assertion that man makes man his prey "because he *must*."

But if, for the sake of argument, we assume that slavery may be justified as a lawful continuance of warfare between the conqueror and the captive,

> Still there is room for pity to abate,
> And soothe, the sorrows of so sad a state. [Ll. 198-99.]

At this point the intrusion of Cowper's religious thinking may seem to have the effect of tempering the expression of his humanitarian passion. It is inevitable in the 1782 volume that the poet should reach a consideration of the greater importance of the bondage of the soul than the bondage of the body. The logical conclusion of such an emphasis might be a feeling that, in spite of all the talk about freeing slaves, one should rather convert the slaves and leave their physical freedom in the hands of God, who is quite capable of bringing about their deliverance when he sees fit:

> Remember, heav'n has an avenging rod—
> To smite the poor is treason against God.   [Ll. 216-17.]

To say that Cowper even teeters on the edge of such a conclusion is to misunderstand his thought. As I have said before, we shall have to avoid applying the same logic to the poet's political and religious thinking. What Cowper is trying to say is clear: Man owes to the Negro something vastly more than physical freedom—freedom from the bondage of ignorance and sin. It is not necessary to wait until physical freedom has been attained for the Negro to give him the other kind of liberty. When the slave is doubly freed, he will sigh no more for Africa, but will realize that "serving a benefactor, I am free."

We cannot overestimate the importance of the Methodist and Evangelical insistence upon the worth of the Negro's soul as a motive force in bringing about the final abolition of slavery. It should be remembered that in the eighteenth century the argument as to whether a Negro had a soul at all was not a closed one. A sentimental regard for the Noble Savage was not alone a potent enough force to bring about freedom for the slaves. One can readily see how much more potent for Cowper's large audience was the poet's assertion

> That souls have no discriminating hue,
> Alike important in their Maker's view;
> That none are free from blemish since the fall,
> That love divine has paid one price for all.

> [Ll. 202-205.]

§ 3

We have mentioned the way in which Cowper flirted with primitivism in *Charity*. It is interesting to observe his attitude toward the Noble Savage in *The Task*, especially in regard to its bearing on his anti-slavery sentiment.

Few people in the century were more interested in the popular volumes of travel and discovery than was the land-locked poet of Olney. To him they provided an exciting and wonderful escape from his melancholia and from the restricted bounds of his little village. To William Unwin he wrote in August, 1784:

Once more, by the aid of Lord Dartmouth, I find myself a voyager in the Pacific Ocean. In our last night's lecture [Cowper read aloud to Mrs. Unwin and Lady Austen] we were made acquainted with the island of Hapaee, where we had never been before. The French and Italians, it seems, have but little cause to plume themselves on account of their achievements in the dancing way; and we may hereafter, without much repining it, acknowledge their superiority in the art. . . . How wonderful, that without any intercourse with a politer world, and having no proficiency in any other accomplishment, they should in this, however, have made themselves such adepts. . . .[36]

The reference here is to Captain Cook's *A Voyage to the Pacific Ocean* (1784), which Cowper borrowed from his noble friend shortly after its publication. In fact, in 1783 and 1784 the poet kept Lord Dartmouth, John Newton, Joseph Hill, and other friends fairly busy supplying his demands for travel books. But his interest in this sort of literature dates from much earlier. He read both Cook's *A Voyage toward the South Pole* and Forster's two volumes on the same voyage shortly after their publication in 1777. He also gives evidence of having read Dr. John Hawkesworth's *A New Voyage Round the World* (1773), a compilation of the journals of Cook, Joseph Banks, and Dr. Solander, all of whom were on Cook's first voyage. He, moreover, read with interest such a book as Henry Swinburne's *Travels through Spain* (1779). Having read the most important volumes of voyages in the Pacific, Cowper had at hand most of the current literature on the South Sea Islands. Professor Fairchild has shown how Hawkesworth, the stay-at-home who compiled the material of Cook and his coadjutors, injected into his work an attitude toward the South Sea Islanders quite different from that of Cook.[37] Hawkesworth's embroidery on his material had a decided tendency to idealize the savage, whereas Cook was as matter of fact in his depiction of savage life as he was humane in dealing with the savages. Cook sees both good and bad in the natives, without giving way to anything like enthusiasm for their "natural virtues."

The statement from Cowper's letter about the adeptness of the Hapaee Islanders may seem to betray an enthusiasm for savage life. The rest of the letter, however, shows that the poet has adopted the cool common-sense attitude of Cook. There are, he observes, striking differences in the attainments of the natives. Some are refined, and some are as rude "as we naturally expect to find a people who have never had any communication with the northern hemisphere." Without idealizing savage life, Cowper, like Cook, is able to see wherein the South Sea Islanders may excel their civilized brothers. As we have seen, he may emphasize the superiority of the savage when he is defending the under-dog. In discussing with Newton the heroism of a Sandwich Islander who, in sacrificing himself to a dead friend, had been mercilessly butchered by our "Christian seamen and mariners," Cowper could arrive at such a statement as: "Proofs of such prowess, I believe, are seldom exhibited by a people who have attained to a high degree of civilization. Refinement and profligacy of principle are too nearly allied to admit of anything so noble. . . . To the production of such heroism undebauched nature herself is equal."[38] But this is rather an attack upon debauched civilization than a glori-fication of undebauched nature, and is no argument that Cowper belongs to the ranks of the primitivists.

To the subject of savage life Cowper comes in the first book of *The Task*. Here he is talking of the blessings of country life,

> Where man, by nature fierce, has laid aside
> His fierceness, having learnt, though slow to learn
> The manners, and the arts of civil life.   [Ll. 594-96.]

It is in the country that "virtue thrives as in her proper soil." The poet's assertion that man is "by nature fierce" prepares the reader for the statements that in "barb'rous climes . . . violence prevails and strength is lord of all" and "War and the chase engross the savage whole." With a quick march we have gone all the way back to Hobbes. The Golden Age of which Pope and many others wrote is demolished. "The state of nature was the reign of God," declared Pope:

> Man walked with beast, joint tenant of the shade;
> The same his table, and the same his bed;
> No murder clothed him, and no murder fed.
> In the same temple, the resounding wood,
> All vocal beings hymned their equal God.
>   [*Essay on Man,* III, ll. 152-56.]

Cowper's statement is a direct refutation of Pope's position:

> War follow'd for revenge, or to supplant
> The envied tenants of some happier spot,
> The chase for sustenance, precarious trust!
>
> [*Task*, I, ll. 609-11.]

He continues concerning the savage:

> His hard condition with severe constraint
> Binds all his faculties, forbids all growth
> Of wisdom, proves a school in which he learns
> Sly circumvention, unrelenting hate,
> Mean self-attachment, and scarce aught beside.
>
> [Ll. 612-16.]

He then turns specifically to the "favour'd isles so lately found," the South Sea Islands. Here Cowper can see possibilities of "but little virtue." Cook had found the license of the Tahitians a matter of distress, and had made many observations of their shameless sexual relationships.[39] Of this Cowper was doubtless thinking when he wrote that the natives in their luxurious ease "lose in morals what they gain in manners." Such people he can but pity. And especially does his pity go out to Omai, one of the most interesting figures in the eighteenth-century scene.[40]

This Noble Savage, brought from the Society Islands to England by Captain Furneaux in 1774, became the center of interest in London and was lionized by the great and near-great. Although Cook did not consider him to be of the finest strain of his own islands, Omai proved remarkably adept at attaining a certain sort of polish. Even Dr. Johnson, far from being a primitivist, was impressed by his manners—which, however, he attributed not to instinct but to his having associated with "genteel company." He was painted by Reynolds and other famous artists, his favor was sought by high-ranking ladies, and George III was amused at being addressed by him as "King Tosh." On his last voyage (1776-1779) Cook took Omai home. The native seemed delighted to return. Loaded with a treasure largely consisting of red feathers, he hoped to improve his social standing in the islands. Cook reports that Omai was not successful in this attempt and that he allowed himself to fall into bad ways through association with evil companions. He is reported to have died about 1780.

In "The Sofa" Cowper pictures Omai, after having found again his "cocoas and bananas, palms and yams," not as enjoying the much-praised life of his "superior" people, but as longing for the civilization that he has left in England and looking sadly upon the "forlorn and abject state" of his own country. Indeed, the poet contends,

> true worth and virtue in the mild
> And genial soil of cultivated life
> Thrive most.   [Ll. 678-80.]

It is true that Cowper hastens to add, "yet not in cities oft." But that is another story.

In the course of the Omai digression, Cowper again attacks the lack of humanitarian aims in Britain's commerce and imperialism:

> Doing good,
> Disinterested good, is not our trade.
> We travel far, 'tis true, but not for nought;
> And must be brib'd, to compass earth again,
> By other hopes and richer fruits than your's.
>   [Ll. 673-77.]⁴¹

The poet returns to the subject of slavery at the opening of the second book of *The Task*. After the famous opening lines, Cowper confesses soul-sickness brought on by his observation that "the nat'ral bond of brotherhood is sever'd."

> [Man] finds his fellow guilty of a skin
> Not colour'd like his own; and, having pow'r
> T' enforce the wrong, for such a worthy cause
> Dooms and devotes him as his lawful prey. [Ll. 12-15.]

Slavery, of course, is not the only evidence of the severing of the bond. Nations are afflicted with narrow nationalism— even "lands intersected by a narrow frith abhor each other." But slavery is still "nature's broadest, foulest blot." The fact that one human being inflicts on another punishment that mercy would forbid to be inflicted on a beast should make man blush and hang his head. The poet then bursts into a passage of typical righteous indignation:

> I would not have a slave to till my ground,
> To carry me, to fan me while I sleep,
> And tremble when I wake, for all the wealth,
> That sinews bought and sold have ever earn'd.
>
> [Ll. 29-32.]

The triumphant efforts of Granville Sharp in the Somerset case had enabled the abolitionists to take up the cry voiced by Cowper: "We have no slaves at home.—Then why abroad?" This idea the poet develops in a passage that must have thrilled those whose patriotism and abolitionist zeal were as closely linked as his own:

> Slaves cannot breathe in England; if their lungs
> Receive our air, that moment they are free;
> They touch our country, and their shackles fall.
> That's noble, and bespeaks a nation proud
> And jealous of the blessing. Spread it then,
> And let it circulate through ev'ry vein
> Of all your empire; that where Britain's pow'r
> Is felt, mankind may feel her mercy too.   [Ll. 40-47.]

The number of lines devoted to slavery in *The Task* is not large. Cowper does not, as in *Charity,* devote himself to answering arguments in favor of the institution. The religious aspects of the question are kept well in the background. There is no argument that the Negro as a Noble Savage should not be subjected to slavery because his state of living may be superior to that of England. Rather is the converse true. The superiority of England's civilization, fostering a freedom of which the nation may be justly proud, should be proved by the extension of her freedom to the whole empire, and even to the whole world. Then British power and British freedom could march hand in hand to a glorious future. To abolitionist sentiment Cowper here gives a dignity and loftiness of poetic expression rarely attained elsewhere.

§ 4

After completing *The Task* in 1784 Cowper, casting about for another project to occupy his energies, decided upon his long-cherished idea of translating Homer. As his letters will show, the translation for a time became so all-engrossing that the affairs of the outside world were pushed out of his immediate range of vision. The fourth mental derangement from January to June, 1787, naturally emphasized his isolation from public affairs. In the meantime, the abolitionists were by no means idle. In May, 1787, the Committee for Abolition was formed and a program of active propaganda was entered upon. Between May, 1787, and the middle of July, 1788, the Committee, according to Clarkson, distributed 51,432 pamphlets or books.[42] That poetry was early looked upon as an effective means of raising revenue for the cause and of disseminating propaganda is shown by the Committee's acceptance, in the month of its foundation, of "the profits" from "The Wrongs of Africa," a poem by a Mr. Roscoe of Liverpool.

Early in 1788 Miss Hannah More—poet, novelist, and litterateur extraordinary to the Evangelicals—wrote *The Slave Trade,* a fairly lengthy propaganda poem that bears evidence of the hastiness of execution admitted by the poet. The piece of verse is interesting not only as a typical anti-slavery poem of the period but as evidence of the complete way in which Cowper had already covered the field.

A brief glance at Miss More's poem[43] will demonstrate the fact. The poet begins with a conventional invocation to Liberty, which she follows with an attempt to contrast liberty and license. There then follows an invocation to Southerne, who was able to evoke humanitarian sentiments in behalf of the Africans. Miss More contends, however, that she will not sing, as Southerne did, of "fictitious woes" but of real woes. As proof for her argument, she borrows from Ramsay's *Essay on the Treatment of African Slaves* the gory tale of Quashi, who, rather than suffer punishment from a beloved master, pins him down in a wrestling match, dexterously manages to cut his own throat, and lets his dead body fall over that of his master. She describes graphically the horrors of the slave trade and appeals to those who love British freedom to think what exile means. A great admirer of Cowper, Miss More does not hesitate to echo his sentiments. Like Cowper, she sees in slavery the degeneration of commerce. She decries the common argument that the Negro's sense of feeling is callous and obtuse. To the savage she gives the assurance that "they are not Christians who infest thy shore" and admonishes them to "depend on God" for deliverance. The rest of this particular passage might have come from Cowper's *Truth:*

> On Him, who made thee what thou art depend;
> He who withholds the means, accepts the end.
> Thy mental night thy savior will not blame;
> He died for those who never heard his name.
> Not *thine* the reckoning dire of light abus'd,
> Knowledge disgrac'd, and Liberty misus'd;
> On *thee* no awful judge incens'd shall sit
> For parts perverted, and dishonour'd wit.
> Where ignorance may be found the safest plea,
> How many learn'd and wise shall envy thee.[44]

The poet then turns on the "White Savage" with the assurance that "God shall vindicate his broken laws." She praises

the humane explorer Cook, and asserts that if all explorers
had been like him,

> Then bless'd Philanthropy! thy social hands,
> Had link'd dissever'd worlds in brother's bands.

After praising Penn and the Quakers for their attitude toward slavery, Miss More calls on Britain to "redeem our
fame." Again like Cowper she inveighs against the "proud
philosophy" that denies to the Negro race a common share
in the powers of our joint humanity, and she argues against
the inconsistency of slavery in a land of liberty.

About the time of the appearance of Miss More's poem,
Cowper's friend, John Newton, entered the field as propagandist with his *Thoughts Upon the African Slave Trade.*
Few people have been better qualified than Newton to serve
the abolitionist cause. Newton's autobiography is an un-
deservedly neglected volume. Written in a series of letters
to the Reverend Mr. Haweis, it reads in parts like pages
from *Captain Singleton, Roderick Random,* and even
Anthony Adverse. The son of a commander in Mediterranean merchant service, Newton first went to sea as a child
on the ships of his father. As a youth he was impressed
into naval service. He then became in turn a sailor on a
slave vessel and a servant to a slave trader on the Plantane
Islands. Here he was strangely persecuted by the black wife
of the slaver. By another master he was treated more kindly
and was given a share in the business. All this time he
was living what he later considered to be an extremely irreligious life. But even after his conversion from his evil
ways, he became captain of a slaving vessel. "During the
time I was engaged in the slave trade," he wrote in the autobiography, "I never had the least scruple as to its lawfulness.
I was upon the whole satisfied with it as the appointment
Providence had worked out for me." While he was captain
of the slaving vessel, he prided himself upon repressing

swearing and profligacy and upon reading the liturgy on Sundays with the crew. He had many adventures and his life was "providentially" saved on occasions too numerous to cite. He had such a passion for self-improvement that he succeeded in educating himself even in the midst of a crowded life. He mastered the first six books of Euclid in Africa, and later taught himself Latin, learning Horace by heart. His tale of adventure is not even without the delicate thread of a love story.

Newton gave up the sea on account of his health. He became surveyor of tides at Liverpool, where, falling under the influence of Whitefield, he decided to take holy orders. When he first made application for orders, he was refused; but through the efforts of Lord Dartmouth he was later accepted. This truly remarkable man became one of the founders of Evangelicalism.

Newton was rector of Olney when Cowper and the Unwins moved there in 1767. He remained the poet's constant companion and spiritual adviser, for better or for worse, until his removal to London in 1780. Just what influence Newton's experience had on Cowper's attitude toward slavery is difficult to ascertain. It is reasonable to believe that Newton probably recounted to the poet some of the horrible details of the trade. It should be remembered, however, that before he went to London Newton was more concerned with fighting the battle of Evangelicalism than with freeing poor Africans. The autobiography certainly could not have been used as an abolitionist pamphlet. It does not delineate the horrors of the traffic and it contains no sweeping condemnation of slavery. Plainly Newton's chief interest was in the spiritual rather than in the humanitarian aspects of his past life. But when he took over the London parishes that the philanthropist, John Thornton, had obtained for him, he soon became associated with such leaders of the abolitionist cause as Clarkson, the Phillipses, Henry Thornton, and Wilberforce.

Newton's *Thoughts Upon the African Slave Trade* is his most important contribution to abolitionist propaganda. It possesses restraint and dignity, and yet at times shows the author's power to depict luridly the horrors of the trade. In originality, however, it is a little disappointing. At times Newton resorts to hearsay stories to the exclusion of his own experiences.

While Miss More and Newton were engaged in their anti-slavery efforts, it occurred to Lady Hesketh that Cowper, who had so far given the most important poetic expression of the century to abolitionist sentiment, should write a poem on slavery. On February 16, 1788, Cowper wrote to his cousin that he had already turned over such a subject in his mind and had half decided to desert Homer for the undertaking; however, he had happened to see an announcement of the forthcoming publication of Miss More's *The Slave Trade* and had dropped his plans. He felt that Miss More, who had "more nerve and energy both in her thoughts and language than half the he-rhymers in the kingdom," could handle the subject sufficiently well. "It occurred to me likewise," he wrote, "that I have already borne my testimony in favour of my black brethren; and that I was one of the earliest, if not the first, of those who have in the present day expressed their detestation of the diabolical traffic in question." He has no doubt, he continues, that some measures will now be taken to alleviate the miseries of the slaves, especially since the nation has been presented the facts and since it is "impossible also to allege an argument in behalf of man-merchandise, that can deserve a hearing."[45] This is a remarkably lukewarm letter for the author of the stirring anti-slavery lines in *Charity* and *The Task*. Cowper says that he would have embarked upon an anti-slavery poem "could I have allowed myself to desert Homer for so long a time as it would have caused me to do them justice"! Taken merely on the surface this statement would suggest a withdrawal from the earlier abolitionist zeal. But we must go deeper. Cowper had not long recovered from the derangement of 1787, and it was extremely painful for him to contemplate suffering. He clings to Homer as a means of escape from his devouring thoughts. He, of course, does not think that Homer is more important than the freedom of the slaves.

The true state of his mind may be seen in a letter written to Newton three days after the one to Lady Hesketh (February 19, 1788). Cowper is concerned about the way in which divine justice may be vindicated in the case of the Negro. A still more puzzling problem—already treated in *Truth*—is the fate of the thousands that have died. The only answer is that God is sovereign and that things not understandable in earthly terms will be understandable in their eternal aspect. That all will be explained hereafter, says the poet, might once have been a cheering thought:

> But in the school of affliction I have learned to cavil and to question; and finding myself in my own case reduced frequently to the necessity of accounting for my own lot by the means of an uncontrollable sovereignty which gives no account of its matters, am apt to discover, what appears to me, tremendous effects of the same sovereignty in the case of others.[46]

The anti-slavery ballads are proof that Cowper could desert Homer for a humanitarian cause.

Cowper's choice of the ballad form for the poems is easily understandable. It is not difficult to see that he felt himself quite incapable of launching into a lengthy poem on the subject. "Boadicea," "The Loss of the Royal George," and "John Gilpin" all attest the ease with which Cowper handled the ballad form. Moreover, he had written "halfpenny" ballads in his Temple days—none of which has come down to us.

The broadside ballad, an early offspring of the invention of printing, developed a lusty popularity in the Elizabethan period. Becoming sophisticated in the eighteenth century, the ballad was applied to politics and satire.[47] Beginning with reflections on the Court or the government (without personal application), the ballads became direct instruments for the expression of party sentiment, and were assumed for comment on current events and for personal satire. The political ballad flourished in the Walpole era, almost every issue of the administration being reflected in ballad verse. In the early part of the century ballads were sold by hawkers and sung by ballad-singers on street corners. Not only were they sung in the streets but in other places of public resort, such as taverns and coffee houses, at bonfires and electioneering meetings. They were also sung in fashionable households, and even served to divert the Court. At the end of the century, much of the popularity of the political ballad had been lost, but the medium still proved to be of some effectiveness in the anti-slavery cause.

The latest complete edition of Cowper's poems—the Oxford edition, of which Sir Humphrey S. Milford is editor—lists and dates the anti-slavery ballads as follows:

1. "The Negro's Complaint"—Feb. (?) 1788.
2. "The Morning Dream"—March (?) 1788.
3. "Sweet Meat"—Early in 1788.
4. "Pity for Poor Africans"—Early in 1788.[48]

"Epigram" is undated and is included with the group solely on the basis of similar subject matter. If one examines the letters, one will immediately discover one objection to Sir Humphrey's dating. In a letter to Lady Hesketh on March 12, 1788,[49] Cowper, though mentioning having read Miss More's "Slavery" (sic) and Newton's anti-slavery tractate, makes no mention of the ballads. Since Lady Hesketh first suggested to Cowper that he write an anti-slavery poem, it is reasonable to believe that, had he written one or more of the ballads at the time, he would have mentioned the fact. It, therefore, seems almost certain that none of the ballads was written before March 12.

On March 17 Cowper wrote to Newton concerning a ballad that he had composed:

An application from a lady, and backed by you, could not be less than irresistible; that lady, too, a daughter of Mr. Thornton's. . . . With modern tunes I am unacquainted, and have therefore accommodated my verse to an old one; not so old, however, but that there will be songsters found old enough to remember it. The song is an admirable one for which it was made, and, though political, nearly, if not quite, as serious as mine. On such a subject as I had before me, it seems impossible not to be serious. I shall be happy if it meet with your and Lady Balgonie's approval.[50]

A request from Newton and Lady Balgonie, then, seems to be the real explanation of Cowper's writing the ballads. The request evidently was specifically for a ballad; and Cowper, who had found the idea of writing a longer poem on slavery unacceptable, doubtless found in the new suggestion a way to perform his duty without overtaxing his mind. Newton's connection with the Committee for Abolition has already been mentioned. Lady Balgonie (afterward the Countess of Leven and Melville) seems to have supported her brother, Henry Thornton, in his very zealous work for the cause. Cowper, then, had written before March 17 one ballad, which he had adapted to a political ballad tune.

In an undated letter to his cousin, General Cowper, the poet wrote:

When the condition of our negroes in the islands was first presented to me as a subject for songs, I felt myself not at all allured to the undertaking: it seemed to offer only images of horror, which could by no means be accommodated to the style of that sort of composition. But having a desire to comply, if possible, with the request made to me, after turning the matter over in my mind as many ways as I could, I, at last, as I told you, produced three, and that which appears to myself the best of those three, I have sent you. Of the other two, one is serious—in a strain of thought perhaps rather too serious, and I could not help it. The other, of which the slave-trader is himself the subject, is somewhat ludicrous.[51]

In his edition of Cowper's correspondence, Wright places this letter between March 12 and 17; however, since it plainly refers to the request of Newton and Lady Balgonie (Lady Hesketh did not suggest *songs*), it must at least be dated on or after March 17. More will be said about the date a little later. The "somewhat ludicrous poem" of which "the slave-trader is himself the subject" is plainly "Sweet Meat," which may therefore be definitely placed among the first of the poems in composition. The problem of what poem is referred to in the letter to Newton and what poem was sent to General Cowper remains.

On March 19 Cowper sent his friend Bagot "The Morning Dream" and ten days later he mentions in a letter to Samuel Rose "The Negro's Complaint," "Morning Dream," and "Sweet Meat." He classifies the first two as "serious." On March 31 he mentions to Lady Hesketh that "Morning Dream" is to be sung to the tune of "Tweedside." On April 14[52] he sent "The Negro's Complaint" to General Cowper.

The poem written at the request of Newton and Lady Balgonie was evidently not "Morning Dream," which was to be set to the tune of the Scottish sentimental ballad "Tweedside," and not to a political ballad tune. The poem sent to General Cowper was certainly not "The Negro's Complaint," for it was sent later. "The Negro's Complaint" seems most likely to have been composed first. The poem sent to General Cowper was evidently "Morning Dream," and the two unsent poems were "Sweet Meat" and "The Negro's Complaint," which at the time Cowper felt to be "too serious." We can, therefore, accept Sir Humphrey Milford's order for the first three poems. The most acceptable dating, however, is as follows:

"The Negro's Complaint"—March 12-17, 1788.
"The Morning Dream"—March 17-19, 1788.
"Sweet Meat"—March 17-19, 1788.

The letter to General Cowper should very probably be dated March 19. The two days between March 17 and 19 would allow for the writing of two ballads; and it would seem likely that it might have occurred to Cowper to send General Cowper "The Morning Dream" on the same day on which he sent it to Bagot.[53]

On March 29 Cowper wrote to Rose in a letter already mentioned:

If you hear ballads sung in the streets on the hardships of negroes in the islands, they are probably mine. I was lately applied to for assistance in that way by a society of gentlemen, enlisted in that laudable service. . . . The subject, as a subject for song, did not strike me much, but the application was from a quarter that might command me, and the occasion itself . . . offered pleas that were irresistible.

The "society of gentlemen" is, of course, the Committee for Abolition, but there is no reason to believe that the Committee had made at the time any kind of formal request to Cowper for ballads. For the "quarter that might command me" we may read Newton. Clarkson, our authority on the functioning of the Committee, gives the following account of the dissemination of "The Negro's Complaint":

This little piece was presented in manuscript to some of his [Cowper's] friends in London; and these, conceiving it to contain a powerful appeal in behalf of the injured Africans, joined in printing it. Having ordered it on the finest hot-pressed paper, and folded it up in a small and neat form, they gave it the printed title of "A Subject for Conversation at the Tea-Table." After this they sent many thousand copies of it in franks into the country. From one it spread to another, till it travelled almost over the whole island. Falling at length into the hands of the musician, it was set to music; and thus found its way into the streets, both of the metropolis and of the country where it was sung as a ballad. . . .[54]

It was not published in any other form until December, 1793, when it appeared in the *Gentleman's Magazine* as "The Complaint, By Mr. Cowper." "The Morning Dream" had appeared in the same magazine in November, 1788.[55]

Cowper's feeling of futility in his efforts is revealed in a letter of April 19, 1788, to Newton. "I fear that neither you nor I," he wrote, "with all our reasoning and rhiming [*sic*] shall effect much good in this matter." The poet has lost faith in the government, which he believes will act only to save its face. Laws will probably be enacted for the humane treatment of Negroes, he feels, but they will not be enforced. Newspapers have reported that planters have passed ordinances to protect lives and limbs from wanton cruelty; but this action, Cowper believes, is only an artifice to avert the impending storm of abolitionist sentiment.

The first three ballads undoubtedly proved the desirability of Cowper as a propagandist for the abolitionist cause, for sometime at the end of May or the first of June, James Phillips, a Quaker bookseller and an original member of the Committee, made, presumably through Newton, a request for an anti-slavery poem. On June 5 Cowper wrote Newton asking him to beg Phillips to release him from the task. Almost two weeks later Cowper wrote to Walter Bagot:

Slavery, and especially negro slavery, because the cruellest, is an odious and disgusting subject. Twice or thrice I have been assailed with entreaties to write a poem on that theme. But besides that it would be in some sort treason against Homer to abandon him for other matter, I felt myself so much hurt in my spirits the moment I entered on the contemplation of it, that I have at last determined absolutely to have nothing more to do with it . . . when man is active to disturb, there is such meanness in the design, and such cruelty in the execution, that I both hate and despise the whole operation, and feel it a degradation of poetry to employ her in the description of it. I hope also that the generality of my countrymen have more generosity in their nature than to want a fiddle of verse to go before them in the performance of an act to which they are invited by the loudest calls of humanity.[56]

This renunciation of propagandist poetry, strong though it may seem, does not have to be taken as final. On June 23 Cowper wrote to Lady Hesketh to announce that the Newtons would arrive in Olney three weeks thence. In the letter he expresses enthusiasm for Pitt on account of his support of Sir William Dolben's bill to increase the comfort of slaves in British ships. "Mr. Pitt," wrote the poet, "has charmed me by the noble manner in which he has taken up the business of the slave trade." The letter also provides evidence that Phillips did not consider the matter of the anti-slavery poem entirely closed. Cowper writes in a postscript that Phillips is sending him by Newton one of the famous cameos then being distributed by Wedgwood in the interest of the abolitionist cause. His pleasure is evident: "I understand that they [the cameos] are not purchasable, which makes it all the more valuable. Wedgwood refused to sell them, affirming that it should never be said of him that he sold a negro." On June 24 he wrote Newton, again expressing enthusiasm for Pitt and the Dolben act. Three days later he wrote to Lady Hesketh that Mr. Rose had seen his ballads, "but not in print": "Where he met with them, I know not. Mr. Bull begged hard for leave to print them at Newport Pagnall, and I refused, thinking it would be wrong to anticipate the nobility, gentry, and others, at whose pressing instance I composed them."[57]

A victory for the abolitionists, however small, was certainly an argument against the futility of the fight; and there is evidence now of Cowper's taking some pride in the ballads done at the behest of "the nobility, gentry, and others." The statement in the letter to Bagot should not, therefore, be construed as precluding the possibility of the composition of "Pity for Poor Africans" after the date of the letter. The only positive evidence for the dating of the poem is its appearance in the *Northampton Mercury* on August 9, 1788. If the ballad had been written, however, when the other three ballads were, it seems almost certain that it would have been mentioned. It seems unlikely that Cowper should have written the poem in the brief period in which the futility of his anti-slavery efforts was uppermost in his mind. There is at least nothing to disprove an assumption that the poem was written at the end of July or even in the first week in August—after the Newtons had come, bringing the cameo from Phillips and the latest news of the abolitionist fight.

The anti-slavery ballads naturally do not represent the poet's best efforts. They do not approach the exquisite perfection of Blake's "The Little Black Boy," written only a little later; but their artistry is not entirely pedestrian. In parts one may feel some of the fine movement of "Boadicea" and "The Loss of the Royal George."

"The Negro's Complaint" is in the form of a monologue. The speaker, a slave, asserts that though his body is enslaved, his mind cannot be; hence, he asks by what right England has made him a slave. He reminds the white man that

Skins may differ, but affection
Dwells in white and black the same.

He next exhorts iron-hearted masters to remember, when
they are enjoying the sweets of the cane, how the backs of
slaves have smarted, and calls upon the same masters to act
as the God he has been told about would have them act.
The fact that God does not approve of slavery, he points
out, is evidenced by the tornadoes that have demolished
colonial settlements.[58] He further asserts that the people
who have enslaved the blacks are not themselves free, for
they are slaves of gold. Finally, he calls upon the whites to
prove their own human feelings "ere you question ours."

"The Morning Dream" is a dream-vision poem. The
poet sees in the steerage of a boat the Goddess of Liberty,
who is on her way "to make Freemen of Slaves." Coming
to a "slave-cultur'd island," the Goddess, in a manner somewhat Spenserian, encounters the demon Oppression and con-
quers him. To the poet this dream presages Britain's freeing her slaves.

In the first part of "Pity for Poor Africans" Cowper
ironically restates the argument that, while slavery is admit-
tedly bad, it is necessary, first, because the production of
sugar and rum is dependent upon slave labor, and, second,
because even though the English should stop buying slaves,
the French, Dutch, and Danes, who were less humane in
the traffic, would continue. If foreigners gave up the trade,
the argument ran, the English might also; but as long as
other nations were getting wealthy in the trade, there was
no reason why England should not share—especially since
her refusal to share would only aid the other slave traders
and would not help the blacks. The second half answers
the argument with the story (which "I saw in print") of a
boy who, urged by his companions to assist in robbing a
poor neighbor's orchard, at first tried to dissuade his com-

panions, but who, seeing that his arguments had no effect
and that his refusal to assist would not benefit the neighbor,
joined in the robbery: "He shar'd the plunder, but pitied
the man."

So much for the "serious" poems. If "Sweet Meat Has
Sour Sauce, or, The Slave-Trader in the Dumps" is "somewhat ludicrous," one must admit that its humor is of a
decidedly grim sort. Again, the form is the monologue. A
slave-trader, feeling that abolition will soon come, offers for
sale his "stock"—i.e., his implements of torture:

> a curious assortment of dainty regales,
> To tickle the negroes with when the ship sails.

Included are chains, cat-o'-nine-tails, whips, padlocks, bolts,
and

> screws for the thumbs
> That squeeze them so lovingly till the blood comes.

One stanza vividly describes the horrible spectacle of slaves
in the hold of a boat "like sprats on a gridiron, scores in a
row." The slave-trader laments giving up an art that he
has very carefully mastered.

§ 5

Cowper began the *Odyssey* in September of 1788, and
again Homer excluded from his thinking most of the affairs
of the world. Almost three years later when he was working on the proof sheets of his translation, he wrote to Lady
Hesketh: "As for politics, I reck not, having no room in my
head but for the Slave Bill. That is lost; and all the rest is
a trifle."[59]

Here an apathetic attitude toward national affairs is evident, but there were spasmodic returns of interest. On
February 20, 1792, for example, Cowper wrote to Newton
in praise of the Sierra Leone Colony for liberated slaves,

which owed its origin to Henry Thornton and Zachary
Macaulay, the father of the historian. But it is a curious
circumstance that causes Cowper to take up his pen once
more in behalf of the abolitionists. A letter that the poet
wrote on April 16, 1792, tells an interesting story:

> I may say with Milton that I am fallen *on evil tongues and
> evil days,* being not only plundered of that which belongs to me,
> but being charged with that which does not. Thus it seems (and
> I have learned it from more quarters than one), that a report is,
> and has been sometime, current in this and neighboring counties,
> that though I have given myself the air of declaiming against the
> Slave Trade in the *Task,* I am in reality a friend to it; and last
> night I received a letter from Joe Rye [the Reverend Joseph
> Jekyll Rye, vicar of Dallington, near Northampton] to inform
> me that I have been traduced and calumniated on this account.
> Not knowing how I could better or more effectually refute the
> scandal, I have this morning sent a copy [of verses] to the North-
> ampton paper [*Northampton Mercury*], prefaced by a short letter
> to the printer, specifying the occasion. The verses are in honour
> of Mr. Wilberforce, and sufficiently expressive of my present
> sentiments on the subject.[60]

This is not the first time that Cowper had been a victim
of local gossip. (Gossip about him and Mrs. Unwin had
occasioned the pronouncement that the poor had little business to judge their betters.) In another letter on April 16[61]
Cowper explains to the Reverend Mr. Rye two bases for the
very unfair conclusion. It should be explained here that
after the abolitionists' failure of 1791 in Parliament the campaign against the use of West Indian sugar and rum, already
begun, was pursued with great vigor by anti-slavery sym-
pathizers. "We use East India sugar entirely," wrote Babington to Wilberforce, "and so do full two-thirds of the
friends of Abolition in Leicester."[62] Clarkson found as he
traveled over the country in 1792 that many had adopted
the ban.[63] But Newton regarded this movement as pre-

mature and likely to alienate moderate men; and Wilberforce decided against making it an essential part of the
campaign. Cowper had apparently adopted the attitude of
Newton. He wrote to Rye:

If any man concludes, because I allow myself the use of sugar
and rum, that therefore I am a friend to the *Slave Trade,* he concludes rashly, and does me great wrong; for the man lives not
who abhors it more than I do. My reasons for my own practice
are satisfactory to myself, and they whose practice is contrary
are, I suppose, satisfied with theirs. . . .

The scandalous report that had reached Rye evidently had
its basis in Cowper's refusal to give up rum and sugar; but
Cowper asserts that even before Mr. Rye's letter arrived there
had been a report that he had read a book on Africa in
which savages were depicted as devouring each other and
that he had decided upon slavery as being preferable to
cannibalism. The basis of this report, Cowper explains,
was the fact that his name did not appear in March, 1792,
on a petition of the people of Olney against the slave trade
to be presented to Parliament.[64] The whole matter could
be cleared up simply: "The single reason why I did not sign
the petition was, because I was never asked to do it; and
the reason why I was never asked was, because I am not a
parishioner of Olney." Cowper was then, of course, living
at Weston, where he had been since November, 1786.

Although the sentiments were doubtless sincere, the
"Sonnet to William Wilberforce, Esq." can be regarded as
little more than the poet's effort to vindicate himself. In a
letter to Lady Hesketh on April 26, 1792, Cowper speaks
of verses "which I found it necessary to publish in the last
Northampton Mercury, attested with my name at length, in
order to clear my character from a calumny that had spread
all over the country concerning my real opinion of the slave
trade." The poem was not without effect, for in the fol-

lowing week's issue of the *Mercury* a complimentary poem to Cowper by one S. M'Clellan appeared.

As further vindication of his sincerity in attacking slavery Cowper wrote and published in the *Mercury* of May 12, 1792, the following epigram:

> To purify their wine some people bleed
> A *lamb* into the barrel, and succeed;
> No nostrum, planters say, is half so good
> To make fine sugar, as a negro's blood.
> Now *lambs* and *negroes* both are harmless things,
> And thence perhaps this wond'rous virtue springs,
> 'Tis in the blood of innocence alone—
> Good cause why planters never try *their own*.

This gruesome bit of verse is Cowper's final poetic expression of anti-slavery sentiment.[65]

Thus, in one great humanitarian effort Cowper appears as an official and, on Clarkson's excellent authority, an effective propagandist. Besides the "great coadjutor" there were numerous other poets who lent their efforts to the fight in the century's last decades. James Hurdis, a minor poet who prided himself on his discipleship to Cowper, entreated his countrymen in 1788 to put away a guilt that would bring vengeance upon them. Mrs. Anna Laetitia Barbauld dedicated a poem to Wilberforce and gave him encouragement amid the first failures of abolitionist efforts in Parliament. Erasmus Darwin attacked slavery in *The Botanic Garden*. In 1794 Southey wrote some spirited sonnets and lyrics against the wicked institution; and in "Religious Musings" of the same year young Coleridge denounced the "hideous trade" that "loud-laughing packs his bales of human anguish." There were others. But above all these Cowper easily towers, for none wrote of slavery more forcefully and earnestly than he; and at the time none wielded an influence that was so wide.

Chapter IV

GOD'S LOVE FOR PAGAN LANDS

§ 1

THE FINAL VERSES of *Truth* present two of the most important theological questions of the century: Can virtue have any merit if it is not founded on Christianity? Are the thousands who are ignorant of Divine Grace to be eternally damned? The increasing consciousness of India's millions and of millions in the jungles of Africa, in the forests of America, and on the islands of the South Sea made the questions highly pertinent. Religious zealotry naturally led many to answer the questions with much finality and callously to postulate damnation for those who by divine accident (or, indeed, even by divine plan) have been denied the Light. Throughout *Truth* Cowper had preached on "Grace" as opposed to "works" and had made a rather thorough castigation of benevolence that is not grounded in Christianity. He had denied exactness of morals and works as sufficient for Salvation. This may seem to be Evangelicalism that is narrow enough, but the ultimate narrowness Cowper takes pains to avoid. He questions the worth of virtue only when it is set up in opposition to Christianity. No lover of mankind in the large such as Cowper was could be satisfied with consigning heathen to perdition, or, at best, handing them over to "uncovenanted mercies" for "ignorance of what they could not know."[1] Cowper's protest against such a conception is a condemnation of religious bigotry:

> Charge not a God with such outrageous wrong!
> Truly, not I—the partial light men have,

My creed persuades me, well employ'd, may save;
While he that scorns the noon-day beam perverse,
Shall find the blessing, unimprov'd, a curse.   [Ll. 520-24.]

It was the Quakers, famous for leading humanitarian endeavor, who seemed first in the seventeenth century to turn from the stern views of predestination and reprobation held by most English Protestants and to argue that integrity and simplicity of heart, wherever they were found among "heathens, Jews, and Turks," were explainable as an evidence of secret unity with God.[2] For the benefit of the heathen Cowper can advance the idea that good must be good wherever it is found, for the Spirit of God is the spring from which all real virtue flows. Wordsworth, looking upon a world blinded to spiritual light by materialism, exclaims:

I'd rather be
A pagan suckled in a creed outworn.

Cowper does not go quite so far; but he is convinced that those "destin'd not to see" stand a better chance of divine mercy than those who are "blind by choice."

The question immediately arises as to whether such a conclusion would not rather engender a laissez-faire attitude toward missionary enterprise than produce true evangelical zeal. That the attitude was not encouraged among Evangelicals is suggested by Thomas Scott's sermon before the Society for Missions to Africa and the East in 1801, in which the famous biblical commentator unequivocally attacked the "antiscriptural sentiment" as cutting "the very sinews" of missionary exertion.[3] In choosing to be nearer the Quakers than Evangelical theologians in his views on the heathen, Cowper plainly allows his humanitarianism to hold his Evangelicalism in check. But instead of cutting the sinews of missionary exertion, his attitude exalts it; for his interest in foreign missions is closely allied to his liberating passion.

The connection between anti-slavery and missionary senti-ment is inevitable. When Cowper inveighs against slavery in *Charity,* he closes with a discussion of a more vicious slavery than that of the body—the slavery of the soul. After the Bastile passage in Book V of *The Task,* one of Cowper's most impassioned pleas for liberty, the poet discusses the freedom of Christianity as superior to political freedom. There is a stirring contrast between the patriot and the Christian martyr:

> A patriot's blood,
> Well spent in such a strife, may earn indeed,
> And for a time ensure, to his lov'd land,
> The sweets of liberty and equal laws;
> But martyrs struggle for a brighter prize,
> And win it with more pain. Their blood is shed
> In confirmation of the noblest claim—
> Our claim to feed upon immortal truth,
> To walk with God, to be divinely free,
> To soar, and to anticipate the skies. [Ll. 714-23.]

Then, just as Cowper wanted to give the political freedom of the Englishman to slaves wherever they were found, he also wanted to give the superior freedom of the Christian to lands in spiritual bondage.

Cowper's religion, as we find it revealed in the poems, is not that of an eremite. It is by no means focussed entirely on the future life. Wesley preached the kinship of clean-liness and godliness, and insisted not only upon preparation for the future life but upon the improvement of living standards in this life. Not enough emphasis has been placed on Cowper's conception of Christianity as a practical force for bringing to the world a superior type of civilization. If he can see brutishness in the lower levels of society, he can also see that the card-playing, fox-hunting, duelling gentry and aristocracy use the conventions of their civilization to cover their inner savagery. In *Tirocinium* Cowper insists upon the kind of education that will produce Christian gentlemen and that will correct the evils of a profligate and decadent society by applying Christian ideals. In Book V of *The Task* he argues against reliance upon philosophy as a means of remaking society, offering in its place the superior means of Christianity:

> Grace makes the slave a freeman. 'Tis a change
> That turns to ridicule the turgid speech
> And stately tone of moralists, who boast
> As if, like him of fabulous renown,
> They had indeed ability to smooth
> The shag of savage nature, and were each
> An Orpheus, and omnipotent in song:
> But transformation of apostate man
> From fool to wise, from earthly to divine,
> Is work for Him that made him. He alone,
> And he by means in philosophic eyes
> Trivial and worthy of disdain, achieves
> The wonder; humanizing what is brute
> In the lost kind, extracting from the lips
> Of asps their venom, overpow'ring strength
> By weakness, and hostility by love.   [Ll. 688-703.]

The Christianity, then, that Cowper wished to send to heathen lands is not only a liberating force, but a civilizing force—"humanizing what is brute in the lost kind." This, indeed, is the ideal of a humanitarian, not that of a mere religionist. Such a vision is a powerful stimulus to evangelical passion:

> who would lose, that had the pow'r t' improve,
> Th' occasion of transmuting fear to love?
> Oh, 'tis a godlike privilege to save! [*Charity,* ll. 224-26.]

Moreover, missions fit beautifully into Cowper's philanthropic ideal for commerce. If the proper function of the merchant marines of the world is to knit together the "unsocial climates" and to make a golden girdle around the globe by genial intercourse and mutual aid, naturally the most priceless thing that the Christian world can give the pagan is its religion of love. Cowper, therefore, writes in *Charity*:

> Let nothing adverse, nothing unforeseen,
> Impede the bark that plows the deep serene,
> Charg'd with a freight transcending in its worth
> The gems of India, nature's rarest birth,
> That flies, like Gabriel on his Lord's command.
>
> [Ll. 131-35.]

§ 2

Although the subject of missions may get into Cowper's verse by way of digression, it does not do so haphazardly. The pedigree of the poet's missionary interest may be traced with some certainty.

There is hardly space or occasion here to outline the history of missionary effort. The expansion of the Christian church is naturally the result of such exertion. Modern missions date from the renewed activity of the Catholic Church brought on by the new outlook given by the Renaissance and by the voyages of discovery, and prosecuted to some extent under the stimulus of the counter-Reformation. The Roman Church was first to grasp the possibilities of expansion in the New World, carrying on the Christianization of Southern, Central, and large parts of North America through the work of the Franciscans, the Dominicans, and most notably the Jesuits.[4]

For many reasons the Protestants were more backward in beginning missionary work. Naturally, their religious organizations were not so well established as those of the Catholics. Moreover, opportunities for imperialistic expansion came earlier to the great Catholic nations than they did to England and Holland. However, when England's

colonization began, the nation at least nominally considered
as a part of its imperialistic program bringing the light to
those "Infidels and Savages" who lived "in Darkness and
miserable Ignorance of the true Knowledge and Worship
of God."[5]

The great English Society for the Propagation of the
Gospel in Foreign Parts has its roots well grounded in the
seventeenth century, although it was not actually founded
until early in the next century. Stimulated by John Eliot's
efforts among the Massachusetts Indians, a group of ministers of the English Church presented to Parliament in
1644 a petition urging the duty of attempting to convert
the natives of North America; and on July 27, 1648, a cor-
poration called The President and Society for the Propagation of the Gospel in New England was established.
This pioneer missionary organization may be considered the
parent of the later organization. Toward the end of the
century the Church of England became interested in supplying the colonies with ministers. Chiefly for this purpose
the S. P. G. was founded in 1701.[6]

The Society for the Promotion of Christian Knowledge
was founded three years earlier. It was not primarily missionary in purpose, but as early as 1709 it established a
connection with the Danish mission to the Hindus at Tran-
quebar and rendered considerable aid to the work. The
Scotch S. P. C. K., founded in 1709, began as a home-mission
society with the purpose of religious and educational work
in the Highlands and in the Scotch islands. Three decades
later this organization was responsible for sending David
Brainerd to America for work among the Indians.

The Danish and the Moravians were far in advance of
the English in mission fields. In 1705 King Frederick of
Denmark founded the mission in India, with which the
S. P. C. K. later coöperated. Denmark also sent Thomas
von Westen to Lapland in 1716 and Hans Egede to Green-

land in 1721. Some of the most remarkable missionary work of the century was done by the Moravians. In 1731 Count Zinzendorf saw two Eskimos in Copenhagen and heard with sadness that Egede's mission in Greenland had to be given up. Members of his party also saw a Negro who told of the suffering of slaves in the West Indies. As a result of both these occurrences, in August of the following year two Moravian missionaries were on their way to the West Indies, and in January, 1733, two other missionaries set out for Greenland. Moravian missions expanded with miraculous rapidity to Surinam, Dutch Guiana, South Africa, and to America, where work was done among the Indians especially in New York and Pennsylvania.[7]

In England the dawning of the great day of foreign missions was delayed until the last decade of the eighteenth century. Olney, Cowper's own village, had the fortune to be one of the most important centers of the spiritual ferment that led to the founding of the first great English Protestant mission.

Roused by Whitefield, a group of Scottish ministers organized in 1744 for a concert of prayer for the spiritual advancement of God's kingdom.[8] The movement spread in England, and in August, 1746, American Christians were invited to join. In the following year Jonathan Edwards published in Boston his *Humble Attempt to Promote Explicit and Visible Union of God's People in Extraordinary Prayer for the Revival of Religion and the Advancement of Christ's Kingdom on Earth*. The movement, however, did not immediately bear important fruit in the field of foreign missions.

Although the Evangelical revival was eventually to furnish powerful incentive for the scattering of the gospel all over the world, we do not wonder that the extension of its field beyond England was slow. In the first place, the revival was born out of a vital need for spirituality in England, and its initial task was to regenerate the homeland. The problems that England itself presented were difficult ones. It is true that at the beginning of their great careers the Wesleys went to Georgia with Oglethorpe; but since they did most of their work among the settlers, their endeavors can hardly be classified as foreign missions. The same is generally true of Whitefield, although his work was broader in scope.

Over thirty years after the publication of Edwards's tract there was great activity among the "Particular" or Calvinistic Baptist ministers of Northamptonshire and adjacent counties. These ministers had organized themselves into an association of fellowship and Christian service and had sought inspiration not only from great English evangelicals but from Jonathan Edwards in America. Olney was one of the strongholds of the organization and was not infrequently its meeting-place. John Sutcliff, the Baptist minister at Olney and a close friend of Newton, was one of its most powerful leaders. To the meetings came William Carey, then a cobbler at Hackleton, and Andrew Fuller, destined to be the first secretary of the great Baptist missionary society.[9] Sutcliff was so tremendously impressed by Edwards's mighty spiritual impulse for the spread of the gospel to all nations of the earth that he caused *An Humble Attempt* to be reprinted, with his own preface, at Northampton in 1789.

The climate of interest in missions that had begun developing in Olney in the last years of the seventies was by no means confined to the Baptists. At least by 1775 John Newton had read Crantz's *The History of Greenland,* translated into English from the original High Dutch in 1767. He acclaimed it a "glorious work" and expressed high praise for the Moravian missionaries who had "hazarded their lives in an extraordinary manner for the sake of Lord Jesus."[10] He probably shared this enthusiasm with Sutcliff; for Carey, whose education was chiefly under Sutcliff's guidance, was later able to acknowledge generously the stimulation of Moravian missions. Thomas Scott stated that he early fell under the influence of the writings of "Edwards, Brainerd, and the New England divines."[11]

The interlinked friendships of Newton, Scott, Sutcliff, and Cowper[12] made it quite natural that the poet should share the enthusiasm for the cause of missions felt by a large number of Northamptonshire and Buckinghamshire ministers. The long passage on missions in *Hope*—the passage that offers Cowper's best claim to the title of "the poet of missions"—definitely links Cowper with the movement that led to the founding of the Particular Baptist Society for Propagating the Gospel among the Heathen, in Kettering on October 2, 1792.[13] The work of this organization in India, especially under William Carey and his coadjutors, is one of the great religious and humanitarian achievements of all time. Whether Cowper knew Carey there seems to be no record. Cowper lived just across the square from Sutcliff when Carey was under the Baptist minister's tutelage at Olney. But we do know that Cowper's poems accompanied the missionary on his momentous voyage to India, and that Carey's journals give evidence of his great admiration for the Olney poet.[14] There is, therefore, every reason to believe that Cowper's zeal for missions and his noble portrait of a missionary hero were an important stimulus to Carey's great work.

§ 3

Cowper's position as the first English poet to champion the new missionary impulse extensively in his verse seems to be unchallenged. It is true that the beginning of the century produced several missionary hymns. In 1719 Isaac Watts's great hymn "Jesus shall reign" was published; and in 1722 appeared William Williams's "O'er those gloomy Hills of Darkness." The Wesleys also wrote several hymns of missionary implication, most of which appeared in the *Collection of Hymns for the Use of the People Called Methodists* in 1780. (Cowper and Newton made the missionary theme no vital part of their own *Olney Hymns*.) The poetry section of the *Evangelical Magazine,* founded in the last decade of the century, seemed to stimulate the composition of hymn-poems on missionary subjects; but in general the development of missionary hymnody in the century was slow.[15]

If the subject of missions was slow in getting into hymns, it naturally had little vogue in other types of poetry. In the first book of *Gotham,* a poem highly admired by Cowper, Charles Churchill had attacked the missionary effort that had come as a part of European imperialism, especially as practiced by Spain and France.[16] The usual procedure, Churchill argued, had been for discoverers and explorers to set up a cross merely as a prologue to the general enslavement of the natives in the new land. Through such a procedure Christians had conquered more than half the globe. Happy indeed was the savage before he knew the bondage and the corruptions of European civilization. Churchill does not belong to the Noble Savage cult; he does not postulate any sort of superior state for the savage—but he anticipates Cowper (if he does not actually influence him) in refusing to leave the savage in complete moral darkness:

> False Lights he follow'd, but believ'd them true;
> He knew not much, but liv'd to what he knew.

We have seen that the accounts of Cook's voyages did not lead Cowper to worship the superior culture of the primitive man; neither did they seem to be, as they were to Carey, a direct inspiration for his missionary zeal. It is true that the account of Omai shows compassion for the savage that has returned to his homeland, but it serves rather as a means of emphasizing the blessings of civilized life and of attacking imperialistic ideals than as a means of suggesting the necessity for taking the Gospel to the South Sea Islanders. It was Crantz's *The History of Greenland*—later to claim the attention of Coleridge and to provide source material for *The Ancient Mariner*—that was the immediate inspiration for the first part of the missionary passage in *Hope*. There can be little doubt that this very interesting book was recommended by Newton and that it had probably been a frequent topic of conversation in Olney.

Crantz did not set out to write a mere history of Moravian mission work in Greenland. He wrote a full and often fascinating account of the geography, natural history, and the inhabitants of the region.

The spectacle of the spread of the gospel to the far ends of the earth—actually still a vision rather than a reality—deeply moved Cowper. His enthusiasm for the work of the Moravians is reflected in his exclamation:

> See Germany send forth
> Her sons . . . . .
> Fir'd with a zeal peculiar, *they* defy
> The rage and rigour of a polar sky,
> And plant successfully sweet Sharon's rose
> On icy plains, and in eternal snows.
>
> [*Hope,* ll. 459-64.][17]

Cowper was justly impressed by the fact that the Greenlanders, according to Crantz's account, offered the supreme test for the regenerative powers of Christianity, and the poet exults in the triumph. The Greenlanders, we are told by Crantz, were not wild and savage in the sense of being grossly brutal or cruel; rather were they a stolid and phlegmatic race. In spite of their lack of obvious savagery, they possessed more characteristics to impress a European with their relation to animals than to impress him with their relation to human beings. Although they lacked many vices of civilization, no little evil lurked behind their passive exterior. What virtue they had, the historian reports, seemed to be instinctive, like that of animals. They showed no compassion, sympathy, or sense of social responsibility. They would, for example, let a man drown rather than save him, and would callously steal from a destitute widow. "Just so it is with the irrational creatures," Crantz writes, "they are insensible to the pleasure or pain of other animals."[18]

One of the most remarkable things about the Greenlanders was that they seemed to have no discoverable form of worship. To Cowper

> They were by nature—atheists, head and heart.
> The gross idolatry blind heathens teach
> Was too refin'd for them, beyond their reach.
>
> .   .   .   .
>
> Not e'en the sun, desirable as rare,
> Could bend one knee, engage one vot'ry there.
>   [Ll. 498 ff.]

Crantz makes a point of correcting a common misconception that the Greenlanders were sun-worshippers; but he does not deny them some conception of a divine being:

. . . a faint idea of a divine Being lies concealed in the minds even of this people, because they directly assent without any objection to the Doctrine of a God and his Attributes, except they are afraid of the consequences of this truth, and so *will not* believe it. Only they suffer their natural sluggishness, stupidity, and inattention to hinder them from attaining just and consistent principles, by a due reflection on the works of creation and on their own timorous forebodings concerning futurity.[19]

When Cowper pictures the Greenlanders as being "dissemblers, drunkards, thieves," he has the full support of his source on only two scores. The poet seems to have an instinctive tendency to associate drunkenness with all flagrant vice. The drunken hero of the chase and the sottish vil-

lager frequently incur his contempt. And under his pen
what a den of vice the tavern becomes! Far from pointing
out drunkenness as one of their important vices, Crantz
observes that the Greenlanders are generally free from this
besetting sin of civilized nations. He does make the following admission: "They have formerly abhorred strong liq-
uors, and called them madwater. But those that have intercourse with the Europeans, would gladly drink if they could
pay for it. They sometimes feign themselves sick, to get a
drink of brandy."[20] Cowper is quick to accept potential
drunkards as drunkards in fact. In spite of Crantz's observation concerning the dances of the Greenlanders that
"they cannot intoxicate themselves, because they have nothing but water to drink,"[21] the poet proceeds to depict—

> The wretch, who once sang wildly, danc'd and laugh'd,
> And suck'd in dizzy madness with his draught. [Ll. 517-18.]

Cowper strikingly sums up the brutishness of the Greenlander before he was subjected to the refining influence of
the Christian missions:

> The full-gorg'd savage, at his nauseous feast
> Spent half the darkness, and snor'd out the rest,
> Was one whom justice, on an equal plan,
> Denouncing death upon the sins of man,
> Might almost have indulg'd with an escape,
> Chargeable only with a human shape.   [Ll. 509-14.]

Crantz's account of the Greenlander's feasting on half-rotten
seal's flesh and on reindeer maw amply justifies most of the
poet's description.

The transformation of these brutish creatures into human
beings whose social relationships were those of a well-
ordered society is to Cowper little short of miraculous. The
"unsightly and rank thistles" had become "myrtle and luxuriant yew." The wretch of bestial proclivities

Is sober, meek, benevolent, and prays,
Feeds sparingly, communicates his store,
Abhors the craft he boasted of before—
And he that stole has learn'd to steal no more.

[Ll. 520-23.]

It is interesting that Cowper emphasizes the social regeneration that has come through spiritual regeneration; whereas
Crantz is inclined to emphasize the phenomena of spiritual
regeneration. The historian writes:

. . . these very people by means of competent instruction, and
through the grace and illumination of the holy Spirit, become so
discreet, attentive, carefully considerate and wise, that they comprehend the greatest mysteries of faith, and realize them in their
souls in an experimental and happy manner, so as to be able to
deliver the most glorious testimonies thereof with spirit and
power.[22]

But Cowper is not so much impressed by the fact that the
almost insensate Greenlander has achieved mystic experiences as he is by the fact that the morally corrupt Greenlander has lost his anti-social habits, improved his manners,
and taken on a recognizable degree of civilization.

When Cowper looks about for a missionary hero, he
quite logically settles upon Whitefield. Following the Wesleys, Whitefield had undertaken a missionary journey to
Georgia in 1738 and had subsequently done evangelical
preaching in New York, Pennsylvania, and in other American colonies. Not only was he the greatest preacher of the
Calvinistic Evangelicals, but he was, as we have seen, the
spiritual ancestor of the Baptist missionary movement. The
spiritual impulse for the missionary ferment in Olney may
be traced from Whitefield to the Scottish ministers, to Jonathan Edwards, to Sutcliff, Scott, and Newton; thence to
Cowper, and finally to Carey. Cowper had doubtless read

with admiration the copy of Dr. Gillies's *Memoirs* of Whitefield that was in his limited library.

The great preacher is eulogized under the name of
Leuconomus. The spectacle of a man of blameless life
assailed by all the forces that evil could muster—ridiculed
in verse in Pope's *Dunciad,* on the stage in Foote's *The
Minor,* and in the novel in Graves's *The Spiritual Quixote*—
gave Whitefield in the eyes of Cowper the aura of the kind
of martyr later eulogized in *The Task.* The poet's crown-
ing praise is naturally for his missionary zeal:

> He followed Paul—his zeal a kindred flame,
> His apostolic charity the same.
> Like him, cross'd cheerfully tempestuous seas,
> Forsaking country, kindred, friends, and ease;
> Like him he labour'd, and, like him, content
> To bear it, suffer'd shame where'er he went.
>
> [*Hope,* ll. 582-87.]

In the history of missionary effort in the century Cowper
occupies a spiritual position between Whitefield and Carey.
Although he, of course, had no part in the organization of
a great missionary project, his championing the missionary
cause entitles him to some consideration along with Sutcliff,
Ryland, Fuller, and Carey as a pioneer in the Northamptonshire movement. Although he had less direct connection
with the foundation of the Church Missionary Society in
1799, among the founders were Henry Thornton and William Wilberforce, who greatly admired his opinions and with
whom he served in the abolitionist struggle.

Cowper presents the missionary cause with remarkable
sanity and lack of religious bigotry. In refusing to postulate
damnation for the heathen, he is able to achieve a more
distinctly humanitarian theory of missions than that of saving the heathen from fire and brimstone, or, conversely, of
giving them the joys of a Christian heaven. In an age in

which political freedom and social welfare were beginning
to be on every tongue, Cowper convincingly presented missionary effort in the light of spiritual freedom and social
regeneration. His vision for the missionary enterprise is no
impractical one, waiting for fruition in a future life. It is
a regenerative ideal for the life of this world. In a perfect
merging of religious and humanitarian zeal, the poet urges
giving the freedom of Christianity to the slaves and the
heathen:

>   a liberty, unsung
> By poets, and by senators unprais'd,
> Which monarchs cannot grant, nor all the pow'rs
> Of earth and hell confed'rate take away:
> A liberty, which persecution, fraud,
> Oppression, prisons, have no power to bind;
> Which whoso tastes can be enslav'd no more.
> 'Tis liberty of heart, deriv'd from heav'n;
> Bought with HIS blood who gave it to mankind.
>   [*Task,* V, ll. 538-46.]

Chapter V

THE CONQUER'D EAST

§ 1

THE CONTRADICTIONS and limitations of Cowper's liberalism
may be the cause of some concern. Why, one may ask,
does he call on the French to tear down the Bastile, and
yet, when the act is a *fait accompli,* why does he seem to
have no sympathy for the Revolution? Even before the
excesses of the "Reign of Terror" opened the eyes of the
liberals in England who had sympathized with the revolutionary party in France, Cowper wrote to Walter Bagot:
"Though you are a Tory I believe, and I am a Whig, our
sentiments concerning the madcaps of France are much the
same. They are a terrible race, and I have a horror both
of them and their principles."[1] One answer to the question
just posed lies in Cowper's instinctive abhorrence of chaos
and mob violence. Although he may urge a slave to rise
up and strike for freedom, he seems in so doing to be thinking in terms of the oppressed individual and his immediate
tyrant. When a whole nation rises up to overthrow the
whole order of its society, Cowper withdraws in some alarm.
He is naturally the type of person who would prefer evolu-
tion to revolution. If possible, reform should proceed from
the top downward. Cowper may conceive of the possible
justification of striking down the tyrant, but hardly of sub-
verting the whole order for which he stands. A second
answer is apparent in the statement quoted from the letter
to Bagot. Abbé Raynal, whom Cowper admired as "a true
patriot" because "the world is his country," had not taught
the poet the lesson of internationalism so well as one might

[113]

infer from Cowper's passage on universal brotherliness. The simple truth is that Cowper did not like the French; and although he could plead for the *oppressed* French as opposed to the French *tyrants,* when those formerly oppressed rose to power Cowper found that he still did not like the French. On January 29, 1793, he wrote to Hayley:

Alas! poor Louis! I will tell you what the French have done. They have made me weep for a king of France, which I never thought to do, and they have made me sick of the very name of liberty, which I never thought to be. Oh, how I detest them! Coxcombs, as they are, on this occasion as they ever are on all. Apes of the Spartan and the Roman character, with neither the virtue nor the good sense that belonged to it.

The positions of oppressed and tyrants have shifted, and the poet's sympathies have shifted with them. It is true, too, that some of Cowper's antipathy for the French may be traced to his patriotism, especially at a time when France was England's chief antagonist.

One may also ask why Cowper's liberalism did not extend to a sympathy for the Americans in their struggle for freedom. As the poet's attitude toward the French reveals, a large part of his "liberalism" is not strictly political liberalism at all but is little more than an extension of the feeling that lies at the basis of his philanthropic thought. When he talks of freedom, he usually thinks of relieving the suffering of those who are not free, whether they are prisoners in the Bastile, slaves in the West Indies, or the hard-pressed industrial laborers of England. He was never an enthusiastic politician. Although he was nominally a Whig, his reactions to national issues were rarely predictable merely on the basis of a party label. He did not always manifest democratic tendencies. He could hold in abhorrence a great popular leader like Oliver Cromwell.[2] Not only did he refuse to regard the Americans as oppressed, and hence worthy of his sympathies as a humanitarian, but he persisted in looking upon them as rebels and upon admitting no extenuation of their conduct. In "The Modern Patriot," in which he attacks Burke's position on both the Catholic and American questions, Cowper writes thus:

> Yon roaring boys, who rave and fight
>   On t'other side th' Atlantic,
> I always held them in the right,
>   But most so when most frantic.
>
> When lawless mobs insult the court,
>   That man may be my toast,
> If breaking windows be the sport,
>   Who bravely breaks the most.[3]

No great perspicacity is needed, however, to see that France is again the real villain of the piece. In "To Sir Joshua Reynolds," probably written in 1781, Cowper attacks the American fight for independence as a product of France's hatred of England. A letter to Newton written on January 26, 1783, sums up beautifully the poet's whole attitude:

. . . the Americans, who, if they had contented themselves with a struggle for lawful liberty, would have deserved applause, seem to me to have incurred the *guilt of parricide,* by renouncing their parent, by making her ruin their favourite object, and *by associating themselves with her worst enemy, for the accomplishment of their purpose.* France, and, of course, Spain, have acted a treacherous, a thievish part. They have stolen America from England, and whether they are able to possess themselves of that jewel or not hereafter, it was doubtless what they intended. . . . America may, perhaps, call her [England] the aggressor, but if she were so, America has not only repelled the injury, but done a greater. As to the rest, if perfidy, treachery, avarice, and ambition can prove their cause to have been a rotten one, those proofs are found upon them.[4]

§ 2

England's struggle for her empire in the last decades of the eighteenth century was over a broad front; and much of the time she was fighting with her back against the wall. For a time "Poor England" was indeed "a devoted deer" beset by the whole world, and as such might well elicit the sympathy that Cowper always kept in store for the oppressed. However, when the poet could see England in the position of the oppressor, the down-trodden and not England received his sympathy. "England, with all thy faults I love thee still" is a fine expression of patriotism, because it means exactly what it says. Cowper was not given to apologizing for his country's position when it was manifestly the wrong one.

In spite of the fact that Cowper felt keenly the loss of the American colonies, he was far from being an imperialist according to the usual conception of the term. So long as British imperialism led to peaceful colonization, the poet had no word of disapproval. Unfortunately, British imperialism of the eighteenth century did not live up to Chatham's ideal—"free institutions and self-government by a free and self-governing people." When imperialism led to aggression, Cowper was quick to protest.

Although the poet insists that man's place is in society where he may develop, he is always ready to suspect

> man, associated and leagu'd with man
> By regal warrant, or self-join'd by bond
> For int'rest-sake.　　　　　[*Task,* IV, ll. 663-65.]

This applies either to war or commerce. Man's duty is to society as a whole, not to a group of which he is a part. Allegiance to a group brings about "defilement not to be endured." Hence, the public plague of "charter'd boroughs"—

> Hence merchants, unimpeachable of sin
> Against the charities of domestic life,

Incorporated, seem at once to lose
Their nature; and, disclaiming all regard
For mercy and the common rights of man,
Build factories with blood, conducting trade
At the sword's point, and dyeing the white robe
Of innocent commercial justice red.   [Ll. 676-83.]

The passage not only reflects what was happening in England with the rapidly expanding Industrial Revolution, but what had been happening in India during the entire course of the century. The situation in India was, along with the slave trade, another evidence that commerce in the century was far from the poet's humanitarian ideal—that of a "golden girdle of the globe," uniting all mankind in universal brotherhood. It was also further proof that "doing good, disinterested good" was not the trade of an imperialistic nation. A letter written on July 13, 1777, to Joseph Hill, apropos of the South Sea Islands, gives Cowper's view of British trade expansion before he wrote the didactic poems and *The Task*: " 'Tis well for the poor natives of those distant countries that our national expenses cannot be supplied by cargoes of yams and bananas. Curiosity, therefore, being once satisfied, they may possibly be permitted for the future to enjoy their riches of that kind in peace."[5]

It was India's bad fortune to offer more valuable bait than yams and bananas. The English exploitation of India dates back to the formation of the East India Company in the reign of Elizabeth, but the great period of the Company's expansion did not come until the eighteenth century. When Clive left India in 1760, after his brilliant exploits, the servants of the Company were virtually, if not legally, the rulers of Bengal and dependent provinces. The puppet Nawab was to collect taxes and hand them over to the English. Since the Company was more interested in results than means, numerous corruptions resulted.[6]

After Clive's departure the exploitation of the internal trade of Bengal was notorious. The Company itself apparently did not gain by this exploitation. Paradoxically enough, employees were getting rich, but the Company's trade was falling off. The fact that the Company paid small salaries encouraged employees to engage in individual speculation. And never before had fortunes been so easily amassed. Clive, who had started out as a penniless clerk, returned to England at the age of thirty-four an enormously wealthy man. When he went back to India in 1764 to clean up abuses, he forbade individual trading and got a supplement for salaries. But abuses did not stop. Although in 1770 the Company was on the very edge of ruin, Englishmen were coming home from India in great numbers to become country gentlemen and to get seats in Parliament. A parliamentary investigation was begun in 1772, and Clive was tried for sins committed before he began his purge of corruptions in Bengal.[7]

In the same year Warren Hastings became governor. He immediately began a reformation of the *diwani* system through which taxes had formerly been collected by natives to the accompaniment of plunder and oppression. At home the government was making some attempt to separate the Company's functions of government and trade. In 1773 Lord North's Regulating Act brought about a unification of India, making the governments of Madras and Bombay subordinate to that of Bengal.

Around 1780 the position of the British in India was made more complicated by the resumption of action by the French. Hastings succeeded in saving India from France, but in raising war revenue he was led into action that later caused him serious trouble. Hastings' arrest of the Rajah of Benares and his forcing the Nawab of Oudh's grandmother and mother (the wealthy Begums) to pay the recalcitrant Nawab's debts furnished the chief material for the famous trial.[8]

In 1783 Lord North returned to power in coalition with Fox. An India Bill presented by Fox would have in some respects completely subverted the charter of the Company[9] and would have replaced the existing Court of Directors and Proprietors by a commission of seven appointed by Parliament. Because it would have placed Indian patronage in the hands of the Whig party for four years, attacks on the bill were violent. Neither the eloquence of Fox nor Burke could save the bill, which was largely defeated by the King. The monarch is said to have "stooped and stooped low to conquer," going to the depths of influencing votes in the House of Lords by threats.

The defeat of the India Bill caused the fall of the coalition government, and the younger Pitt became prime minister. His India Bill passed into law in 1784. This Act provided for a board of control, including a Secretary for India with a seat in the cabinet. The close relations of the Secretary and the Governor-General did much in transferring the sovereign power to the home government. Although it, of course, did not correct all abuses, the plan proved workable and was used for seventy years.

Thus the period between 1772 and 1786 represents one of the most crucial epochs in the history of British India. If one wishes to see how important the affairs of India were during these years and how closely they were wrapped up with political and party relations, one has only to glance through the pages of Cobbett's *Parliamentary History* for the period. There were two severe parliamentary investigations of the East India Company, one in 1772 and the other in 1781; each was followed by a great statute and an attack on a great individual.[10] As the first investigation was followed by the attack on Clive and Lord North's Act of 1773, after 1781 came Pitt's Act and the impeachment of Warren Hastings.

In this crucial period of Indian affairs an exponent of better government for India might have political motives, humanitarian motives, or both. One does not expect to find a political cast in Cowper's attitude on the Indian situation. In turning toward the East, he maintains the feeling, already discussed in connection with his anti-slavery poetry, that the freedom of the Englishman should be extended to the far ends of the earth—"In Afric's torrid clime, or India's fiercest heat." Although his treatment of corruptions in India is not so extended as his attack on slavery, the poet shows his keen awareness of the situation and again dares to speak out boldly as a champion of the oppressed.

Expostulation provides the first example of Cowper's strong feeling. The poem is a sort of jeremiad in which the poet, taking upon himself a mantle similar to that of the Hebrew prophet, warns England that, although she has been favored like the Jews, her heedlessness will cause "the unique awfulness of ruin" to fall upon her as it did upon the chosen people. Like Israel of old, England deals in robbery and wrong: oppression "grinds" her poor, slavery flourishes in her colonies, corruption is rampant in her church. The poet does not wonder that the nation has fallen upon evil days, and calls upon England to judge herself. In warning England that "no success attends on spears and swords unblest," he arrives at the situation in India. This he analyzes with remarkable compactness and force:

> Hast thou, though suckled at fair freedom's breast,
> Exported slav'ry to the conquer'd East,
> Pull'd down the tyrants India serv'd with dread,
> And rais'd thyself, a greater in their stead?
> Gone thither arm'd and hungry, return'd full,
> Fed from the richest veins of the Mogul,
> A despot big with pow'r obtained by wealth,

And that obtain'd by rapine and by stealth?
With Asiatic vices stor'd thy mind,
But left their virtues and thine own behind;
And having truck'd thy soul, brought home the fee,
To tempt the poor to sell himself to thee?   [Ll. 364-75.]

Thus, in the year of the second parliamentary investigation Cowper wrote the rather popular story of hundreds who went to India penniless and returned to buy seats in Parliament.

The tradition to which Cowper had obviously fallen heir is interesting. Very little national pride and not much confidence had been bestowed upon India. As early as 1764 British policy in India had been attacked in verse by Charles Churchill. In *Gotham,* he contended, in anticipation of Burke's impassioned charges years later,

                    that by no act
Which Nature made, that by no equal pact
'Twixt man and man, which might if justice heard,
Stand good; that by no benefits conferr'd,
Or purchase made, Europe in chains can hold
The sons of India, and her mines of gold.
Chance led her there in an accursed hour;
She saw, and made the country hers by power.[11]

In 1772 a great storm of popular disapproval, the accumulation of several years, had broken on Clive.[12] The "nabobs," as the Anglo-Indians were called, were unpopular for many reasons. The gentry and aristocracy were inclined to scorn them as *nouveaux riches,* for they generally had no family background and breeding. Then, too, as Lord Macaulay has pictured them, they were overbearing in manners. It began to be whispered that their great wealth was obtained by extortion and tyranny of the worst sort. Of the 1772 investigation Horace Walpole wrote: "Such a scene of tyranny and plunder has been opened as makes one shudder!

. . . We are Spaniards in our lust for gold, and Dutch in our delicacy of obtaining it."[13]   The *Annual Register* of 1772 reported that the Select Committee had exposed "a scene of rapacity, iniquity, and cruelty."[14]   Chatham wrote in 1773, "India teems with iniquities so rank as to smell to earth and heaven."[15]   The "nabob" was satirized on the stage and in verse.   Samuel Foote's *The Nabob* was produced in 1772; and in 1773 appeared *The Nabob: or Asiatic Plunderers,* a satirical poem "in the manner of Pope," which warns of retributive justice.   Pamphlets painting the misdeeds of the Company's servants as emulating the atrocities of the Spaniards in Mexico gained popularity.[16]

It was quite natural that the slave traffic and the India question should become associated.   Wesley wrote in 1776:

It [the slave traffic] is a trade of blood, and has stained our land with blood! And is the East India trade a jot better? I fear not. They seem very nearly allied. For though here is no leading into captivity, as in the former; yet the refined iniquity practised there, of fomenting war among the natives, and seizing the chief of the plunder, has been as conspicuous to the serious and attentive. What millions have fallen by these means, as well as by artificial famine! O earth cover not their blood![17]

The temper of the *Monthly Review* in February, 1781— the month before the lines in *Expostulation* were written— is revealed in the bluntly terse review of *A State* [*sic*] *of the British Authority in Bengal:*

Two words seem to comprehend the whole history of British transactions in the East Indies,—*accusation* and *vindication:* thus would it have happened, had printing been as common as it is with us, while the Spaniards were plundering, torturing, and butchering the innocent natives of Mexico and Peru.[18]

Before Cowper wrote *The Task* there had been such a graphic description of Indian affairs as that of Burke's great speech on Fox's Bill:

Young men (boys almost) govern there, without society and without sympathy with the natives. They have no more social habits with the people than if they still resided in England,—nor, indeed, any species of intercourse, but that which is necessary to make a sudden fortune, with a view to a remote settlement. Animated with all the avarice of age and all the impetuosity of youth, they roll in one after another, wave after wave; and there is nothing before the eyes of the natives but an endless, hopeless prospect of a new flight of birds of prey and passage, with appetites continually renewing for a food that is continually wasting. Every rupee of profit made by an Englishman is lost forever to India. With us are no retributory superstitions, by which a foundation of charity compensates, through ages, to the poor, for the rapine and injustice of a day. With us no pride erects stately monuments which repair the mischiefs which pride had produced, and which adorn a country out of its own spoils. England has erected no churches, no hospitals, no palaces, no schools; England has built no bridges, made no high-roads, cut no navigations, dug out no reservoirs. Every other conqueror of every other description has left some monument, either of state or beneficence, behind him. Were we to be driven out of India this day, nothing would remain to tell that it had been possessed, during the inglorious period of our dominion, by anything better than the orang-outang or the tiger.[19]

In the first book of *The Task,* begun in the year of Fox's Bill, Cowper turns for a few indignant lines to those who have fabulously enriched themselves by their depredations:

> thieves at home must hang; but he that puts
> Into his overgorg'd and bloated purse
> The wealth of Indian provinces, escapes.   [Ll. 736-38.]

In the famous opening passage of the fourth book the poet inquires—

> Is India free? and does she wear her plum'd
> And jewell'd turban with a smile of peace,
> Or do we grind her still?   [Ll. 28-30.]

The letters are more revelatory of the poet's sentiments on the very important question. Cowper supported Fox's India Bill—as a humanitarian is perhaps sometimes likely to do—a little uncritically. He acknowledged its blemishes, but he was unable to see how serious they really were. A letter written to Newton on December 15, 1783, makes his position clear:

I know not what are your sentiments upon the subject of the East India Bill. This, too, has frequently afforded me matter of speculation. I can easily see that it is not without its blemishes; but its beauties, in my eye, are much predominant. Whatever may be its author's views, if he delivers so large a portion of mankind from such horrible tyranny as the East has so long suffered, he deserves a statue much more than Mongolfier, who, it seems, is to receive that honour. Perhaps he may bring our own freedom into jeopardy; but to do this for the sake of emancipating nations so much more numerous than ourselves, is at least generous, and a design that should have my encouragement, if I had any encouragement to afford it.[20]

Almost a month later he writes to William Unwin advocating the annulment of the East India Company's charter as a corrective of corruptions in India. The eloquence of the letter makes one feel that Cowper might almost have imagined himself as speaking from the floor of the House of Commons. The cumulative power of his rhetoric, rising to an impressive climax, may be seen in the following excerpt:

[The charter of the East India Company] constitutes them a trading company, and gives them an exclusive right to traffic in the East Indies. But it does no more. It invests them with no sovereignty; it does not convey to them the royal prerogative of making war and peace, which the king cannot alienate if he would. But this prerogative they have exercised, and, forgetting the terms of their institution, have possessed themselves of an immense territory, which they have ruled with a rod of iron, to which it is impossible they should ever have a right, unless such a one as it is a disgrace to plead,—the right of conquest. The potentates of this country they dash in pieces like a potter's vessel, as often as they please, making the happiness of thirty millions of mankind a consideration subordinate to that of their own emolument, oppressing them as often as it may serve a lucrative purpose, and in no instance, that I have ever heard, consulting their interest or advantage. That government, therefore, is bound to interfere, and to unking these tyrants, is to me self-evident. And if having subjugated so much of this miserable world, it is therefore necessary that we must keep possession of it, it appears to me a duty so binding upon the legislature to rescue it from the hands of those usurpers, that I should think a curse, and a bitter one, must follow the neglect of it.[21]

Thus was the oratory ringing in Parliament echoed in the far reaches of Olney. Never had Cowper been nearer Burke in style or sentiment.

Again, on January 25, 1784, Cowper wrote a letter to Newton which shows that his feelings were still running at a high pitch:

I would abandon all territorial interest in a country to which we can have no right, and which we cannot govern with any security to the happiness of the inhabitants, or without the danger of incurring either perpetual broils, or the most insupportable tyranny at home:—that sort of tyranny, I mean, that flatters and tantalizes the subject with a show of freedom, and in reality allows him nothing more; bribing to the right and left, rich enough to afford the purchase of a thousand consciences, and consequently strong enough, if it happen to meet with an incorruptible one, to render all the efforts of that man, or of twenty such men . . . romantic, and of no effect. . . . I distrust the court, I suspect the patriots, I put the Company entirely aside, as having forfeited all claim to confidence in such a business, and see no remedy, of course, but in the annihilation, if that could be accomplished, of the very existence of our authority in the East Indies.[22]

Although George III's superficial piety seems at times to have misled Cowper, for several years he had been under no delusions concerning the monarch's position on the matter of British liberty. In letters to William Unwin written on February 13, and May 8, 1780, Cowper had discussed the similarities and dissimilarities of George III and Charles I. The failure of the India Bill and the consequent failure of the North-Fox coalition ministry caused Cowper to attack both the King and the younger Pitt—for whose father the poet had had almost unbounded admiration. Cowper wrote to Newton in February, 1784, as follows:

Stuartism, in my mind, has been the characteristic of the present reign; and being, and having always been somewhat of an enthusiast on the subject of British liberty, I am not able to withhold my reverence and good wishes from the man, whoever he be, that exerts himself in a constitutional way to oppose it. The son of Lord Chatham seems to me to have abandoned his father's principles. . . . I fear much that he is the tool of mischievous purposes, and that his unrelaxing steadiness, too much resembling that of a certain personage, will bring down a storm upon himself and upon the nation.[23]

In another letter written to Newton on the following March 8, he resumes his attack on the Crown, with special reference to the King's highly reprehensible political maneuvering. "The patronage of the East Indies will be a dangerous weapon in whatever hands," the poet concludes; "I had rather, however, see it lodged any where than with the Crown. In that event, I should say adieu forever to every hope of an uncorrupt representation and consequently to every hope of constitutional liberty for the subject."[24] If this sounds more like politics than humanitarianism, we should not forget that Cowper the humanitarian urged complete freedom for India. Cowper the Whig may also speak his mind!

§ 3

By the time of the great impeachment trial of Warren Hastings, Cowper was beginning to feel with less vehemence on public questions. This fact we have already seen in his attitude toward the anti-slavery poems. Only if one does not know Cowper the man, will one have any cause to wonder that the poet did not follow up his support of Burke's position on the India Bill with continued support for Burke's attack on Hastings. It is not difficult to see, as several critics have pointed out, that Cowper seemed ever willing to relax generalizations in favor of the particular whenever his friendships were involved. "Bishops in general might be lazy and useless, but not his friend Bishop Bagot; Deans as a rule worldly, but not Dean Cowper; College Dons triflers or topers, but not the poet's brother";[25] pluralism was objectionable but not if it was practiced by William Unwin; tobacco was to be denounced until it was smoked by "the smoke-inhaling Bull"; physicians were incompetent and were paid for "length'ning out disease," but such a physician Dr. Cotton was not; and so on. We are, therefore, not greatly surprised that Cowper refused to allow himself to be misled by the same sort of logic that caused Burke, ignorant of many of the circumstances with which Hastings had to cope, to picture Hastings as a monster whose rule was an ineradicable blot upon his country's fame. Lord Macaulay was certainly not wholly wrong in feeling that the poet "could image to himself Hastings the Governor-General only as the Hastings with whom he had rowed on the Thames and played in the cloister, and refused to believe that so good-tempered a fellow could have done anything very wrong."[26] There might also have been another reason for Cowper's attitude; that is, the poet's instinctive tendency to go to the rescue of the underdog. The alleged oppressor of India, against whom some of the nation's most brilliant and powerful voices were crying for vengeance, was now himself oppressed. Even if Hastings had not been a school friend, Cowper might have been able to say "Poor Hastings!" with the same fervor that he said "Poor Louis!"

But we do not have to explain Cowper's attitude entirely on the basis of his instinct and his essential benevolence. We may allow him a reasonable amount of perspicacity. Fanny Burney, who also knew Hastings as a friend and who reported the famous trial in her brilliant gossipy way, wrote at the outset, "I cannot believe Mr. Hastings guilty; I feel in myself a strong internal evidence of his innocence drawn from all I have seen of him; I can only regard the persecution as a party affair."[27]   Indeed, the trial had become too quickly a party question.   More than that, it had become too obviously one-sided.   Sir Philip Francis had for so long poured his venom into Whig ears that the Whigs painted Hastings as a complete monster of iniquity.   The fact was not unapparent, however, that while evidence was being dug up against him, Hastings was too busy in India to trouble much about a defense.[28]   As the trial proceeded, not even an idealistic statesman like Burke escaped some of the malignant and mean aspects of the case.   There is no reason to believe that Cowper was completely blind to these facts.

Cowper's early attitude toward the trial, as revealed in a letter to Lady Hesketh of February 16, 1788, is somewhat surprising for the amount of interest the poet evinces in the purely dramatic aspects.   As Fanny Burney, Joseph Farington, and the periodical literature of the time report the trial, it was a great show with impressive pageantry of statesmen and people of fashion, and with Burke lashing himself into such a fury as to cause some of his fashionable auditors to faint.[29]   Cowper wrote:

I recommend it to you, my dear, by all means to embrace the fair occasion, and to put yourself in the way of being squeezed

and incommoded a few hours, for the sake of hearing and seeing
what you will never have an opportunity to see and hear hereafter,—the trial of a man who has been greater and more feared
than the great Mogul himself. Whatever we are at home, we
certainly have been tyrants in the East; and if these men have,
as they are charged, rioted in the miseries of the innocent, and
dealt death to the guiltless with an unsparing hand, may they
receive a retribution that shall in the future make all governors
and judges of ours, in those distant regions, tremble! While I
speak thus, I equally wish them acquitted. They were both my
schoolfellows, and for Hastings I had a particular value.[30]

In the same month, one observes, Cowper's desire to say
something in defense of his former schoolmate found indirect expression in the "Sonnet addressed to Henry Cowper, Esq., Clerk Assistant to the House of Lords," praising
his cousin for his eloquence in defense of Hastings. The
poem was published in the *Gentleman's Magazine* for April,
1788, with the author's identity hidden under the signature
"T. H."

As the trial dragged on, gradually bringing the physical
and financial ruin of Hastings, Cowper's sympathy was completely won for the defendant. Early in the trial Miss Burney had been touched by the overwhelming odds against
Hastings, and Erskine had pictured the "terrible, unceasing,
exhaustless artillery of warm zeal, matchless vigour of understanding, and devouring eloquence . . . pouring forth upon
one private unprotected man."[31] In the spring of 1792 Cowper was ready to go to the defense of his friend. On May 5 he
wrote Lady Hesketh, sending the lines "To Warren Hastings,
Esq.": "I wish much to print the following lines in one of
the daily papers. Lord S.'s vindication of the poor culprit
in the affair of Cheit-Sing has confirmed me in the belief
that he has been injuriously treated, and I think it merely
an act of justice to take a little notice of him."[32] The poem
is as follows:

HASTINGS! I knew thee young and of a mind,
While young, humane, conversable, and kind,
Nor can I well believe thee, gentle THEN,
Now grown a villain, and the WORST of men.
But rather some suspect, who have oppress'd
And worried thee, as not themselves the BEST.

But this generous, if naïve, gesture did not serve its purpose.
As Miss Burney felt it expedient on account of her connections at court to maintain discreet "silence and sorrow,"
Lady Hesketh with important court connections seems to
have frowned upon having her talented cousin commit himself so definitely. The poem did not appear until Hayley
printed it in 1803.

Whatever may have been the route by which he arrived
at it, Cowper's final analysis of the trial has the distinction
of being justified by history. Although he deplored Hastings' suffering, the poet would doubtless have been pleased
if he could have known fully the effect that the trial had
in succeeding years as a deterrent for officials who were
inclined to play tyrant.

§ 4

Not only in "the conquer'd East" but in England was
legal justice in need of champions. Cowper's poetry on
prison and legal reforms at home is not merely an additional evidence of the catholicity of his humanitarian interests. It is not a matter of his championing a movement far
removed from his actual sphere of living. Only a few miles
away in Bedfordshire the first great English prison reformer
began his work and his first research took him to Huntingdon, where Cowper had lived after he left St. Albans.
Moreover, Cowper's friends were interested in prison work.
To his beloved William Unwin, the poet wrote on November 4, 1782:

I congratulate you on the discharge of your duty and your conscience, by the pains you have taken for the relief of prisoners. You proceeded wisely, yet courageously, and deserved better success. Your labours, however, will be remembered elsewhere, when you shall be forgotten here; and if the poor folks at Chelmsford should never receive the benefit of them, you will yourself receive it in heaven.[33]

The Evangelicals had been quick to lend their support to the growing protest against the inhumanities of the penal system. John and Charles Wesley began their religious labors in the prison at Oxford. John Wesley's *Journal* throws much lurid light on prison conditions. "I know not, if . . . there could be anything like it on this side of hell," Wesley observed of the Ludgate and Newgate prisons. The Conference of 1778 formally regarded it a duty of preachers to visit prisoners. Interest in reforming a highly corrupt penal system and a very illogical criminal code, however, antedated the great religious revival.

Cowper did not need his legal training at the Temple to be conscious of what Bentham was to attack as "the lawless science of the law"; but this training doubtless helped to impress upon him the inconsistencies of the English criminal code and the corruptions of the penal system. The administration of justice (if, indeed, it may be so called) in the eighteenth century presents two aspects equally incredible: the illogic of the criminal code and the corruption of magistrates and juries. Thus the law through its rigid inhumanity and its defective administration was capable both of bringing about oppression and encouraging license.

The age was one in which the only cure for crime seemed to be the gallows. London of the eighteenth century has been described as a city of gibbets and pillories. In Finchley Common, at Tyburn, or in the marshes below Purfleet, gallows dangled their hideous corpses to the breeze. Much has been said about the "rubricks of blood" that disgraced English statute books until after the end of the century. Until 1811, for example, stealing in a dwelling house to the extent of forty shillings was a capital offense. In 1776 the number of capital offenses was estimated in Parliament at 154 and by Blackstone at 160. Ten years later Romilly contended that they had increased considerably.[34] Besides being brutal, the code was inconsistent. It was possible to steal without being a thief, and yet to be guilty of a capital offense without intention of theft or violence. The severity of the law led to the reluctance of juries to convict for small offenses; and it was often preferable to be tried for a capital offense rather than a misdemeanor.

Cowper's first concern in the matter of reforming the criminal code is not, however, for the anomalous laws governing capital offenses. In *Expostulation* he protests against "Oppression labouring hard to grind the poor," not a little of which, we are led to believe in *Charity,* is the practice of throwing debtors into prison. In this protest Cowper had distinguished predecessors.

Although the Reverend Dr. Thomas Bray had begun his prison work some twenty-five years earlier, the first notable prison reformers of the century were General Oglethorpe and Lord Perceval, the outstanding members of the Parliamentary Committee of 1729 to investigate jails. The Committee exposed flagrant abuses at the Fleet and Marshalsea prisons and secured some ameliorative legislation—most notably an act that released many debtors from prison.[35] Although the investigation aroused popular indignation, it occasioned no sweeping reforms. More important were the endeavors of Bishop Berkeley and Oglethorpe in the founding of colonies for debtors in Bermuda and Georgia. The work of Oglethorpe won the praise of Pope and Thomson. Thomson's enthusiastic eulogy of the Jail Committee in *The*

Seasons doubtless furnished Cowper a precedent for his poetic treatment of prison reforms:

> And here can I forget the generous band,
> Who, touch'd with human woe, redressive search'd
> Into the horrors of the gloomy jail—
> Unpitied, and unheard, where Misery moans;
> Where Sickness pines; where Thirst and Hunger burn,
> And poor Misfortune feels the lash of Vice?
>
> [*Winter,* ll. 359-64.]

Thomson depicts vividly the tyrannous jailers snatching "the lean morsel from the starving mouth" and tearing "from the cold wintry limbs the tattered weed." He also calls for reforms in the code itself:

> The toils of law (which dark insidious men
> Have cumbrous added to perplex the truth,
> And lengthen simple justice into trade).

In the mid-century artist and novelist had joined hands in depicting the miseries of imprisoned debtors and the widespread corruption of the penal system. Hogarth, Smollett, and Fielding have left valuable records. Fielding, whose experience as a barrister and as Magistrate of Bow Street Court gave him a scholar's understanding of legal confusion and prison conditions, was the most indefatigable champion of legislative and prison reforms of the mid-century.[36] He used novels, plays, and pamphlets for his purpose. *Amelia* alone is an invaluable source book of information on the outrageous condition of prisons, the tyranny of bailiffs and jailers, the ignorance and corruption of magistrates, and the difficulties and inconsistencies of law enforcement. To the deplorable lot of debtors Fielding drew attention in *The Champion* and in *Jonathan Wild.* Henry Brooke argued the inhumanity of imprisonment for debt in *The Fool of Quality.*

Cowper's immediate inspiration for his passage in *Charity* seems to have been a speech made by Edmund Burke on the hustings at Bristol in 1780 "upon certain points relative to his Parliamentary conduct," a part of which is a noble defense of the statesman's support of Lord Beauchamp's bill for reforming the legal process concerning the imprisonment of insolvent debtors. That Cowper often followed Burke's speeches closely we have ample evidence. As we have seen, the poet and the statesman did not always agree. Although the American question was a point of violent disagreement, Cowper had read Burke's speech on "Economical Reform" in February, 1780, and had expressed his approval.[37] He was later to echo Burke's opinions on the India question. In his Bristol speech Burke had pointed out that one of the capital faults in English law with relation to civil debt was

. . . that every man is presumed solvent. A presumption, in innumerable cases, directly against truth. Therefore, the debtor is ordered, on a supposition of ability and fraud, to be coerced his liberty until he makes payment. By this means, in all cases of civil insolvency, without a pardon from his creditor, he is to be imprisoned for life:—and thus a miserable mistaken invention of artificial science operates to change a civil into a criminal judgment, and to scourge misfortune or indiscretion with a punishment which the law does not inflict on the greatest of crimes.[38]

Cowper, too, argues that prisons should be restricted to the function for which they were designed: "to bind the lawless, and to punish guilt." Although as a moralist and social philosopher he is willing to attribute poverty largely to indolence, as a humanitarian interested in legal reforms he is inclined either to place a Calvinistic interpretation on insolvency and regard it as a visitation of Providence, or to treat debt as being often an evidence of the triumph of guile over honesty, for neither of which has society any right to exact a toll. Cowper concludes—

Let just restraint, for public peace design'd,
Chain up the wolves and tigers of mankind;
The foe of virtue has no claim to thee—
But let insolent innocence go free.

[*Charity,* ll. 286-89.]

Burke's praise of John Howard, the greatest single force
for prison reform in the century, is more strikingly reflected
in Cowper's verse. When Howard, who had been living as
a country gentleman at Cardington, became in 1773 High
Sheriff of Bedford (a county adjoining Cowper's Buckinghamshire), he set about the reformation of the Bedford jail.
His investigation extended immediately to neighboring
Huntingdon and Cambridge, where he found evils similar
to those in Bedfordshire.[39] In 1774 he gave evidence before
a parliamentary committee on jail conditions. The result
was that two beneficent acts were passed—one regulating
sanitary conditions and another governing the exacting of
jailer's fees from men who had not been indicted or who
had been acquitted. This was the beginning of his single-
handed battle for prison reforms—a struggle that lasted until
his death in Russia in 1790, a martyr to his cause. He inves-
tigated most of the county jails and hundreds of bridewells
in England; moreover, his investigation of jails and lazarettos on the continent was of great significance.[40] It was
in pursuit of his study of "jail fever" that he was mortally
stricken. His epoch-making volume was *The State of Prisons in England and Wales,* which he brought out and sold
at a small cost in 1777.

Burke pays eloquent tribute to Howard's magnificent
humanitarianism:

I cannot mention this gentleman without remarking that his
labours and writings have done much to open the eyes and hearts
of mankind. He has visited all Europe—not to survey the sump-
tuousness of palaces, or the stateliness of temples; not to make

accurate measurements of the remains of ancient grandeur, nor
to form a scale of the curiosity of modern art; not to collect
medals, or collate manuscripts:—but to dive into the depths of
dungeons; to plunge into the infection of hospitals; to survey the
mansions of sorrow and pain; to take gage and dimensions of
misery, depression, and contempt; to remember the forgotten, to
attend to the neglected, to visit the forsaken, and to compare and
collate the distresses of all men in all countries. It was a voyage
of discovery; a circumnavigation of charity. . . . He will receive,
not by retail but in gross, the reward of those who visit the
prisoner; and he has so forestalled and monopolized that branch
of charity, that there will be, I trust, little room to merit by such
acts of benevolence hereafter.

The contagious quality of Burke's eloquence on this subject
is seen in a letter written by Sir Samuel Romilly, one of the
century's great legal reformers, on May 22, 1781, shortly
before Cowper began writing *Charity:* "What a singular
journey!—not to admire the wonders of art and nature, not
to visit courts and ape their manners; but to dive into dungeons, to compare the misery of men in different climates,
to study the art of mitigating the torments of mankind."[41]
Cowper's fine tribute to the great reformer plainly borrows
from Burke:

> To quit the bliss thy rural scenes bestow
> To seek a nobler amidst scenes of woe,
> To traverse seas, range kingdoms, and bring home,
> Not the proud monuments of Greece or Rome,
> But knowledge such as only dungeons teach,
> And only sympathy like thine could reach;
> That grief, sequester'd from the public stage,
> Might smooth her feathers and enjoy her cage;
> Speaks a divine ambition and a zeal,
> The boldest patriot might be proud to feel.
> Oh that the voice of clamor and debate,
> That pleads for peace till it disturbs the state,

Were hush'd in favor of thy gen'rous plea—
The poor thy clients, and heav'n's smile thy fee!

                [*Charity,* ll. 299-312.]

After the eulogies of Burke and Cowper it became the fashion to praise Howard. The ode of Hayley, who later became Cowper's friend and first biographer, had, of course, come earlier.[42] Mrs. Inchbald's *Such Things Are* is said to contain a part modelled on Howard. On July 28, 1787, Wesley wrote enthusiastically of him in his journal, calling him "one of the greatest men in Europe." Miss Anna Seward called him "the matchless philanthropic hero," and Dr. Darwin paid tribute to him in *The Botanic Garden* (1789).

In Book I of *The Task* Cowper protests against the absurd lack of logic in the criminal code and also the laxities of law enforcement. These he treats, significantly enough, as the first blot on the fame of London. Of law enforcement in general he makes an extremely pertinent comment. To him it seems, as indeed it was, "more prompt t' avenge than to prevent the breach of law." Moreover, it is a legal code that regulates the poor without regulating the rich. Here is a serious fallacy. The irony that a man who steals a loaf of bread becomes a convict while the man who steals an empire becomes a hero must be as old as civilization; but there is a freshness in Cowper's protest in spite of the triteness of the subject. The law, he finds

        is rigid in denouncing death
On petty robbers, and indulges life
And liberty, and oft-times honour too,
To peculators of the public gold.
. . . thieves at home must hang; but he, that puts
Into his overgorg'd and bloated purse
The wealth of Indian provinces, escapes.   [Ll. 732-38.]

If Cowper deplores the existence of the "rubricks of blood" a little less strongly than others have done, it is because he refuses to sentimentalize the criminal. For fleshly weaknesses he often shows little sympathy. The noose is none too good for the chicken thief who steals in order to drink and who in his drunkenness neglects his wife and children. With sexual irregularities he has little patience. In the following century Thomas Hood extended his humanitarian sympathy to the prostitute. Not so, Cowper. This fact is strongly revealed in his anonymously printed *Anti-Thelyphthora* (1781), an attack on his cousin Martin Madan's sincere but highly ill-advised *Thelyphthora; or, a Treatise on Female Ruin,* a work on the biblical sanctions for polygamy. The two-volume treatise was the result of Madan's observation of fallen women at the Lock Hospital, of which he was chaplain, and was an attempt to find some remedy for the flagrant evil of prostitution. Following its publication in 1780, the *Gentleman's Magazine* literally teemed with replies to the work and with reviews of books and pamphlets attacking Madan. After Cowper had written his attack, he was not proud of it and was glad to preserve its anonymity throughout his life; but he never swerved from his position. In Book III of *The Task,* for example, he finds that the nation has departed from the time-honored ideals of domestic happiness and that as a result

> prostitution elbows us aside
> In all our crowded streets; and senates seem
> Conven'd for purposes of empire less
> Than to release th' adultress from her bond.
> Th' adultress! what a theme for angry verse!
>
> [Ll. 60-64.]

If Cowper does not insist upon more legal pressure on the vice, he insists upon more social pressure and upon unequivocal condemnation of the loss of virtue in womanhood.

It must be admitted that the attack would have been more effective had it been written from London instead of from Olney!

Later in Book III the poet returns to a consideration of other laxities in law enforcement. Time was, Cowper writes, when

> he that sharp'd
> And pocketted a prize by fraud obtain'd
> Was mark'd and shunn'd as odious. He that sold
> His country, or was slack when she requir'd
> His ev'ry nerve in action and at stretch
> Paid, with the blood that he had basely spar'd,
> The price of his default. But now—yes, now
> We are become so candid and so fair,
> So lib'ral in construction, and so rich
> In Christian charity, (good natur'd age!)
> That they are safe, sinners of either sex,
> Transgress what laws they may.   [Ll. 86-97.]

In the very year in which *The Task* appeared Martin Madan, ever a controversialist, published his *Thoughts on Executive Justice,* in which he insisted upon a return to the rigorous enforcement of the criminal law. The work provoked the brochure of Sir Samuel Romilly called *Observations on a late Publication, entitled 'Thoughts on Executive Justice'* and was a stimulus to much of Romilly's valorous work in reforming the criminal code. Romilly admitted that the work was "in truth, a strong and vehement censure upon the judges and the ministers for their mode of administering the law, and for the frequency of the pardons that they granted"; but, he argued justly, the code itself was at fault and the insistence upon an impossible code was the wrong course to take. Cowper, however, was not so much writing with an eye on the bloody enforcement of the law among all classes as he was with his eye on laxities of the law in the upper strata of society, where it was easiest to escape. He had already pointed out the lack of logic in punishing the poor and allowing the rich to evade punishment.

In the eighteenth century the office of justice of the peace had fallen into contempt on account of the disreputable character of the office holders. The original arrangement had been that in rural districts gentlemen should serve without pay; but when duties became arduous, justices were allowed to appropriate fees of people charged before them. The "trading justices" became notorious.[43] Inefficiency of lawyers and corruption among magistrates were not satirized in the century more effectively than by Fielding in Lawyer Scout of *Joseph Andrews* and in Jonathan Thrasher, Esq., of *Amelia*. To the gallery of eighteenth-century magistrates Cowper adds his portrait of the "plump convivial parson," who, laying aside both "his rev'rence and his worship," is inefficient both out of habitual sloth and the fear of retribution from the gang to which "th' audacious convict" before him belongs. Nor does the cloth keep him above bribery:

> Examine well
> His milk-white hand; the palm is hardly clean—
> But here and there an ugly smutch appears.
> Foh! 'twas a bribe that left it: he has touch'd
> Corruption! Whoso seeks an audit here
> Propitious, pays his tribute, game or fish,
> Wild-fowl or ven'son; and his errand speeds.
> [*Task*, IV, ll. 606-12.]

In Cowper's vision of the reign of love in the final book of *The Task* the corruptions of the English legal system are not forgotten. The passage is remarkable because it represents in essence the ideals toward which Sir Samuel Romilly, Sir James Mackintosh, Jeremy Bentham, Sir Robert Peel, and Lord Brougham strove in Cowper's own century and in the succeeding one. The poet sees a world

Where violence shall never lift the sword,
Nor cunning justify the proud man's wrong,
Leaving the poor no remedy but tears:—
 Where he that fills an office shall esteem
Th' occasion it presents of doing good
More than the perquisite;—where law shall speak
Seldom, and never but as wisdom prompts
And equity; not jealous more to guard
A worthless form, than to decide aright:—
Where fashion shall not sanctify abuse,
Nor smooth good-breeding (supplemental grace)
With lean performance ape the work of love!

                                    [Ll. 843-54.]

Here again Cowper has achieved the poetic expression of a
lofty humanitarian ideal with all the dignity and beauty
that the subject commands. There are in it a quiet sublimity and an artless perfection rarely attained by a poet
outside the first rank. Cowper is rightly called a religious
poet; but it is remarkable how often a humanitarian rather
than a purely religious impulse carries him to the highest
reaches of his art.

Chapter VI

SWORDS UNBLEST

§ 1

THE CONCEPTION of Cowper as a hermit-like pietist nowhere fits more poorly than it does with his attitude toward war. Particularly as a youth, he was swept away with enthusiasm over the glorious victories of the Seven Years' War. Boscawen's success off the coast of Portugal, Hawke's demolition of Conflans, and Wolfe's conquest of Quebec stirred his truly English heart. It is true that all this came before St. Albans, and the Huntingdon and Olney years, but he never ceased to feel pride in England's defiance of the world. We shall, therefore, be disappointed if we expect of Cowper anything like a philosophy of passive resistance or adherence to a rigid interpretation of Christian teachings about war. His religion, his patriotism, his politics, and his common sense are all determining factors in his attitude toward the use of coercion and force. Through his poetry and his letters between 1779 and the completion of *The Task* we may see the development of an anti-war theory that has its culmination in Book V of *The Task*. The steps in the development are not clearly marked. But there is apparent a general trend of growth toward something that may be labeled, perhaps somewhat ineffectually, "revolutionary."

If ever a century provided reason for a reaction against the stupidity and horror of war, it was the eighteenth century. There were wars and rumors of wars in remarkable profusion—wars on land and sea, wars on the Continent, in India, in Egypt, in America. But never did martial zeal glow more warmly than it did in England, and never was the chip more delicately poised on the nation's shoulder. The cause of the War of Jenkins' Ear was not merely that of the incident giving the war its name; nevertheless, the name is suggestive of the slight provocation necessary to produce a conflict. There seemed to be an element of savage delight in the prospect of war, which to the national mind stood for expansion and progress. Peace seems to have suggested apathy and retrogression. Brilliant military exploits thrilled the nation and filled it with patriotic frenzy. Most of the horror of war was forgotten. A colossal struggle for empire was on; and the dramatic elements—the gold braid, the brass buttons, the romantic tales of valor and adventure —effectively obscured the spilled blood and the dying groans of the battlefields.

That there were no peace movements in the century occasions no great surprise; but theories of peace had begun to spring up in Europe.[1] The *grand dessein* presented in 1638 to Henry IV by Sully, the great minister of the French monarch, was the starting point of several schemes of international tribunals and federations that were offered as preventives of war. In 1693 the Quaker, William Penn, published *Towards the Present and Future Peace of Europe*. Since George Fox and eleven other Quakers issued their famous declaration against war in 1660, the Quakers had been the leading exponents of abolishing war even for self-defense. In 1713 the Abbé Castel de Saint-Pierre presented another scheme based on Sully. The two essays of Rousseau, *L'État de Guerre* and *Jugement sur le Projet de Paix Perpétuelle,* were published between 1753 and 1758. Finally, in the last decades of the century Bentham published *A Plan for an Universal and Perpetual Peace,* in which he arrived at a conception of a United States of Europe; and Kant wrote his *Zum Ewigen Frieden.*

The plans for international concert cannot themselves interest us here, but some of the ideas of their designers will be of importance to our purpose. Rousseau, with his lofty conception of the natural man, argued that man is by nature peaceful and timid ("*naturellement pacifique et craintif*")[2] and that wars are the consequence of the greed and rivalry of nations. With the Abbé de Saint-Pierre, he agrees that wars are matters not between individuals but between states —or, to put it another way, not between nations but between princes and cabinets. Here he is pointedly at variance with the conception of the state held by Grotius, the great seventeenth-century Dutch jurist and "father of international law," and by Hobbes, whose whole theory of the natural man Rousseau, of course, opposes. Rousseau further maintains that war is not justifiable on the grounds of destroying life, for territorial expansion, or for any material benefits. It can only be waged to maintain the freedom of one state against the aggression of another. Outside these limits it is murder and brigandage. On this point, Rousseau was more nearly in agreement with Grotius, who gave the chief "just" causes of war as self-defense and defense of one's property and who quoted Augustine in condemnation of aggression and imperialism: "Without justice what are empires but so many robberies?"[3] In his attempt to inculcate international-mindedness, Bentham was also to attack conquest and imperialism as robbery, going so far as to advocate that England and France give up their colonies and found no more.[4]

In seventeenth-century France, Pascal and La Bruyère had continued the ridicule of war in the Rabelaisian vein.[5] Voltaire carried the same strain over into the next century; whereas Montesquieu framed his objections to war on a more seriously reasoned basis, and the Encyclopedists, led by Diderot, were able to arrive at a conception of the modern interdependence of the whole world. In England no one ridiculed war so effectively as Dean Swift in "A Voyage to the Houyhnhnms."

In the early part of the century peace did not seem to be a good theme for poetry, for the poets were too busy singing the glorification of British liberty to the shame of the French.[6] Sir Andrew Freeport is described in the second *Spectator* paper as a gentleman who "will tell you that it is a stupid and barbarous way to extend dominions by arms, for true power is to be got by arts and industry." Here, indeed, is a theory of peace entirely compatible with Whig glorification of commerce. But when Britain's commercial supremacy and its all-important wool industry were threatened, there was no time to talk idealistically of peace. Young denounced war in *Imperium Pelagi* (1730) only because it was "the death of commerce and increase." A little earlier in the poem he had sung of Britain's "honest wars" in pursuing her commercial career. As the century goes on and England's struggle for empire continues, we find a statesman like William Pitt confessing on one occasion that he loved "honourable war." Even after the middle of the century one finds somewhat infrequently a poem like Beattie's *Ode to Peace,* which mourns the departure of peace from Albion and cites Ambition as the cause:

> Where sordid gold the breast alarms,
> Where cruelty inflames the eyes of Pride,
> And Grandeur wantons in soft Pleasure's arms!

It is true, however, that Brown attacked Whig commercialism in the *Estimate* and Churchill attacked European imperialism in his satires.

Dr. Johnson, hardly a pacifist, made a significant step toward a realistic treatment of war. In 1771 he wrote in *Thoughts on the late Transactions respecting Falkland's Islands:*

The wars of civilized nations make very slow changes in the system of empire. The public perceives scarcely any alteration but an increase of debt; and the few individuals who are benefited are not supposed to have the clearest right to their advantages. If he that shared the danger enjoyed the profit, and after bleeding in battle grew rich by the victory, he might shew his gains without envy. But at the conclusion of a ten years war, how are we recompensed for the death of multitudes and the expense of millions, but by contemplating the sudden glories of paymasters and agents, contractors and commissaries, whose equipages shine like meteors, and whose palaces rise like exhalations?

The importance of the point of view is not to be discredited by the fact that the pamphlet is a political one now chiefly remembered for its powerful invective against Junius.

Although Wesley had warned those in power of the dangers of the struggle, he supported the government (as his *Calm Address to Our American Colonies* of 1775 shows) when war with America became inevitable. But in 1776 the horror of war caused him to write his *Seasonable Address to the Inhabitants of Great Britain,* in which he deplores all conflict. As theologians both John Wesley and John Newton look upon warfare as proof of the depravity of man. In the famous treatise on "Original Sin," Wesley brands war as evidence "of the utter degeneracy of all nations from the plainest principles of reason and virtue," and finds it particularly inconceivable that Christian should war against Christian.[7] Newton shows complete agreement in the sermon on the "Extent of Messiah's Spiritual Kingdom":

War is followed as a trade, and cultivated as a science; and they who, with the greatest diligence and success, spread devastation and ruin far and wide, and deluge the earth with blood, acquire the title of heroes and conquerors. Can there be a stronger confirmation of what we read in Scripture concerning the depravity of man?[8]

Wesley stands with Swift and Rousseau in conceiving of war as between princes rather than nations:

... a man, who is King of France, has a quarrel with another man, who is King of England. So these Frenchmen are to kill as many of these Englishmen as they can, to prove the King of France is in the right. Now, what an argument is this! What a method of proof! What an amazing way of deciding controversies!

His conclusion is that "men in general can never be allowed to be reasonable creatures, till they know not war any more." Eyes were now being opened to the illogic of war.

§ 2

When Cowper left London in 1763 on account of his mental derangement, England had successfully concluded the Seven Years' War and seemed sure of her rank as first nation in the world; but when the poet again became actively interested in the affairs of the world in the last half of the seventies, the position of England was most precarious.[9] Not only was she the object of universal hatred, but the victories of her opponents were becoming alarming and the disintegration of her empire had set in. We are not surprised that Cowper's instinctive patriotism and his equally instinctive sympathy for the oppressed tended to lead him to champion the justice of England's cause. That he did not always do so uncritically, however, will be apparent.

One of his first poetic utterances of the ideal of brotherly love as an antidote to conflict, personal and national, comes in the moral fable, "The Nightingale and Glow-worm," written in February, 1780:

> Hence jarring sectaries may learn
> Their real int'rest to discern;
> That brother should not war with brother,
> And worry and devour each other.

The moral is commonplace, and its application is not strictly to war. A more important pacifistic sentiment is to be found

in the same year in "Boadicea." Although the deeply patriotic sentiments may tend to obscure other impressions, the
poem is instinct with the idea that bloody aggression is always doomed to divine punishment and that the expansion
and growth of a nation is possible without war.

Table Talk, the first of the didactic poems in point of
position in the 1782 volume, opens with an attack on war
as an instrument of kings' selfish desire for glory. The attack, however, has more elements of conventional patriotism
than it has of true pacifism, coming as it does at a time when
England's back was to the wall and when Cowper was dis-
satisfied with the inefficiency with which the war in America and the campaign against France were being carried on.

The poem itself, cast in the conversational form of an
Horatian satire, is, as Cowper puts it, "a medley of many
things." Mr. J. C. Bailey sees as its dominant idea the need
of character in public men; whereas Sir George Trevelyan
regards it as a satire on the Opposition. At least the first
part of the poem is a defense of England's part in the general European embroilment. At the outset, Cowper makes
it clear that one should not condemn war too unequivocally.
He does not pose as too much of an idealist. Here he accepts the Evangelical idea of war as an evidence of man's
depravity without protesting against the fact. Knowing that
men are by nature fierce, avaricious, and proud, he does not
hope for freedom from war until human nature is funda-
mentally changed. War is not without its justification. Justice is an ample reason for war. If a war has been entered
upon for the sake of justice, then all honor to him who
refuses to yield until justice has been accomplished. Indeed,
at this point Cowper can make the martial assertion that
the man who is not moved by tales of valor in warfare on
the side of justice "is base in kind and born to be a slave."
(For *justice* one may read *England*.)

But infamy should visit a monarch who for ambition
would lay a country waste:

> Chief monster that has plagu'd the nation yet:
> The globe and sceptre in such hands misplac'd,
> Those ensigns of dominion, how disgrac'd! [Ll. 38-40.]

The "royal mastiff" that Cowper depicts as "panting at the
heels" of an attacked nation could be the monarch of any
one of England's enemies; it could hardly be George III,
with whom at the time Cowper in his rather relentless attitude toward the American "rebellion" sided against the powerful Whig Opposition. In the poet's delineation of the ideal
king, a generous gesture seems plainly to be made in the
direction of the British monarch. It will be observed that
the pacifism of Cowper's ideal monarch is founded on the
high-sounding principles that most modern pacifists justly
brand as ineffectual. But the poet is always sincere, even
when both his logic and his idealism are subject to criticism.
His monarch is expected

> To touch the sword with conscientious awe,
> Nor draw it but when duty bids him draw;
> To sheathe it in the peace-restoring close
> With joy beyond what victory bestows. [Ll. 77-80.]

If "justice" is the most legitimate reason for a king's
leading his people into war, for the people themselves freedom is the most legitimate object of warfare. In spite of
his failure to sympathize with the American Revolutionists,
a fight for freedom usually appealed to the poet's imagination:

> they, that fight for freedom, undertake
> The noblest cause mankind can have at stake.
>
> [Ll. 285-86.]

Cowper's interest in naval affairs is seen in two poems
of 1779—"On the Trial of Admiral Keppel" and "An Ad-

dress to the Mob on Occasion of the Late Riot at the House of Sir Hugh Palliser"—in which he defends first Keppel and then Palliser in the famous trial in which Keppel was the accused and Palliser was the accuser. The human interest of the trial seemed to appeal to Cowper more than the actual issues involved. By the time Cowper wrote *Table Talk* he had begun to see the evils of inefficiency and lack of morale in the British navy. He was then of the opinion that naval commanders had failed and were failing to exert themselves properly to preserve the honor of their country. He, therefore, attacks

> admirals, extolled for standing still,
> Or doing nothing with a deal of skill;
> Generals, who will not conquer when they may,
> Firm friends to peace, to pleasure, and good pay.
>
> [Ll. 192-95.]¹⁰

The turn that the poem finally takes is rather typical of Cowper's reasoning. If his patriotism causes him to defend England, his Evangelicalism causes him to speak in condemnation of England. He is conscious of no contradiction: he is merely thinking on different planes. Dr. John Brown, according to the poet's way of thinking, had attacked the effeminacy, folly, and lust of the nation without seeing the real cause of what he attacked. Cowper offers sin as the reason for the nation's decay. The nation has now forgotten God in war and in peace, and wars have been sent as a scourge. England's failures on land and on sea the poet no longer explains on the basis of the inefficiency of commanders; he now explains them as a matter of God's punishment.

The attack on lack of organization and courage in the navy is resumed in *Expostulation*. Cowper reiterates the contention that God's visitation of wrath on the nation is to be explained by the fact that England in the pride of her success in previous wars has taken due credit from God, and warns

That no success attends on spears and swords
Unblest, and that the battle is the Lord's. [Ll. 352-53.]

But a condemnation of the nation's godlessness does not argue for a relaxation of the poet's patriotism. A letter to Newton in March, 1781—the same month in which *Expostulation* was being written—shows characteristically how Cowper can merge his patriotism and his religion: ". . . wherever there is war, there is misery and outrage; notwithstanding which it is not only lawful to wish, but even a duty to pray for the success of one's country."

Charity, as we have seen elsewhere, presents a condemnation of the bloody aggression of Spain in the New World, depicting Cortez as the arch-villain. At the end of the poem the poet visualizes a Utopian civilization in which love will be the dominant force and in which "slaying men will cease to be an art."

Sometime during the year in which he was writing the didactic poems,[11] Cowper wrote "Heroism" (called "Aetna" in the letters), a poem which in a measure repeats some of the ideas of *Table Talk,* but which shows a keener analysis of the causes and nature of war. Like *Table Talk* it presents an attack on war as an instrument of glory and gain. Again, Cowper pictures the ruthless tactics of monarchs, writing in blood the merit of their cause, invading peaceful lands—"their only crime, vicinity . . ."—murdering the inhabitants, and laying waste their fields. He now sees clearly that national honor and justice are more often excuses than reasons for war, and that the true reason for war is economic: the avaricious desire of one monarch for the wealth of another. A ravaged nation will slowly rebuild; then

Increasing commerce and reviving art
Renew the quarrel on the conq'rors' part;
And the sad lesson must be learn'd once more,
That wealth within is ruin at the door.

Monarchs, asserts the poet in a particularly ill-fitting figure, are Aetnas, always ready to spew destruction on the
unsuspecting.

The passionately patriotic closing lines of the poem assure
one that England is "a heav'n protected isle" and that
George III is no volcano. But the patriotic bias does not
keep the poem from showing significant development in
Cowper's anti-war sentiment.

§ 3

In 1783 Cowper was not so firmly convinced of the blessings of "a George's reign" as he was when he wrote the
closing lines of "Heroism." Before the year was over he
was to turn into a staunch opponent of the King's position
on the India Bill. Early in the year he commented with
fine irony on the proposed terms of the Treaty of Versailles
and of the patching up of friendship between the kings of
France and England. Here one can see that the poet has
accepted whole-heartedly Rousseau's position that war is
not between nations but between kings and cabinets, and
that he now allots to George III his full share in the heinous
chess game of international affairs:

I give you joy of the restoration of that sincere and firm
friendship between the Kings of England and France, that has
been so long interrupted. It is great pity, when hearts so cor-
dially united are divided by trifles. Thirteen pitiful colonies,
which the King of England chose to keep, and the King of
France to obtain, if he could, have disturbed that harmony which
would else, no doubt, have subsisted between those illustrious
personages to this moment. If the King of France, whose greatness of mind is only equalled by that of his Queen, had regarded
them, unworthy of their notice as they were, with an eye of
suitable indifference; or, had he thought it a matter deserving in
any degree his princely attention, that they were, in reality, the
property of his good friend the King of England; or, had the

latter been less obstinately determined to hold fast his interest in them; or could he, with that civility and politeness in which monarchs are expected to excel, have entreated his Majesty of France to accept a bagatelle, for which he seemed to have conceived so strong a predilection, all his mischief had been prevented. But monarchs, alas! crowned and sceptered as they are, are yet but men; they fall out, and are reconciled, just like the meanest of their subjects. I cannot, however, sufficiently admire the moderation and magnanimity of the King of England. His dear friend on the other side of the channel has not indeed taken actual possession of the colonies in question, but he has effectually wrested them out of the hands of their original owner; who, nevertheless, letting fall the extinguisher of patience upon the flame of his resentment, and glowing with no other flame than that of sincerest affection, embraces the King of France again, gives him Senegal and Goree in Africa, gives him the islands he had taken from him in the West, gives him his conquered territories in the East, gives him a fishery upon the banks of Newfoundland; and, as if all this were too little, merely because he knows that Louis has a partiality for the King of Spain, gives to the latter an island in the Mediterranean, which thousands of English had purchased with their lives; and in America, all that he wanted, at least all that he could ask. No doubt there will be great cordiality between this royal trio for the future: and though wars may, perhaps, be kindled between their posterity, some ages hence, the present generation shall never be witnesses of such a calamity again. I expect soon to hear that the Queen of France, who, just before this rupture happened, made the Queen of England a present of a watch, has, in acknowledgment of all these acts of kindness, sent her also a seal wherewith to ratify the treaty. Surely she can do no less.[12]

In another letter to Newton, Cowper is willing to make some concessions to the Calvinistic point of view and to explain the unfavorable terms of the treaty as the punishment of Providence visited on a sinful nation. "But," he asserts, "when I consider the peace as the work of our ministers, and reflect that with more wisdom, or more spirit, they might perhaps have procured a better, I confess it does not please me. . . . I do not think it just that the French should plunder us, and be paid for doing it; nor does it appear to me that there was an absolute necessity for such tameness on our part. . . ."[13] This expression of disgust is typical of Cowper's impatience with what he considers to be false humility. Cowper's Calvinism, as we have seen before, is not the kind that can accept every evil as a punishment of God for sin. When he can trace tyranny to the selfishness and vainglory of princes, or even to that of human beings, he is not inclined to advocate "kissing the rod" or "turning the cheek." A great deal of light is thrown on his attitude toward the Treaty of Versailles by a letter written two years earlier than the letter just quoted. In advising William Unwin about the proper course to take in a dispute in which he is involved, the poet's exegesis on the scriptural exhortation is illuminating:

"If a man smite one cheek, turn the other." "If he takes thy cloak, let him take thy coat also." That is, I suppose, rather than on a vindictive principle avail yourself of that remedy that the law allows you, in the way of retaliation, for that was the subject immediately under the discussion of the speaker. Nothing is so contrary to the genius of the Gospel as the gratification of resentment and revenge; but I cannot easily persuade myself to think that the author of that dispensation could possibly advise his followers to consult their own peace at the expense of the peace of society, or inculcate a universal abstinence from the use of lawful remedies, to the encouragement of injury and oppression.[14]

It is no credit to a man or a nation to fail to insist upon rights.

The opening lines of Book II of *The Task* show how Cowper's abhorrence of slavery led him to a conception of the evils of nationalism, the spirit that pits man against man in hatred and warfare:

> Lands intersected by a narrow frith
> Abhor each other. Mountains interpos'd
> Make enemies of nations, who had else
> Like kindred drops, been mingled into one.
> Thus man devotes his brother, and destroys. [Ll. 16-20.]

The poem continues with a plea for brotherly love among nations on the basis of their common fellowship in sorrow.

This is the broad view, and it works well for the anti-slavery argument. But Cowper is not able to hold it when he again thinks of the conduct of the war against France and of the Treaty of Versailles. In the same book in which he projects an internationalism of brotherly love, he makes a more scathing attack than he did in *Table Talk* and *Expostulation* on the inefficiency of the English army and navy. What shall we do with the contradiction? The most obvious explanation is that Cowper simply did not let the ideal obscure the real. He mourns "the pride and av'rice that make man a wolf to man" and hopes for a state of society in which such base motives will be removed. But if a wolf is actually in one's path, the thing to do is to deal with it with as much credit to oneself as possible. One cannot achieve right by letting wrong prevail.

In the attack on the army and navy Cowper follows closely the lead of Brown's *Estimate*. Of the army he writes:

> How, in the name of soldiership and sense,
> Should England prosper, when such things, as smooth
> And tender as a girl, all essenc'd o'er
> With odours, and as profligate as sweet;
> Who sell their laurel for a myrtle wreath,
> And love when they should fight; when such as these
> Presume to lay their hand upon the ark
> Of her magnificent and awful cause?   [Ll. 225-32.]

The poet bemoans the fact that England has not produced another general like his boyhood hero, Wolfe, or another

statesman like the elder Pitt. The satire on the navy is
even more bitter (ll. 255-63).

The succeeding passage shows how poorly Newton had
convinced Cowper that the proper attitude toward the
Treaty of Versailles was one of Christian submission. The
poet continues his biting irony. There is no argument for
turning the cheek here. France has caused England's loss
of America, has "pick'd the jewel out of England's crown":

> And let that pass—'twas but a trick of state!
> A brave man knows no malice, but at once
> Forgets in peace the injuries of war,
> And gives his direst foe a friend's embrace.
> And, sham'd as we have been, to th' very beard
> Brav'd and defied, and in our own sea prov'd
> Too weak for those decisive blows that once
> Ensur'd us mast'ry there, we yet retain
> Some small pre-eminence; we justly boast
> At least superior jockeyship, and claim
> The honours of the turf as all our own!   [Ll. 267-77.]

This is not the effeminate Cowper that Hazlitt limned!

If poor organization and shallow military ideals have
brought inefficiency to the officers in the army, Cowper
finds that "universal soldiership" has had equally devastating
effects on the "meaner class." Arms, Cowper concludes in
Book IV of *The Task:*

> through the vanity and brainless rage
> Of those that bear them, in whatever cause,
> Seem most at variance with all moral good,
> And incompatible with serious thought. [Ll. 619-22.]

Cowper presents a delightful description of the transformation of the rustic into a soldier. The humor does not detract
from the seriousness with which the poet regards the problem. The simple, sheepish countryman, whose "introverted
toes" and dull wit make him at first a hay-foot-straw-foot

subject for the sergeant, at last attains the superficial airs
of a soldier. When his "three years of heroship" are over,
he

> Returns indignant to the slighted plough.
> He hates the field, in which no fife or drum
> Attends him; drives his cattle to a march;
> And sighs for the smart comrades he has left.
>   [Ll. 645-48.]

But the exterior change is not all. The evil habits of drinking and gambling acquired in the army ruin him for life.
All his simple goodness is gone, never to be recaptured.

In peaceful society, Cowper asserts, man finds full opportunities for development; but the poet has developed a deep
mistrust for man "leagu'd with man" for purposes of war.
Not only does he see how the system of universal soldiership can corrupt the rustic, but he also sees now that the
general effect of war on the morality of the individual is
one of its most vicious aspects:

> the field of glory, as the world
> Misdeems it, dazzled by its bright array,
> With all its majesty of thund'ring pomp,
> Enchanting music, and immortal wreaths,
> Is but a school where thoughtlessness is taught
> On principle, where foppery atones
> For folly, gallantry for ev'ry vice.   [Ll. 684-90.]

It is in Book V of *The Task* that Cowper expresses his
most important anti-war sentiment in a revolutionary passage attacking the tyranny and vainglory of princes. From
a discussion of the fabulous ice palace of the Tsarina Elizabeth, he concludes that "great princes have great playthings," and launches into a spirited discussion of war as a
game that princes play, making mankind their sport. It is
only through the stupidity of mankind, the poet insists, that

such a condition is made possible. If men were wise, they would not allow their sovereigns such costly sport.

For his explanation of the origin of war Cowper achieves an interesting blend of biblical legend and Rousseauistic philosophy. War may be traced ultimately to Cain, the first murderer. From him sprang "the first artificer of death," Tubal, the Vulcan of the Hebrew legend. After the flood the seeds of murder remained in the breast of men. When Babel was confounded, the various nations were allotted land by just division. As long as the nations ploughed their own fields and attended to the reaping of their harvests, peace reigned in the world. But

> The tasted sweets of property begat
> Desire of more, and industry in some,
> T' improve and cultivate their just demesne,
> Made others covet what they saw so fair.
> Thus war began on earth.   [Ll. 224-28.]

Here we recognize an idea propounded vigorously by Rousseau: that the concept of property is the root of war.[15] Locke, of course, had suggested the idea to the French philosopher. Cowper's idea that war is traceable to the grouping of individuals into political units is also Rousseau's.

At first warfare was crude and irregular, the poet continues. At length a valorous warrior was chosen leader; and eventually he who could lead best in battle was deemed best fit to govern in times of peace. Thus kings came into being. The commons, themselves powerless to attain leadership, set their king on a pedestal, and

> by degrees, self-cheated of their sound
> And sober judgment, that he is but man,
> They demi-deify and fume him so,
> That in due season he forgets it too.
> Inflated and astrut with self-conceit,
> He gulps the windy diet.   [Ll. 264-69.]

Thenceforth, to the king the people are as mere cattle, "drudges born to bear his burden," and he deems "an easy reck'ning" ten thousand lives lost in a battle to achieve fame and glory for him. With further revolutionary zeal Cowper contemptuously presents the irony of men trembling before the gods that they have created. Such a phenomenon is remarkable enough in barbaric society, but it is still little less than incredible in an enlightened age. Can it be logical, asks the poet, that a man who is like all other men should feel that he is the only freedman and should arrogate to himself the power to make war when and with whom he pleases —to give

> His thousands, weary of penurious life,
> A splendid opportunity to die?   [Ll. 319-20.]

Further on we shall see that this attack on war and tyranny is written with an eye on France. The Bastile passage is deservedly famous. But Cowper no longer feels that he must handle George III with too much deference. He dares to point a warning finger at the monarch on the English throne:

> But recollecting still that he is man,
> We trust him not too far, King though he be,
> And king in England, too, he may be weak,
> And vain enough to be ambitious still.   [Ll. 335-38.]

In his letters Cowper had already accused George of Stuartism.

It is true that Cowper did not follow through his enthusiasm for the French Revolution after he had finished *The Task,* and that a few years later Lady Hesketh, with her eye on the laureateship, had him writing commendatory verses to the King and Queen; but we have no reason to doubt the sincerity of this significant attack on war.

If we had only the didactic poems, we could not argue very strongly for the importance of Cowper's anti-war sentiment. As one would expect, he accepts the Christian's duty to promote peace. He begins with the feeling that war is all but ineradicable and that it is, on occasions, just. In summing up the natural rights of war, he is likely to employ such a conventional label as *justice,* or to defend warfare "when the battle is the Lord's" without providing any apparatus for determining whether it is actually God's or the Devil's. We have ample evidence, however, that he was by no means blind to the possibility of England's injustice. He condemns unequivocally any war to gain fame or territory. The intensity of his protest against aggression and exploitation is illustrative of the distance between his position and that of the panegyrists who in the early decades sang of Britain's commercial and territorial expansion. This feeling alone makes him important as a humanitarian. Although he can visualize a Utopian society in which love is law, he realizes the necessity for facing a sinful world in which avarice is a dominant motive. In such a world he is inclined to feel that an argument for universal abstinence from the use of force might encourage rather than discourage injury and oppression. Here, he rules out sentimentality for common sense. Moral or physical weakness in a nation or a man does not win the poet's sympathy. So far, Cowper has not gone beyond the position of such a seventeenth-century thinker as Grotius.

"Heroism" shows the beginning of the assumption of Rousseau's essential point of view. The first step toward this revolutionary conception is the discovery of the economic reasons for war, and the discovery that national honor and justice are often excuses for aggression. In *The Task* Cowper manifests a marked resentment of the fact that wars are playthings of princes and governments, and that people are pawns in the hands of those that govern them. If in *Table Talk* he speaks of the necessity of the king's touching the sword with "conscientious awe," in *The Task* he denies

the real right of kings to make war at all. He has learned
Rousseau's lesson well. Of no little importance is the way
in which *The Task* presents the devastating effect of warfare
on the nation's morals. Cowper can only hint at internationalism as a basis of peace. He was naturally not political
economist enough to foreshadow such a scheme of international concert as that which Bentham was formulating when
The Task was being written. His chief value as a pacifist lies
in the way that he was finally able to strip war of its glory
and idealism and to present its causes, motives, and effects
with telling realism. If Cowper's anti-war sentiments should
seem commonplace, it is well to remember that no other
poet in the century had laid such a solid foundation for a
pacifistic philosophy, that Cowper's pacifism antedated that
of Blake, Godwin, Coleridge, and Southey, and that concentration of pacifistic sentiments sufficient to cause a peace
movement did not come in England until the next century.[16]

Chapter VII

A SHORT VIEW OF EDUCATION

§ 1

ALTHOUGH in the eighteenth century continental Europe was the scene of much activity in the field of educational reform, England was notoriously backward in the development of her educational system.[1] One does not doubt that a great amount of the ignorance and depravity found in all levels of English society during the century is traceable to the inadequate instruction given in childhood and early youth. England had not lacked educational theorists or destructive critics of her deficient system. The preceding century had produced John Locke, whose influence on Rousseau was great, in spite of the fact that the French theorist discredited the disciplinary idea of education. Critics of the kind of education available in English public schools and universities were legion. It seems, however, to have been difficult for either destructive or constructive critics to stimulate action. One must wait for the Evangelical revival to see any very definite traces of interest in improving education. The work of John Wesley was revolutionary. However narrow the Evangelical ideas and ideals of education may seem to those who would discount the value of religious instruction, they proved a powerful force in sweeping out ignorance and slothfulness.

No one would want to call Cowper an important educational theorist. He was not capable of constructing a complete educational philosophy, and he wisely made no attempt to do so. However, as a critic of a deficient system, he occupies a distinguished place in the tradition of William

Law, John Wesley, and Hannah More. This fact we may accept in spite of Professor Hartmann's conclusion that Cowper's *Tirocinium* represents an honest opinion but that it is worthless as reform literature. Such a conclusion happens to be consequent upon a laborious proof that "Cowper's *Schilderungen aus seiner Schulzeit sind unzuverlässig und übertrieben, die vorgeschlagenen Gegenmittel nicht anwendbar*"![2] The *non sequitur* is easily apparent. One might almost as justifiably say that *The Shortest Way With Dissenters* and *A Modest Proposal* are ineffective reform literature because they do not portray existing conditions with literal accuracy and because the remedies they suggest are impracticable. We shall not be primarily concerned here with the accuracy or inaccuracy with which Cowper pictured the schools of his time, although the matter will naturally have to receive some consideration. In regard to Cowper's exaggeration Professor Hartmann has painstakingly proved the obvious; unfortunately, the German scholar placed inferior emphasis on a vastly more important matter, the relevancy of the criticism. It is significant that even today a critic like Mr. Hugh Fausset can write in the introduction to his volume of selections from Cowper: "I have excluded with some regret *Tirocinium, or A Review of Schools* because the protest which he made against the competitive system and other defects of the public schools is still unhappily relevant."[3]

However, an attestation of the value of *Tirocinium* as reform literature should come from a period nearer Cowper's own. A striking refutation of Professor Hartmann's contention is inherent in the anonymous tract, "A Reply to the Most Popular Objections to Public Schools, with Particular Reference to the Tyrocinium of Cowper," which appeared in *The Pamphleteer* in August, 1814. The author writes:

There is a magical power in the Tyrocinium of Cowper, which has awakened in the finest and purest bosoms a deep-rooted prejudice against Public Seminaries of Education; it abounds with so many sweet and natural images, it speaks so touchingly to the inmost sensibilities of the soul, it treats the subjects with so conversational a grace, and yet with a solemnity so awfully affecting, that even where it fails to dissuade the parents from the course they feel to be rational and expedient, it makes them tremble with anxiety, accuse themselves of a cruel policy, and regard their child almost as a victim and a sacrifice.[4]

The mere necessity of a public attack upon Cowper's educational ideas, together with those "promulgated in the *Edinburgh Review*," argues fairly conclusively that *Tirocinium* was regarded as effective reform literature.

It is rarely easy to trace with certainty the sources of Cowper's ideas. However, a study of the background of his views on the purpose and ideals of education will serve at least to place him in the educational thought of his century. We should not expect Cowper to be highly original; but he can, as we have already seen, be credited with giving very effective poetic expression to ideas already current. If we must look to the Evangelical revival for the rebirth of interest in education, we shall have to consider that prodigious dynamo, John Wesley, one of the most important educational thinkers in the century. Wesley's influence on Cowper's educational thought cannot be estimated with exactness. There are fewer direct references to Wesley in Cowper than one would ordinarily suspect, even though Cowper and Wesley did belong to different schools of Evangelical thought.[5] But since a great many of the ideas of the two men concur, it is reasonable to believe that the influence of the older man on the younger, whether direct or indirect, was important. Many of the educational ideas of both Wesley and Cowper are to be found in William

Law, the saintly mystic whose general influence over the titan of the Evangelical revival is well established. Wesley's knowledge of Milton's *Tractate of Education* and Rousseau's *Émile* (which he found to be "the most empty, silly, injudicious thing that ever a self-conceited Infidel wrote") we may also assume for Cowper, who by no means had Wesley's contempt for Rousseau's educational novel. Both men probably knew Locke's *Thoughts on Education*.[6] Cowper's constant contention that the existing system of education produces effeminacy is directly traceable to John Brown's *Estimate*.

Unlike Milton, Cowper was not able to ground his observations on education on his experience both as student and tutor; but a letter to Joseph Hill, written on July 6, 1776, shows that Cowper was at that time considering taking "two, three, or four boys under my tuition, to instruction."[7] "One half laughs and half shudders," wrote Professor Saintsbury, "to think what would have happened if the notion . . . had been carried out."[8] Cowper, it is true, was hardly fitted for managing an "academy."

Just as Locke's immediate cause for writing his *Thoughts on Education* was a desire to advise a friend on the education of his children, Cowper was stimulated to educational thought by a desire to give advice to William Unwin on the education of his son, John. The letters that he wrote to Unwin in 1780 may be regarded as studies for *Tirocinium*. On September 7, 1780, the poet wrote to insist that students should not be given Latin and Greek too young lest they grow to dislike study: "The mind and the body have . . . a striking resemblance of each other. In childhood they are both nimble, but not strong: they can skip and frisk about with wonderful agility, but hard labour spoils them both." The earliest training, Cowper felt, should be allotted to writing and arithmetic, together with geography, which was "imperfectly, if at all, inculcated in the schools." (Lord Spencer's son, the poet suggests, got a fine grasp of geography through a puzzle map.) If the student begins Latin and Greek at eight or nine, it is soon enough. He should not go to the university until he is fifteen, "a period, in my mind, much too early for it, and when he can hardly be trusted there without the utmost danger to his morals." This type of criticism with moral emphasis, rather than the preceding criticism on the student's curriculum, is to be most typical of Cowper's educational thought. Further on, Cowper maintains that one should "bridle in" rather than push a bright boy. In contending that the process of early education should be pleasurable, Cowper might have been on the side of either Locke or Rousseau, who concurred on this point. But the suggestion of bridling is definitely contrary to Rousseau's ideas. The fundamental disagreement of Locke and Rousseau is on the point made by Locke that the purpose of education is to thwart and thus through discipline to control the natural tendencies of the child.[9] To this idea Wesley also subscribed; and one will notice that an insistence upon discipline is distinguishable in most of Cowper's educational thought.

A second letter written ten days later[10] continues the subject. Here Cowper advances some of the arguments for education in the home that are later to appear in *Tirocinium*: in public schools morals and religion are too little attended to; a boy in public schools will come under the influence of evil companions; a child who is sent away from home at an early age will be weaned away from parental affection and authority.

A third letter of October 5, 1780, opens with a criticism of the neglect of instruction in English in favor of instruction in Latin, a deficiency which the poet maintains may be remedied by home instruction. Further, he denies that a public education is an effectual remedy for shyness. Rather, the poet contends, does it tend to produce shyness. He continues by attempting to refute the argument that friendships made at school are lasting and beneficial. In his own case, he asserts, not one friend has survived ten years' time.

Already the argument against the public school has assumed considerable proportions, but it has not taken on the religious fervor or the satirical sharpness that it is to acquire in Cowper's poetry.

§ 2

In the year of the letters on the education of John Unwin, Cowper began *The Progress of Error,* in which a consideration of education in general is continued in verse. Before we treat the poem directly, it is necessary to consider briefly the type of educational theory against which Cowper reacted.

The Enlightenment of the early eighteenth century brought in a contempt of authority and an exaltation of reason that rapidly developed from a healthful reactionary sentiment to a narrow formalism.[11] It is this kind of formalism against which Rousseau reacted in insisting that the senses were not always to be depended upon and that reason was not always infallible. To Rousseau the emotions or inner sentiments were to be followed as the only true guides. Voltaire was, of course, the incarnation of all that Rousseau revolted against.

If the rationalistic movement had no influence upon schools in England, it did have important influence upon private education in the upper classes.[12] In spite of the fact that, as Sir Charles Strachey has insisted, the letters of Lord Chesterfield are written to one person for one purpose and should not be regarded as a kind of "Popular Educator,"[13] they are still the best repository of those educational ideals that seem to characterize the Enlightenment. They advocate an education in worldly wisdom and one in which there is a higher appreciation of manners and courtliness than of virtue and seriousness. Lord Chesterfield's system seems to encourage a smattering of all kinds of knowledge, to be entirely materialistic, and to aim at the development of a nature capable of rendering all decisions in the light of reason. Good breeding, or decorum, is characteristically described by the noble lord as something "more than manners and less than morals, without which the most virtuous may often be detested, and with the aid of which the deformity of vice and falsehood may to some extent be softened."

To the twentieth-century mind the immorality of Chesterfield's philosophy is not so monstrous as it was to Dr. Johnson and to Cowper. Dr. Johnson's statement that Chesterfield's letters taught "the morals of a whore and the manners of a dancing master" is perhaps better explained on the basis of a personal prejudice than on that of the critic's sound judgment. He later saw fit to modify the opinion considerably. If Chesterfield admitted that dissimulation is allowable, and if he recommended flattery as a means of getting along in the world, we must not forget that he held essential truth in high esteem. "Do not mistake me," he wrote on October 16, O. S. 1747, "and think that I mean to recommend to you abject and criminal flattery: no, flatter nobody's vices or crimes: on the contrary, abhor and discourage them. But there is no living in the world without a complaisant indulgence for people's weaknesses, and innocent, though ridiculous vanities."[14] It is quite true that Chesterfield recommended irregular attachments with married women as a part of a gentleman's education; but, although this advice may be inexcusable, it is to be found in only a few letters.[15] In general, the moral laxities of Chesterfield's plan for educating his son are perhaps more fairly chargeable to the age than to the man. But the important consideration is that moral laxities, whatever the source, were easily apparent.

Along with Rousseau's revolt against rationalism came another revolt of a different sort, the Evangelical revival. Wesley was keenly aware of the pitfalls of Reason and felt it his Christian duty to quell the menace that was threatening the nation and its educational system, worming its deadly way into the universities.[16] Milton's theory of education as a means of repairing the ruins of man's fall had been reflected in William Law's statement that "the only end of education is to restore our rational nature to its proper state."[17] "The grand end of education," according to Wesley, is to cure the diseases of human nature.[18] Wesley's theory of education is, of course, founded on the theological doctrine of man's depravity and is as far removed as the poles from the idea of the inherent goodness of man held by a rationalistic religion like deism. To Wesley a religion built upon rationalistic principles could lead only to pride and love of the world. The functions of true education should be vastly different: "The bias of nature is set the wrong way: Education is designed to set it right. This, by the grace of God is to turn the bias from self-will, pride, anger, revenge, and the love of the world, to resignation, lowliness, meekness, and the love of God."[19]

Cowper has the same fear of the corrupting influence of Reason that Wesley has—a fear that at times seems to lead him into a narrow contempt for learning. But this contempt, viewed rightly, is not so damning an evidence of narrowness as it may at first appear. In *Truth,* as we have already seen briefly, the poet regards learning as a snare, and Voltaire looms large as an example of what learning without "grace" will do (ll. 301-30). The cottager in her ignorance of worldly learning is far happier, for she knows the truths of the Bible:

> Oh, happy peasant! Oh, unhappy bard!
> His the mere tinsel, her's the rich reward. [Ll. 331-32.]

Voltaire, possessed with an infinity of worldly wisdom, is lost in error.

In *Charity* the poet clarifies his position. Philosophy, he feels, may lead man into the secrets of nature and enrich him. From philosophy man may get a "bosom charg'd with rich instruction, and a soul enlarg'd." Knowledge in itself is not to be scorned, for "all truth is precious, if not divine." But the danger lies in making knowledge an end in itself and in forgetting that

> reason still, unless divinely taught,
> What e'er she learns, learns nothing as she ought.
>   [Ll. 337-38.]

When knowledge is an end in itself, it can lead only to pride. Here is the real basis of Cowper's distrust of learning. The poet would agree with Francis Bacon, who in "Of Atheism" argues that those who have imperfectly mastered their fields are most likely to lose sight of the First Cause in a welter of second causes. "The lamp of revelation," the poet continues, shows that whatever man has attained in knowledge, he is still the "progeny and heir of sin." If he is thus taught, his pride vanishes and he is capable of attaining true philosophy. But if man does not rely upon an "unerring guide,"

> Whether he measure earth, compute the sea,
> Weigh sun-beams, carve a fly, or spit a flea—
> The solemn trifler, with his boasted skill,
> Toils much, and is a solemn trifler still.   [Ll. 353-56.]

In the second book of *The Task* we find that Cowper's belief in Providence leads him logically into contempt for "the spruce philosopher," and for science and philosophy that discover causes but have no control over effects (ll. 189-97). In "The Garden" there is a passage in which the attack upon formal scholarship and scientific research is

reminiscent of the *Dunciad,* although the basis of the attack
is rather far removed from Pope's:

> Some write a narrative of wars, and feats
> Of heroes little known; and call the rant
> An history: describe the man, of whom
> His own coevals took but little note;
> And paint his person, character, and views,
> As they had known him from his mother's womb.
>
> .   .   .   .
>
> .   .   .   .   Some drill and bore
> The solid earth, and from the strata there
> Extract a register, by which we learn
> That he who made it, and reveal'd its date
> To Moses, was mistaken in its age.
>
> .   .   .   .
>
> Great contest follows, and much learned dust
> Involves the combatants; each claiming truth,
> And truth disclaiming both.   And thus they spend
> The little wick of life's poor shallow lamp,
> In playing tricks with nature, giving laws
> To distant worlds, and trifling in their own.   [Ll. 139 ff.]

It is not surprising that Cowper should be out of sympathy
with discoveries when they tend to discredit revelation. He
is chiefly concerned, however, with the *futility* of such
learning rather than with its vicious nature. If one accepts
the premise that the salvation of the soul is the most important thing in life, it is easy to regard all knowledge that
does not lead to the great end of existence as a matter

> Of dropping buckets into empty wells,
> And growing old in drawing nothing up.
>
>   [Ll. 189-90.]

Cowper's meaning should not be construed to be that man's
study should be confined to matters of the soul. His con-

cern is, after all, merely with the proper balance between one's learning and one's relationship with God.

If the poet is eager to insist that learning should not be a barrier to God, he is equally eager to insist that one should arrive at a conception of God through revelation rather than through Reason or Nature:

> God never meant that man should scale the heav'ns
> By strides of human wisdom.   [Ll. 221-22.]

These might almost have been the words of the "affable archangel" to Adam when the mortal pupil oversteps the bounds of proper inquiry. Cowper is in agreement with Milton's position in *Paradise Lost* on the point that one should seek God rather than learning; for too often, as Cowper puts it, the more one learns of Nature, the more one tends to overlook Nature's author. But if philosophy is "baptiz'd in the pure fountain of eternal love," it "has eyes indeed." With divine inspiration one may truly understand the phenomena of the universe, for "all truth is from the sempiternal source of light divine" (II, ll. 499-500).[20] Such, feels the poet, was the understanding of Newton and of Milton, both learned men whose immense knowledge did not prove a barrier between them and God. Cowper's position should now be clear: so long as one's learning does not keep one from God or prevent one from preserving humility before God it is not to be held in contempt.

There is a final word in the last book of *The Task*. Here Cowper makes his striking distinction between knowledge and wisdom:

> Knowledge dwells
> In heads replete with thoughts of other men;
> Wisdom in minds attentive to their own.
> Knowledge, a rude unprofitable mass,
> The mere materials with which wisdom builds,
> Till smooth'd and squar'd and fitted to its place

Does but encumber whom it seem'd t'enrich.
Knowledge is proud that he has learn'd so much;
Wisdom is humble that he knows no more.

[VI, ll. 89-97.]

§ 3

It is rather significant that in *The Progress of Error*
Cowper begins his disquisition on education with an attack
on Lord Chesterfield. In the twenty-eighth chapter of *A
Serious Call* William Law had closed his discussion of education with the delineation of an ideal father, Paternus, who
educated his son in his own house, bringing him up in
humility and in the love of God. The desire of Paternus
to have "truth and plainness" as "the only ornament" of his
son's language, and to have him modest in dress and tem-
perate in appetite provides an interesting contrast to the
educational ideas of Chesterfield. Cowper satirized the
Earl under the name of Petronius. Although there is no
proof that Cowper was consciously setting his portrait of
Petronius over against Law's Paternus, the points of contrast in the two "characters" may not be entirely accidental.

Cowper plainly felt that Chesterfield represented the
epitome of everything bad in a system of education based
on a rationalistic philosophy. The personal attack is
vigorous:

Thou polish'd and high-finish'd foe to truth,
Grey-beard corrupter of our list'ning youth,
To purge and skim away the filth of vice,
That, so refin'd, it might the more entice,
Then pour it on the morals of thy son,
To taint *his* heart, was worthy of *thine own.*

[Ll. 341-46.]

Chesterfield was, of course, dead when these lines were
written; but to Cowper the sad fact was that his ideals of
education were not interred with his bones. Cowper felt

that he could complain, with the same justice with which Law had earlier complained, of an educational system that tended to develop the pride of the child, to encourage ideals of position, and to neglect the true Christian virtues.

The system of education that had already begun developing among the Evangelicals was designed to correct the evils of the rationalistic approach. Wesley held that the soul was sick by nature, having brought into the world with it such diseases as pride, atheism, love of the world, and self-will. Since children are not free from the penalty of Adam's disobedience, they are subject to diseases just as adults are. The sermon "On the Education of Children" includes several diseases not mentioned in the sermon on "Original Sin." These include "anger, a deviation from truth, a proneness to speak or act contrary to justice, and unmercifulness."[21] We have already seen that Wesley's theory was that education should be a cure for the inbred diseases. He believed, citing youthful saints, that children are capable of developing a deeply religious life. He naturally insisted that everything in a child's education should be subordinated to those things that were directly connected with his religious development; and everything possible was to be done at home and in school to lead him to salvation. Wesley does not fail to indicate that responsibility rests on the parents for playing an active part in the religious education of their children.[22] In his own school he sought not only to correct deficiencies in ordinary training but to give his students training in religion. He furthermore attempted to provide the rigid discipline that he deemed necessary for the proper upbringing of children, his theory being that if children were to submit to God when they grew older they must learn to submit to discipline in their youth.[23]

To return to *The Progress of Error,* we find Cowper in complete agreement with Wesley in insisting that a child should be given the correct religious and moral training in his earliest years. It is this period in which the child is most impressionable and in which the mind falls into the mould of false or true education. The poet is also in agreement with Wesley in the matter of discipline. If a child is treated with too much tenderness, he will not be strong; and

> without discipline, the fav'rite child,
> Like a neglected forester, runs wild.   [Ll. 361-62.]

Cowper then turns to a criticism of the shallow educational ideals of his century. Far from giving a child training in discipline and morals,

> We give him some Latin, and a smatch of Greek;
> Teach him to fence and figure twice a week;
> And, having done, we think, the best we can,
> Praise his proficiency, and dub him man.   [Ll. 365-68.]

From the public school the young man goes to Oxford or Cambridge. After he has finished there, he is ready to embark with a tutor on a European tour. The Grand Tour as a means of putting polish on a youth's education had been attacked many times before Cowper. Ascham, Elyot, and Lyly, among others, had two centuries before warned of the debaucheries into which a student might fall in Italy. In the eighteenth century perhaps the most brilliant attack on the Grand Tour is that of Pope in the *Dunciad*. Abroad, Pope's youth

> The stews and palace equally explored,
> Intrigued with glory, and with spirit whored;
> Tried all *hors-d'œuvres,* all *liqueurs* defined,
> Judicious drank, and greatly-daring dined.
>   [IV, ll. 315-18.]

In *Spectator* No. 364 Addison attacked the practice of sending a youth "crying and snivelling into foreign countries," accompanied by a tutor, to see things to no more advantage than a child gets from "staring and gaping at an amazing variety of strange things." "Estimate" Brown also attacked travel as a means of education, feeling that "while Wisdom and Virtue can find no place" in the student on tour, "every Foreign Folly, Effeminacy, or Vice, meeting with a correspondent Soil, at once takes Root and flourish [sic]."[24] The opinion of Adam Smith is equally unequivocal.[25]

It will be observed that Cowper does not here waste any time in attacking the universities. That attack he reserves for a later occasion. With Lord Chesterfield still uppermost in his mind, he is eager to pour his venom on the Grand Tour. No one seems to have observed the close relationship between Cowper's satire and Chesterfield's letters. It should be noticed that young Philip Stanhope, who was Cowper's junior by only one year, was a schoolmate of the poet at Westminster. Whether or not Cowper knew the boy, there seems to be no record. Stanhope left the school in 1746 (Cowper was in residence from 1741 to 1749) for Germany, Switzerland, and Italy in the company of a tutor, Walter Harte, the son of a former Canon of Bristol who lost all his preferments at the time of the Revolution.[26] The fact that Mr. Harte lacked the "Graces" that Lord Chesterfield was eager for his son to acquire has often been remarked upon. Young Stanhope's own "awkward bashfulness, shyness, and roughness" were apparent even to his father.[27] In Cowper's satire the youth sets out "with rev'rend tutor, clad in habit lay." In the light of what we have just seen, it seems more than a mere coincidence that Cowper should have described his two travelers as "the gosling pair, with awkward gait, stretch'd neck, and silly stare." (*Progress of Error*, ll. 379-80.) Cowper depicts his tutor as being used by the student "to tease for cash, and quarrel with all day." Although Chesterfield's letters do not leave with us the impression that young Stanhope was a contentious lad, we do find evidences of Stanhope's borrowing from Harte.

"Mr. Harte informs me," wrote the Earl, "that he has reimbursed you part of your losses in Germany; and I consent to his reimbursing you of the whole, now that I know you deserve it."[28] Cowper's satirical thrust at the

> memorandum-book for ev'ry town,
> And ev'ry post, and where the chaise broke down,
> [Ll. 373-74.]

was clearly inspired by the kind of advice to be found in the following passage from Chesterfield's letters:

To be serious; though I do not desire that you should immediately turn author, and oblige the world with your travels; yet, wherever you go, I would have you as curious and inquisitive as if you did intend to write them. I do not mean that you should give yourself so much trouble, to know the number of houses, inhabitants, signposts, and tomb-stones, of every town that you go through; but that you should inform yourself, as well as your stay will permit you, whether the town is free, or to whom it belongs, or in what manner: whether it has any peculiar privileges or customs; what trade or manufactures; and such other particulars as people of sense desire to know. And there would be no manner of harm, if you were to take memorandums of such things in a paper book to help your memory.[29]

Continuing, the travelers

> Discover huge cathedrals, built with stone,
> And steeples tow'ring high, much like our own;
> But show peculiar light by many a grin
> At popish practices observ'd therein.   [Ll. 381-84.]

For this thrust the letters offer an interesting source. On September 21, O. S. 1747, Chesterfield wrote:

I received, by the last post, your letter of the 8th, N. S., and I do not wonder that you are surprised at the credulity and superstition of the Papists at Einsiedlen [sic], and at their absurd stories of their chapel. But remember, at the same time, that errors and mistakes, however gross, in matters of opinion, if they are sincere, are to be pitied, but not punished nor laughed at.

The "gosling pair" become typical sight-seers and buyers of souvenirs. Finally, the student comes home. For this event the poet has saved two of his most brilliant couplets:

> Returning, he proclaims, by many a grace,
> By shrugs, and strange contortions of his face,
> How much a dunce that has been sent to roam
> Excels a dunce that has been kept at home. [Ll. 413-16.]

Before digressing Cowper fires a final broadside at Chesterfieldian ideals of education:

> Accomplishments have taken virtue's place,
> And wisdom falls before exterior grace;
> We slight the precious kernel of the stone,
> And toil to polish its rough coat alone.
> A just deportment, manners grac'd with ease,
> Elegant phrase, and figure form'd to please,
> Are qualities that seem to comprehend
> Whatever parents, guardians, schools intend.
> Hence an unfurnish'd and a listless mind,
> Though busy, trifling; empty, though refin'd;
> Hence all that interferes, and dares to clash
> With indolence and luxury, is trash;
> While learning, once the man's exclusive pride,
> Seems verging fast towards the female side.
> [Ll. 417-30.]

§ 4

No one can doubt that the great English universities were at a low moral and intellectual ebb in the eighteenth century. To this fact there are many testimonies. In his "Essay on Modern Education" Swift wrote that he had heard "more than one or two persons of high rank declare that they could learn nothing more at Oxford or Cambridge than to drink ale and smoke tobacco."[30] Dr. Johnson reveals the laxity of discipline in the Oxford of his own day —a day when he could excuse his absence from a tutorial period by fearlessly telling his tutor that he had preferred to slide in Christchurch meadow![31] Adam Smith complained, "In the University of Oxford, the greater part of the public professors have, for these many years given up altogether even the pretense of teaching."[32] John Brown also attacked idleness among university professors. "They make their Court," he wrote, "to idle Sons and weak Mothers, in Proportion as they suffer their wealthy Pupils to live, and return, laden with Ignorance and Vice."[33] Brown urged more supervision of students and more earnestness in the colleges, making a plea for fewer teas and parties and less attention to cards. Gray, Gibbon, and later Southey all testified to the worthlessness of their university education. Cowper had his most direct contact with university life through his brother John, whom he at times visited at Cambridge. The poet had doubtless heard the kind of account that Wilberforce gave of his entrance into St. John's, Cambridge, in 1776, some years after John Cowper's death:

On the very first night of my arrival I was introduced to as licentious a set of men as can well be conceived. They were in the habit of drinking hard and their conversation was in perfect accord with their principles. Though often mingling in their parties I never relished their society—indeed, I was often horror-struck at their conduct and felt miserable.[34]

In the second book of *The Task* Cowper turns to the lack of discipline in the universities. Discipline is personified as a kindly, paternal old man who once dwelt in "colleges and halls" and whose occupation was to encourage goodness. Learning grew under his care. As a master, he was severe only when one of his charges overleapt the limits of control. But, through neglect, Discipline had died, and the schools had become

                    a scene
Of solemn farce, where Ignorance in stilts,
His cap well-lin'd with logic not his own,
With parrot tongue perform'd the scholar's part,
Proceeding soon a graduated dunce.
Then compromise had place, and scrutiny
Became stone blind; precedence went in truck,
And he was competent whose purse was so. [Ll. 735-42.]

The kind of education provided by the universities was reflected in the students, whom Cowper pictures with grim
earnestness as

            gamesters, jockeys, brothellers impure,
Spendthrifts, and booted sportsmen, oft'ner seen
With belted waist and pointers at their heels
Than in the bounds of duty.   [Ll. 751-54.]

One need have no fear that the world will teach them vice
when they leave the walls of the college; for in college, although the place masquerades as an abode of science and
learning, they acquire all the evil to be acquired.

   In the matter of fixing the blame, Cowper asserts that
the students themselves are not so much at fault as the university.   In a figure suggestive of *Beowulf*, the poet feels
that he has "track'd the felon home, and found his birth-
place and his dam."   Undoubtedly, the source of the nation's
corruption is in its universities, which like "the muddy beds
of Nile" spawn "a race obscene" to pollute all England—

            and the cause itself
Of that calamitous mischief has been found:
Found, too, where most offensive, in the skirts
Of the rob'd pedagogue.   [Ll. 820-23.]

Here again is the poison of rationalism that Wesley deprecated in the universities.

   In the midst of his attack, Cowper finds need to pause
for an exception.   The sweeping condemnation of college

men and colleges should not include his brother, John Cowper, who was uncorrupted at Cambridge; nor must it include John's college, Ben'et (Corpus Christi), "in which order yet was sacred." The tribute is one of great dignity and is marked with none of the bad taste apparent in Cowper's account of John's conversion to the "true light" in *Adelphi*. It will be observed that the whole attack on the universities in *The Task* is on a plane of high moral indignation rather than on that of religious enthusiasm, which in *Adelphi* caused the poet to take this somewhat conflicting point of view: "He [John] lamented the dark and Christless condition of the place [Cambridge], *where learning and morality were all in all,* and where, if a man were possessed of all these qualifications, he neither doubted himself, nor did anybody else question the safety of his state."[35] The difference between the point of view of *Adelphi* and that of *The Task* is characteristic of the poet's changed thought. In *The Task,* Cowper is more the Christian moralist than the Evangelical enthusiast. Certainly, the fact that almost every criticism of the universities made by Cowper is corroborated by contemporaries argues that the attack on the universities in *The Task* is not merely one of a religious zealot. In spite of some tendency toward exaggeration, it shows the sanity rather of a serious social critic who sees to what ends materialism or license can lead a university or a nation. The charges are not a good deal more severe than those of Brown's *Estimate,* from which Cowper may have got some inspiration for his satire. Both the attack on the Grand Tour and that on the universities are barbed enough to make one wonder why a critic like Goldwin Smith[36] should deny to Cowper his just due of satirical vigor.

§ 5

Cowper's treatment of the various stages of the educational process does not seem to take those stages chronologically. Although there is an attack upon educational ideals and the Grand Tour in *The Progress of Error,* there is no extended attack on the public schools or the universities. The universities are reserved for *The Task,* and the public schools are finally "reviewed"—much to their discredit—in *Tirocinium.*

However, as it has already been hinted, the inception of *Tirocinium* came four years before its actual completion. The first letter written to Unwin on the education of his son is a rather practical one and barely mentions the moral and religious aspects of a child's training. In the ten days intervening between the first and second letters the ideas of the moral and religious hazards of a public school education seem to have taken shape in Cowper's mind. The link between the second letter and the attack on the educational ideals of the Enlightenment written in the following December (1780) as a part of *The Progress of Error* is clear. But it is difficult to determine exactly when the idea occurred to Cowper that he might make an extended attack upon the public schools. From December, 1780, to July, 1781, he was busily engaged in writing the first and more sober didactic poems. In July Lady Austen came to Olney, and a different note appears in his poetry. *Conversation* and *Retirement* are much lighter in tone than their predecessors. The fact that Cowper could write to Newton, toward whom he usually maintained marked soberness of style, the charming "Hop O' My Thumb" letter is another evidence of the change that had come over the poet. When Lady Austen returned to London in October, a serious note is again perceptible in his correspondence.

On August 25 Cowper wrote to William Unwin congratulating him on the arrival of a second son—one of the "two sons" mentioned in the dedication of *Tirocinium.*[37] *Retirement* was completed on October 2 with a sigh of relief from the author.[38] On November 7 Cowper wrote to

Newton: "Having discontinued the practice of verse-making for some weeks, I now feel quite incapable of resuming it; and can only wonder at it, as one of the most extraordinary incidents in my life, that I should have composed a volume."[39] But on November 27 he wrote again to Newton:

> Mrs. Unwin having suggested the hint, I have added just as many lines to my poem lately mentioned as make up *the whole number two hundred.* I had no intention to write a round sum, but it happened so. She thought there was a fair opportunity to give the Bishops a slap; and as it would not have been civil to have denied a lady so reasonable a request, I have just made the powder fly out of their wigs a little.[40]

That *Tirocinium* is here indicated there can be little doubt. On October 20, 1784, Cowper wrote in a letter to Unwin, informing him that *Tirocinium* was to be inscribed to him: "Two years since, I began a piece which grew to the *length of two hundred lines,* and there stopped. I have lately resumed it, and (I believe) shall finish it."[41] In spite of the discrepancy in time, the specific reference to the length serves as a reasonably safe index. The reference to the Bishops' wigs probably indicates Cowper's attack on rationalistic religion and "knavish priests" in the first two hundred lines of the poem. It does not seem likely that *Tirocinium* should have been begun before November 7, 1781. At any rate, two hundred lines of it seem to have been completed in some form by November 27. It is rather remarkable that the tone of the opening lines is closer to that of the earlier poems—especially the insistence upon early religious education in *The Progress of Error* and the attack upon deism in *Truth*—than it is to *Conversation* and *Retirement*.

Just why Cowper laid the poem aside is not apparent. At any rate, we hear no more about it until 1784. In this year it was completed between November 8 and 20,[42] just in time for publication with *The Task.*

Adam Smith was not so much concerned about the public schools as he was about the universities. "In England," he wrote, "the public schools are much less corrupted than the universities. In the schools the youth are taught, or at least may be taught, Greek and Latin; that is, everything which the masters pretend to teach, or which it is expected that they should teach."[43] But other contemporary comments convince us that conditions in the public schools were by no means good. From the seventeenth century the schools had steadily lost their hold on the socially distinguished, and the nobility and gentry had increasingly educated their sons at home under private tutors. Fielding's comment on the public schools in *Tom Jones* is doubtless true, in spite of the fact that the novelist satirizes the tutorial system in Thwackum and Square. Mr. Allworthy, we are told,

. . . having observed the imperfect institution of our public schools, and the many vices which boys were there liable to learn, had resolved to educate his nephew, as well as the other lad, whom he had in a manner adopted, in his own house, where he thought their morals would escape all that danger of being corrupted to which they would be unavoidably exposed in any public school or university.

The great schools like Eton, Harrow, Winchester, and Westminster were charged with giving the student a mere trifle of classical learning at an enormous expense. Westminster, Cowper's own school, had a reputation for roughness. Chesterfield had a low opinion of the school as a place where one might acquire "the more decorative portion of a gentleman's education." In one letter he speaks to his son of "that *curious* infelicity *of diction,* which you acquired at Westminster";[44] and in another he states that "Westminster is undoubtedly the seat of illiberal manners and brutal behavior."[45]

If schools were intellectually and morally deficient, they

naturally gave very little attention to religion. Wesley found the public schools to be "nurseries of all manners of wickedness"; consequently, he concerned himself with instructing parents about the kind of schools to which they should send their children. No schools, he insists, can be satisfactory except those in which the masters have for their goal the Christian ideal of education as a preparation for heaven.[46] These schools must, therefore, provide specific religious instruction. It is easy to believe that such schools were rarities. To meet the need Wesley founded the Kingwood School for Methodist boys. The objections raised by Wesley to existing boarding schools definitely anticipate Cowper's position: First, most boarding schools were in large towns, which offered too many distractions; moreover, the town children might corrupt the religion of the boarding students. Second, the schools were not sufficiently exclusive in admitting students; thus were chances of corrupt morals and religion increased. Third, in many schools the masters were not concerned about the religious welfare of their charges. Finally, many schools offered only the most superficial type of instruction. Arithmetic, writing, geography, and "chronology" were neglected; Greek and Latin were imperfectly taught.[47]

Several explanations have been offered for Cowper's severe attitude toward public schools in *Tirocinium*. In telling of the poet's well-known experience with a boy-tyrant at Dr. Pitman's school in Market Street, Hertfordshire, Southey remarks: "The tyranny under which Cowper suffered there, made, as it well might, a deep and lasting impression on him; and to this it is that the strong dislike with which, in the latter part of his life, he regarded all schools, must be ascribed."[48] The anonymous writer in *The Pamphleteer*, undoubtedly misled by Hayley's erroneous assignment of the "boy-tyrant" to Westminster, assumed that Cowper's "weak constitution" and his "hereditary derangement" made him unfit for the "agitation of Westminster School" and, consequently, that his years there "were filled with inexpressible bitterness. . . . He saw all objects relating to the scene of his internal miseries," the writer concludes, "through a false and gloomy medium, and thus was wholly unfit for correctly portraying them."[49]

The second opinion is clearly erroneous. Southey exonerates Westminster of the blame for shaping Cowper's views on education. In spite of the school's reputation for roughness, Cowper's own testimony on the point of his happiness there seems sufficiently explicit. In a letter to Unwin written in 1786 he spoke of his school life as "a period of life in which, if I had never tasted true happiness, I was at least equally unacquainted with its contrary."[50] Canon Benham remarks, ". . . his life at Westminster seems to have been a happy one. He not only became an excellent scholar, but was a good cricketer and football player; and was popular with both masters and boys."[51] His love for one of his teachers, Vinny Bourne, continued throughout his life, and he was able to praise Dr. Nichols for the care that he took in preparing students for confirmation. Although one may admit that the tyranny endured by Cowper at Market Street may have made an indelible impression on him, one would hardly like to attribute *Tirocinium* to such a circumstance. It is logical to believe that the years of relative happiness at Westminster might have tended to soften the impression.

In the light of what Cowper had to say about education in other places than in *Tirocinium,* the true explanation seems apparent. In a period in which the Evangelicals were vitally interested in improving education, it is almost impossible that Cowper, who was broadly interested in humanitarian endeavor, should not have been infected by the movement. No one need believe that in *Tirocinium* Cowper set out to reflect accurately his own school experience.

The poem represents the attitude of a man who had developed a philosophy of religious and moral education, and who was eager to enter the crusade against corruptions in education that were obvious on every hand. Since he took a very serious view of the problem, it is not entirely unnatural that he should have reflected his own school experience "obliquely ... in the mirror of an ideal."[52] We may agree with Southey that "when Cowper accused himself as a juvenile proficient in the 'infernal art of lying,' he imposed upon himself in a far greater degree than he ever imposed upon an usher, for lying is certainly not one of those vices which are either acquired or fostered at a public school."[53] This self-accusation was made in a period when the poet's "enthusiasm" was considerably greater than it was when he wrote *Tirocinium,* but it is illustrative of the kind of unconscious exaggeration that is consequent upon the poet's high seriousness. There is no real reason why we should not expect a modicum of *conscious* exaggeration in *Tirocinium,* for exaggeration is, after all, a legitimate weapon of satire. The fact that Cowper was happy at Westminster should strengthen the effect of his sincerity.

On November 8, 1784, Cowper wrote to the Reverend William Bull:

The Task, as you know, is gone to the press: and since it went I have been employed in writing [i. e., completing and revising] another poem, which I am now transcribing, and which, in a short time, I design shall follow. It is intituled [sic] Tirocinium, or a Review of the Schools: the business and purpose of it are, to censure the want of discipline, and the scandalous inattention to morals, that obtain in them, especially the largest; and to recommend private tuition as a mode of education on all accounts; to call upon fathers to become tutors of their own sons, where that is practicable; to take home a domestic tutor where it is not; and if neither can be done, to place them under the care of such a man as he to whom I am writing; some rural parson, whose attention is limited to few.[54]

The poem opens with a restatement of the ideals of Christian education in slightly different terms from those used by the poet elsewhere. It is man's soul, says Cowper, that gives him "his right of empire over all that lives." This soul is possessed of three handmaidens: Memory, to amass wisdom for its benefit; Fancy, to delight it; and Judgment, to guide it. Man's majesty over all created things is proof of his immortality. If man has no soul, he is of all creatures of least worth. Proof enough of the existence of the Deity is found in Nature, which reflects the attributes of God. If all inanimate creation reflects the attributes of the Creator, how much more logical it is to expect man, the crown of creation, to live to God's praise:

> This once believ'd, 'twere logic misapplied
> To prove a consequence by none denied
> That we are bound to cast the minds of youth
> Betimes into the moulds of heav'nly truth,
> That, taught of God, they may indeed be wise,
> Nor ignorantly wand'ring miss the skies.   [Ll. 103-8.]

The poet next seeks to emphasize the importance of early religious education. Most children have for their earliest reading the hornbook (containing, of course, the Lord's Prayer), Bible stories, and Bunyan's *Pilgrim's Progress*. If such reading could be continued, all would be well. But the artless piety of youth is lost when the child is subjected to the snares and deceptions of the world. Taught by "babblers called Philosophers" the young student is induced to blaspheme the creed of his childhood. This kind of argument naturally sounds a little curious to the modern ear, but it will not sound curious if we remember that it is merely a sequel to the attacks on rationalism in *The Progress of Error* and *Truth*. Cowper sees quite logically that even the child is not immune to the dangers of a system of thought that can lead only to deism, if indeed it does not lead to out-and-out atheism. He sees the

"young apostate" neglecting prayer, denying the inspiration
of the scriptures, and learning to put his faith in Reason:

> And thus, well-tutor'd only while we share
> A mother's lecture and a nurse's care;
> And taught at schools such mythologic stuff,
> But sound religion sparingly enough;
> Our early notices of truth, disgrac'd,
> Soon lose their credit, and are all effac'd.
>
> [Ll. 195-200.][55]

Thus end the first two hundred lines—doubtless the earlier
section—of the poem.

The newer section begins with a vigorous attack upon
the schools, with an emphasis upon the *moral* rather than
the *religious* aspects of life in them. Unless one wishes his
son to be "a sot or dunce, lascivious, headstrong; or all these
at once"—the poet asserts—the son should be kept away
from schools. In the schools boys are boys only in years;
"in infidelity and lewdness" they are men. At a public
school students learn before they are sixteen that "authors
are most useful pawn'd or sold" and that the "knowledge
of the heart" is best acquired in the taverns.

> There waiter Dick, with Bacchanalian lays,
> Shall win his heart, and have his drunken praise,
> His counsellor and bosom-friend shall prove,
> And some street-pacing harlot his first love. [Ll. 214-17.]

Schools keep their students too long, especially when discipline is lax. The young boys are subjected to the bad
influence of older boys over a long period of time and attempt to ape them in their wild escapades, their petty lar-
ceny, and their brawls. Colleges complete the miseducation.

As Cowper refused to place the burden of the blame for
corruption in the universities on university students, he also
refused to place the burden of blame on the public school
students: "for public schools 'tis public folly feeds." The

moral and religious apathy or the uncritical attitude of the patrons, who prefer to follow the "establish'd mode" rather than to think, is the root of the trouble. At least for the purpose of stressing parental obligations, Cowper is willing to assert that the schoolmasters themselves are perhaps not entirely to blame for the evils; but he can have little respect for their enduring evils out of fear of losing what little power they have over the students. ("Ye connive at what ye cannot cure.")

Since we know "that these *menageries* all fail their trust," the poet asks, why do we still send our sons to them? If the reason is a sentimental attachment to "the play-place of our early days," perhaps the weakness is forgivable. At this point the poet remembers with tenderness and warmth his own school days in perhaps the most famous passage in the poem:

> The little ones, unbutton'd, glowing hot,
> Playing our games, and on the very spot;
> As happy as we once, to kneel and draw
> The chalky ring, and knuckle down at taw.
>
> [Ll. 304-7.]

But this sentimental attachment too often leads the father to set before the child all the follies of his school days, his petty larcenies and naughty pranks:

> Retracing thus his *frolics,* ('tis a name
> That palliates deeds of folly and of shame)
> He gives the local bias all its sway;
> Resolves that where he play'd his sons shall play.
>
> [Ll. 332-35.]

His wish will be fulfilled to a degree that perhaps he does not anticipate. In the schools the pert will be "made perter, and the tame made wild."

Having discarded sentimental attachment as an unsound basis for choosing a school, Cowper turns to a much more

reprehensible motive—that of the forming of profitable
social contacts for one's children. Samuel Foote in the first
act of *The Author*[56] and Thomas Day in *Sandford and Merton*[57] satirized this frequently encountered type of social
climbing. Cowper looks with contempt upon the same
kind of practice. In the public schools, he finds, the rich
learn the wastefulness that we condemn in the less fortunate.
Public schools, he maintains ironically, are quite suitable
for the rich. But why should modest families with high
aspirations for their children send them to public schools?
The trouble is that these high aspirations are too often of
the wrong sort; they are material rather than spiritual:

> The father, who designs his babe a priest,
> Dreams him episcopally such at least;
> And while the playful jockey scours the room
> Briskly, astride upon the parlour broom,
> In fancy sees him more superbly ride
> In coach with purple lin'd, and mitres on its side.
>
> [Ll. 364-69.]

It is true that if students are sent where they will have contacts with "peers and sons of peers" their chances for material success will be increased, but they will be increased at a
cost of the loss of appetite for scholarship and true religious
zeal. Cowper is particularly scornful of the use of contacts
with the nobility as stepping stones to advancement in the
church. To the parent who believes that "the parson knows
enough who knows a duke," the poet exclaims, "Egregious
purpose! . . . barb'rous prostitution of your son." Furthermore if one looks at the matter from a purely practical
point of view, Cowper argues, one cannot ignore the fact
that the friendships formed in the school may not be so
profitable as they seem to promise. Therefore, it is in every
way the better part of wisdom to teach children to abhor
"connexions form'd for int'rest"—

> Than set your son to work at a vile trade
> For wages so unlikely to be paid.   [Ll. 456-57.]

From an attack on pride in parents the poet passes to a public-school evil that engenders pride and hatred in children. In Chapter XVIII of *A Serious Call,* Law writes as follows of the dangers of "emulation" in public schools:

> How dry and poor must the doctrine of humility sound to a youth, that has been spurred up to all his industry by *ambition, envy, emulation, and a desire of glory, and distinction!* And if he is not to act by these principles when he is a man, why do we call him to act by them in his youth? . . . when children are taught to bear no rival, they are plainly and directly taught to be envious. For it is impossible for any one to have this scorn of being outdone, and this *contention* with *rivals* without *burning* with envy against all those that seem to excel him, or get any distinction from him. So that what children are taught is rank envy, and only *covered with the name of a less odious sound.* . . . I know it is said in defence of this method of education, that ambition and a desire of glory, are necessary to excite young people to industry; and that if we were to press upon them the doctrines of humility, we should deject their minds and sink them into dulness and idleness.[58]

With the last contention Law states his grounds for disagreement. Cowper's attack on emulation is so similar as to suggest that the poet had Law's chapter in mind when he wrote. To the poet, emulation

> Ranks as a virtue, and is yet a vice;
> Or rather a gross compound, justly tried,
> *Of envy, hatred, jealousy, and pride—*
> Contributes most perhaps t' enhance their fame;
> And *emulation* is *its specious name.*
> Boys, once *on fire* with that *contentious zeal,*
> Feel all the rage that female *rivals* feel.
>
> .   .   .   .
>
> Each vainly magnifies his own success,

Resents his fellow's, wishes it were less,
Exults in his miscarriage if he fail,
Deems his reward too great if he prevail,
And labours to surpass him day and night,
Less for improvement than to tickle spite.

[Ll. 465 ff.]⁵⁹

Like Law, Cowper grants that the spur of emulation is powerful, but there are so many attendant evils that the end is vitiated by the means.

Large schools have been condemned. Are small schools better? For an answer Cowper falls back on Pope's dictum about government: "What'er is best administered is best." After all, the question is not whether a school is large or small, but whether boys "may *learn,* while *morals* languish." Cowper gave the same kind of advice that Wesley gave on the choice of schools. Both large and small schools, Cowper asserts, have the same faults. Again, the *bête noire* is the "rob'd pedagogue," of whom the poet paints a picture that is indeed unflattering. He is little more than a cormorant, swayed "through motives of mere lucre," taking credit for a student's success but assuming no responsibility for his failure.

The next division of the poem is devoted to more constructive criticism—the possible solutions open to parents who are concerned about the kind of education their children will have.

The important rôle of the father in the educational process has been emphasized by numerous educational theorists. Both Montaigne and Locke insisted upon the father's part in disciplining and moulding the child's early life, and both preached the advantages of a home education. Law embodied his idea of the father's part in the education of his children in the "character" of Paternus, and Wesley showed himself keenly aware of the responsibility resting on parents especially for religious education. Rousseau has much to say on the matter:

Comme la véritable nourrice est la mère, le véritable précepteur est le père.... Un père, quand il engendre et nourrut des enfants ne fait en cela que le tiers de sa tâche. Il doit des hommes à son espèce; il doit à la société des hommes sociables; il doit des citoyens à l'État. Tout homme qui peut payer cette triple dette et ne fait pas, est coupable, et plus coupable peut-être quand il la paye à demi. Celui qui ne peut remplir les devoirs de père n'a point droit de le devenir.[60]

No doubt Cowper's reading of *Émile*, as well as his reading of *A Serious Call*, is reflected in his ideal of "father, and friend, and tutor all in one." Why should one "resign into a stranger's hand," asks the poet, a duty that "God and nature and your int'rest" delegate to one? ("*Voilà la fonction*," exclaimed Rousseau, "*que vous confiez tranquillement à des mercenaires.*")

In seeking to emphasize the necessity for the father's functioning as tutor, Cowper makes a digression which seems to have been suggested by the same section of *Émile* from which we have just been quoting. Rousseau wrote—

Les enfants, éloignés, dispersés dans des pensions, des couvents, dans des collèges, porteront ailleurs l'amour de la maison paternelle, ou, pour mieux dire, ils y rapporteront l'habitude de n'être attachés à rien. Les frères et les sœurs se connaîtront à peine. Quand tous sont rassemblés en cérémonie, ils pourront être fort polis entre eux; il se traiteront en étrangers. Sitôt qu'il n'y plus d'intimité entre les parents, sitôt que la société de la famille ne fait plus la douceur de la vie, il faut bien recourir aux mauvaises mœurs pour y suppléer. Où est l'homme assez stupide pour ne pas voir la chaîne de tout cela?

Cowper dramatizes the idea in an appealing picture of a boy who has just returned from school:

Arriv'd, he feels an unexpected change;
He blushes, hangs his head, is shy and strange,

No longer takes, as once, his fearless ease,
His fav'rite stand between his father's knees,
But seeks the corner of some distant seat,
And eyes the door, and watches a retreat,
And, least familiar where he should be most,
Feels all his happiest privileges lost.   [Ll. 567-74.]

Putting the argument in a positive form, Cowper asserts that the "num'rous follies . . . in the mind and heart of every boy" require the admonition of a father for their correction. Even the boy's pastime requires supervision of an affectionate sort. The "public hacknies in the schooling trade" will give training in "conjugated verbs and nouns declin'd"; but the father who exercises any ingenuity will avoid the dry and unpleasant discipline of the schools, providing for his son the kind of education that Paternus gave to his son in *A Serious Call,* that Rousseau elaborates in *Émile,* and that Thomas Day, following Rousseau, champions in his highly sentimental *Sandford and Merton:*

To lead his son, for prospects of delight,
To some not steep, though philosophic, height,
Thence to exhibit to his wond'ring eyes
Yon circling worlds, their distance, and their size,
The moons of Jove, and Saturn's belted ball,
And the harmonious order of them all;
To show him in an insect or a flow'r,
Such microscopic proof of skill and pow'r,
As, hid from ages past, God now displays
To combat atheists with in modern days.   [Ll. 630-39.]

Furthermore, the heart of the youth is to be inspired by the example of the noble ancients or, better, by living worthies. We may thus see that Cowper accepts from Rousseau's educational theory one of the methods that we now look upon as being most characteristically Rousseauistic. The fact that Law had projected the same sort of plan with an intensified religious emphasis unknown to

Rousseau may easily have influenced Cowper's acceptance of the idea. Certainly, the religious emphasis of Cowper's plan is on the side of Law. A relaxation of discipline is not implied. Instruction, the poet concludes, should be "solid" rather than "too weighty," and "not forbidding sport."

The ideal tutor is, then, the father; but if he is "professionally tied" and cannot be directly responsible for his son's education, the first alternative is the right sort of hired tutor. Locke wrote of the tutor or governor:

> I would from their first beginning to talk, have some discreet, sober, nay wise person about children, whose care it should be to fashion them aright, and keep them from ill, especially the infection of bad company. I think this province requires great sobriety, temperance, tenderness, diligence, and discretion, qualities hardly to be found united in persons that are to be hired for ordinary salaries, nor easily to be found anywhere.[61]

No emphasis is placed here on Chesterfield's "Graces." Cowper's delineation of the proper sort of tutor seems almost a verse rendering of Locke:

> Behold that figure, neat, though plainly clad;
> His sprightly mingled with a shade of sad;
> Not of a nimble tongue, though now and then
> Heard to articulate to other men.
>
> .   .   .   .
>
> Prepar'd by taste, by learning, and true worth
> To form thy son, to strike his genius forth;
>
> .   .   .   .
>
> Safe under such a wing, the boy shall show
> No spots contracted among grooms below.
> Nor taint his speech with meannesses design'd
> By footman Tom for witty and refin'd.
>
> .   .   .   .
>
> Are such men rare? perhaps they would abound
> Were occupation easier to be found.   [Ll. 664 ff.]

When a good tutor is found, the poet recommends that he should be treated with great deference and consideration.

The final alternative is to place the child in the hands of a pious country clergyman who has not more than two students in this care. Here in quietness and in virtuous toil the boy may attain the "settled habit and decided taste" that a Christian gentleman should have. The conditions for such an alternative seem extraordinarily drastic: the household of the parents must be a very den of worldliness, unfit for student or tutor. One wonders whether Cowper knew Day's incomparable Mr. Barlow, a minister-tutor who succeeded admirably in making a prig of Tommy Merton by just such training as Cowper suggests. Fortunately, the poet's friend, the "smoke-inhaling" Bull—much less of a prig than Mr. Barlow—is suggested as the ideal clergyman-tutor.

In conclusion, Cowper states that he is under no illusions about the possible efficacy of his message. He expects his advice to fall on many deaf ears, but he has reason to hope that here and there it will prevent an erroneous choice. He calls upon those of "life's middle state," where, he believes, resides "two thirds of all the virtue that remains," to see the debauchery into which the age has fallen as a result of its faulty educational ideals. Milton in *Of Education* found the corrupt products of the educational system of his own age to be divines "ambitious and mercenary," lawyers who had not been fed on "the prudent and heavenly contemplation of justice and equity," "unprincipled statesmen, and others, lastly, of a more delicious and airy spirit," who "retire themselves, knowing no better, to the enjoyments of ease and luxury, living out their days in feast and jollity."[62] Cowper finds

> great commanders making war a trade,
> Great lawyers, lawyers without study made;
> Churchmen, in whose esteem their blest employ

Is odious, and their wages all their joy.

. . . .

Fops at all corners, lady-like in mien,
Civeted fellows, smelt ere they are seen.   [Ll. 821 ff.]

The poet issues a final warning against taking such a
risk as a public school involves. "Send him not to school,"
he urges. "No—guard him better." What then is to be
done to public schools? Are they all to be leveled to the
ground? The poet's answer is not quite so drastic:

> though I would not advertise them yet,
> Nor write on each—*This Building to be Let,*
> Unless the world were all prepar'd t' embrace
> A plan well worthy to supply their place;
> Yet, backward as they are, and long have been,
> To cultivate and keep the MORALS clean,
> (Forgive the crime) I wish them, I confess,
> Or better manag'd, or encourag'd less.   [Ll. 915-22.]

An extended analysis of the way in which Cowper's religious bias or moral earnestness caused him to exaggerate
actual conditions or to argue somewhat illogically is really
not necessary. After all, the exaggerations and inconsistencies are rather obvious. "It cannot be gainsaid," commented Southey on Cowper's account of his "irreligious"
school life in the *Memoir,* "that our boarding-schools are
unfavorable to those devotional feelings, the seeds of which
have been sown in early childhood, and destructive of those
devotional habits which have been learned at home; that
nothing which is not intentionally profane can be more
irreligious than the forms of religion which are observed
there, and that attendance of school boys in a pack at public worship, is worse than perfunctory." Southey, however,
pointed out that Cowper's accounting for the decay of the
child's devotional habits by saying that the duties of a
schoolboy precluded religious life is hardly good reason-

ing. A better explanation is that the school age is a time
when the animal part of a boy's nature is in the ascendency
over the intellectual and spiritual parts.[63] The eighteenth
century had a way of regarding children as little men and
women. Wesley has been accused of an almost complete
misunderstanding of the meaning of childhood. Cowper,
too, does not always have a full understanding of childhood
when his thought is guided by religious enthusiasm or when
he is engaged in impassioned dialectic. This observation
is not negated by the fact that the poet was often able to
recapture his own childhood days with remarkable tenderness and vividness for artistic purposes.

That the recapturing of a past experience and the
evaluating of the same kind of experience for the purpose of dialectic are not always in agreement is beautifully
attested by a seeming contradiction in Cowper's view on
"emulation." In *Table Talk* the poet remembered with
naïve pride the very thing that he was to castigate in
Tirocinium:

> At Westminster, where little poets strive
> To set a distich upon six and five,
> Where discipline helps op'ning buds of sense,
> And makes his pupils proud with silver pence,
> I was a poet too.   [Ll. 506-10.]

This instance alone should suggest how his entire school
experience underwent a transformation when placed under
the microscope of his earnest inquiry. From one point of
view, the whole attack upon emulation in *Tirocinium* is
exaggerated. "That any advancement whatever can be
made without emulation," the anonymous critic of *The
Pamphleteer* remarked with some justice, "will only be
maintained in the wildest reveries of Madame de Staël, who
actually fancies she has seen five hundred children never

excited by either hope or fear, reward or punishment, making the most rapid advances in every kind of knowledge, from the influence of some inward and mysterious principle."[64] But it must be seen that an argument for an education that would produce Christian humility and obliterate worldly pride would naturally fasten upon the principle of competition as a vital point of attack.

No one would be expected to believe that the products of the schools were quite so bad as Cowper said they were. Professor Hartmann takes some trouble to point out that among Cowper's schoolmates who attained fame and useful service were Robert Lloyd, Warren Hastings, Elijah Empey, George Colman the Elder, Charles Churchill, Bonnell Thornton, and George Cumberland.[65] (He might with a great deal more appropriateness have mentioned Lord Dartmouth, whose service to the Evangelical cause was outstanding.) The anonymous critic cites Leigh Hunt, Coleridge, and Charles Lamb of Christ's Hospital to prove that fine feelings may be nourished by the schools.[66] This kind of evidence Cowper himself would have admitted readily —but not as a refutation of his argument:

> And, if it chance, as sometimes chance it will,
> That, though school-bred, the boy be virtuous still;
> Such rare exceptions, shining in the dark,
> Prove, rather than impeach, the just remark.   [Ll. 839-42.]

Both the critic of *The Pamphleteer* and Professor Hartmann object to the remedies proposed by Cowper on the score of their impracticability. "The ability of maintaining a private tutor," wrote the earlier critic, "is confined to a very limited circle, and all the middling orders of society . . . are compelled either to suffer their children to grow up without any learning at all, or to send them to school. . . ." Professor Hartmann repeats the criticism, adding that a home education would lack many things that a school education would afford and would limit the student's horizon.[67] These criticisms are not unjust. It should be remembered, however, that the inception of the idea in Cowper's mind was the desire to advise his friend Unwin, a minister who probably had the leisure to educate his sons. It is true that the whole poem cannot be regarded as addressed directly to Unwin—it is really advice for the world at large; but the original idea doubtless had much to do with suggesting the "remedies" that Cowper proposed. Perhaps Cowper's deep concern about existing conditions inclines him toward idealism, rather than realism; nevertheless, Cowper had distinguished precedent for advocating home education, whether by father or tutor. And if practicability is the sole criterion for reform literature, not only *Tirocinium* but *Émile* will have to be cast overboard. What Cowper, of course, did fail to do was to show how the schools themselves might be improved.

Mr. Gilbert Thomas has argued the very interesting thesis that the emphasis on paternal instruction in *Tirocinium* is in a sense the poet's indictment of his father's failure to give him the proper education. As Mr. Thomas observes, the Reverend John Cowper plays a very minor part in his son's letters and poetry. We are told that he was fond of poetry and that he "succeeded well in ballad writing."[68] Cowper also describes him as "most indulgent." The one allusion to him in the *Memoir* concerns the fact that he gave his son a "vindication of self-murder" to read. Since Cowper was sent away to boarding school at an early age, he had little contact with his father. What Cowper means by saying that his father was indulgent may be questioned. "'Indulgence' towards a child," writes Mr. Thomas, "may imply anything from parental indifference that takes the line of least resistance to the positive spoiling that is hardly less dangerous than repression." We have no proof of any sort of deep bond between father and son. We do know that, though Cowper constantly paid tribute in his verse to those whose friendship or memory he treasured, the only tribute to his father is in the closing lines of "On the Receipt of My Mother's Picture." Although it does not seem possible to take Mr. Thomas's argument to demonstration, it is quite possible that Cowper's emphasis on the responsibility of father and his plea for home education were colored by his own experience.

In spite of some digressions and looseness of structure, *Tirocinium* is Cowper's most successful effort at sustained thought. It is blessed, as few of Cowper's long poems are, with a beginning, middle, and end. The poem represents the final and most complete statement of the poet's educational ideals, the growth of which we have traced through the years of his greatest creative activity. These ideals, reflecting a repugnance for rationalistic philosophy and a deep-seated conviction of the necessity for inculcating humility as a Christian virtue, are decidedly the educational ideals of the entire Evangelical movement. If Locke held that the end of education is the formation of character, Wesley and Cowper held that the end of education is the formation of Christian character. Although Cowper did not treat educational problems with the completeness with which Wesley treated them, he did give expression in his poetry to the most important principles that Wesley set forth in his sermons and put into practice in his schools. *Tirocinium* must, therefore, be regarded as an important monument in the Evangelical campaign for improved educational aims and methods. To continue the summary at the expense of some repetition, the poem is essentially one of protest; and its strength as such is not to be minimized by the fact that the remedies it suggests are open to criticism on the grounds of impracticability. The objection that it exaggerates actual conditions should also not be allowed to reflect seriously on its worth. It is true that there are exaggerations; but in every really important phase of the attack on the schools the poet's judgment is amply corroborated by contemporary records. The poem's efficacy as reform literature is to some extent attested by the necessity for a public attempt to refute its charges twenty-eight years after its first appearance.

§6

Although Wesley was widely interested in the religious education of the young, one of the most important movements of the century grew up outside his immediate influence. The Sunday School movement was not entirely original with its founders, Robert Raikes and the Reverend Thomas Stock, but these men are responsible for its effective initiation. With the purpose of overcoming vice, ignorance, and squalor, Robert Raikes in 1780 set up a school in Sooty Alley in the manufacturing center of Gloucester. Six months later another school was established in Southgate Street. From this point expansion was rapid, and soon there were Sunday Schools throughout England, Wales, Ireland, and Scotland. The movement was attacked by some members of the upper classes, but it received the support of several noblemen and of Wesley. The Methodists were largely responsible for the rapid spread of the movement. The original schools proposed by Raikes were designed for the instruction of children and adults in religion and in the rudiments. Reading and the Catechism were taught, and teachers were paid a shilling a Sunday. The Methodists had voluntary teaching staffs, and seem to have been responsible for the gradual abandonment of the secular aspects of the instruction.[69] In 1785 a Sunday School Society was founded. Within a decade this organization distributed nearly one hundred thousand spellers, twenty-five thousand testaments, and over five thousand Bibles. Moreover, it trained some sixty-five thousand people in its thousand schools.[70]

Lord David Cecil's statement that Cowper was one of the "prime movers" in establishing the Olney Sunday School in 1785 seems perhaps a trifle stronger than the recorded facts warrant.[71] We do know, however, that the movement received Cowper's hearty moral support. He wrote to Newton on September 24, 1785, telling of a visit that he had had from the Reverend Thomas Scott, who as curate was interested in raising a fund for establishing a Sunday School in his Olney parish. Of the movement Cowper wrote:

It is a wholesome measure, that seems to bid fair to be pretty generally adopted, and for the good effects that it promises, deserves well to be so. I know not, indeed, while the spread of the gospel continues so limited as it is, how a reformation of manners, in the lower class of mankind, can be brought to pass; or by what other means the utter abolition of all principle among them, moral as well as religious, can possibly be prevented. Heathenish parents can only bring up heathenish children; an assertion no oftener or more clearly illustrated than at Olney; where children, seven years of age, infest the streets every evening with curses and with songs, to which it would be unseemly to give their proper epithet. Such urchins as these could not be so diabolically accomplished, unless by the connivance of their parents. It is well, indeed, if in some instances their parents be not themselves their instructors. . . . It is, therefore, doubtless an act of the greatest charity to snatch them out of such hands before the inveteracy of the evil shall have made it desperate.[72]

The somewhat reluctant retraction of the theory of home education so dear to his heart in *Tirocinium* is quite typical of Cowper's habit of keeping his thinking for different levels of society in separate compartments. A theory of work absolutely essential to the welfare of the lower classes need not be applied to higher social strata; and a theory of home education designed for those of "middle estate" also has its own particular limits. In *Tirocinium,* as Professor Goldwin Smith pointed out, Cowper did not see as an alternative for home education a good day school, where superior instruction could be obtained with no sacrifice of home affections.[73] But it was not difficult for him to see how remarkable a force the Sunday School would be for those whose home environment was unhealthful.

Chapter VIII

THE GROANS OF NATURE

§ 1

Auguries of Innocence, To a Mouse, The Ancient Mariner, and *Peter Bell* are evidence enough that to the poets who were writing the "new" poetry at the end of the eighteenth century kindness to animals was a very important theme. But it was by no means a new theme; and those who would like to look upon it as essentially "romantic" will have to reckon with the fact that it has its roots firmly fixed in classicism. Indeed, the neo-classicist par excellence of the English Augustan Age made an important contribution to this phase of humanitarian thought; and a literary interest in animal life developed so rapidly in the eighteenth century that by the time Cowper, Blake, Burns, and Wordsworth became conscious of the groans of nature the theme of compassion for suffering animal life was already respectably established.[1] In fact, it is possible to regard Cowper's sympathy for animal suffering as one of the least original phases of his humanitarian thought.

An effort to trace all the sources of interest in lower animal life in the century may lead into a labyrinth. On the other hand, simplification of the problem by limitation to too few sources might prove equally dangerous. On the face of the matter, it may seem a little absurd to attempt any explanation whatsoever. Does not humanitarianism find its source in human nature? Certainly, we are not to believe that Thomson and Pope were the first men whose sensibilities revolted at the brutalities of hunting. One will remember that it was Shakespeare, not Cowper, who wrote

[206]

And the poor beetle that thou tread'st upon
In corporal sufferance feels a pain as great
As when a giant dies.[2]

The personality of the poet must, indeed, have some consideration in the matter. It is easy to see, for example, how
Pope, Burns, Cowper, and Coleridge might have developed
in the hard school of physical and mental suffering a state
of mind that lent itself with peculiar readiness to benevolence toward lower animal life. If, however, we realize
that we are dealing not merely with personal attitudes toward animal life but with the literary expression of these
attitudes, we shall find it necessary to probe beyond the
individual personality.

Addison's protest against "a very barbarous Experiment"
in *Spectator* No. 120 suggests the importance of the practice
of vivisection,[3] which had developed rapidly at the end of
the seventeenth century and at the beginning of the eighteenth, in calling the attention of the reading public to the
sufferings of the animal creation. Other forms of obvious
cruelty to animal life, such as bullbaiting and cockfighting,
were also drawing protests throughout the century.[4] A
revulsion from flagrant brutality, however, is still not an
adequate explanation of sensibility to animal suffering as a
literary phenomenon.

There are many other important sources of the century's
literary interest in the "brute creation." An attempt to
estimate their relative importance is difficult. At any rate,
we may be reasonably sure that some of the major influences
were the humanitarian philosophy of Montaigne, the humanitarian philosophy that was inherent in the Oriental
tale, and that which was a part of the very important
philosophical system of Lord Shaftesbury. These are not
yet all. Beyond them we must consider the influence of
the humanitarian ideas of the ancients, with which every

humanist had ample contact. We must also consider the importance of the development of science in giving man a better understanding of the universe and in increasing the significance of all forms of life. Then, too, we shall not forget that the interest in animal life is a part of the expanding aesthetic interest in all external nature. After the middle of the century we shall find that further impetus was given the interest in animal life by that great stimulus for all humanitarian endeavor, the Evangelical revival.

Montaigne's long and important influence on English literature did not suffer eclipse in the early eighteenth century. Pope proudly admitted that he "housed" with Montaigne. No one can read "Of Custom," "Of Cruelty," and "An Apology of Raymond Sebond" without finding in them almost every humanitarian sentiment in regard to animal life that later found expression in eighteenth-century prose and verse. Indeed, these essays are direct sources for Pope's important contribution to humanitarian literature, the *Guardian* essay, No. 61. The following passage from "Of Custom" not only furnishes Pope with a point for his essay but it anticipates the account in *Tatler* No. 112 of cruel young Dicky and adumbrates the treatment of cruelty in children in Shaftesbury's *Characteristics:*

> Some mothers think it great sport to see a child wring off a chickens necke, and strive to beat a dog or cat. And some fathers are so fond-foolish that they will conster as a good Augur or fore-boding of a martiall mind to see their sons misuse a poor peasant, or tug a lackey that doth not defend himself . . . yet are they the true deeds or roots of cruelty, of tyranny, and of treason. In youth they bud, and afterward grow to strength, and come to perfection by means of custom.[5]

In "Of Crueltie" the essayist again tells how he cannot endure seeing a chicken's neck pulled off or "a pigge stickt." "I cannot endure a seelie dew-bedabled hare to groane," he writes, "when she is seized upon by the houndes."[6] In the same essay he continues:

As for me I coud never so much as endure, without remorse and grief, to see a poore, sillie, and innocent beast pursued and killed, which is harmelesse, and void of defence, and of whom we receive no offence at all. And as it commonly hapneth, that when the Stag begins to be embost, and finds his strength to faile him, having no other remedie left him, doth yeeld and bequeath himself unto us who pursue him, with tears suing to us for mercie,

> . . . *questuque cruentus*
> *Atque imploranti similis*
> With blood from throat, and tears from eyes,
> It seems that he for pity cryes

was ever a grievous spectacle unto me. I seldom take any beast alive, but I give him his libertie.

Here is sufficient literary authority for all the tears shed by deer in eighteenth-century verse, not to mention authority for the groans of other forms of animal life. Neither Pope, Thomson, nor Cowper could say a great deal more about the cruelty of hunting. Montaigne continues by pointing out that the killing of the first beast was but a prelude to the murder of the first man. In the same essay he deplores sports in which animals "tug, mangle, and enteare one another." "An Apology of Raymond Sebond" shows us a Montaigne who can muse upon the apish tricks of his cat as Cowper does, and who can perceive "what excellency beasts have over us."

The Oriental romances gave some popularity to the attitude of the Brahmin toward animal life and to the fascinating subject of metempsychosis.[7] One may find evidence of Oriental respect for and glorification of animal life in any number of the tales from the *Arabian Nights*,[8] the *Persian Tales,* and the *Chinese Tales* which were "translated" during the century.

An interesting example of the treatment of humanitarian ideas from the Oriental, or rather pseudo-Oriental, point of view is to be found in the very popular satirical romance of Giovanni Paolo Marana, *The Turkish Spy:*

> The historians say that the first inhabitants of earth, for above two thousand years, lived together on vegetable products, of which they offered the first fruits to God—it being deemed an inexpiable wickedness to shed the blood of an animal, though it were in sacrifice, much more to eat of their flesh. To this end they relate the first slaughter of a bull to have been made at Athens . . . and the bull being flea'd, and fire laid on the altar, they all assisted at the new sacrifice. . . . In the process of time a certain priest, in the midst of the bloody sacrifice, taking up a piece of the broiled flesh that had fallen from the altar on the ground, and burning his fingers therewith, suddenly clapped them into his mouth to mitigate the pain . . . and hence this species of gluttony was taught to mortals.[9]

Here is a source for Lamb's famous essay; here is also a prototype for Pope's Flamen who first tasted living food.[10]

It seems not to have been unusual to find in such a volume as *The Blossoms of Morality* (1789), a book of moralized Oriental tales for children, a story like that of the good vizier Alibeg, who is unjustly exiled and who lives in contentment as a hermit among his affectionate domestic animals. Oriental tales of transmigration and reverence for animal life furnish the basis for the protest against cock-fighting in *Tatler* No. 134. Steele writes that in many "wise nations of the East"

> . . . nothing was more frequent than to see a dervise lay out a whole year's income in the redemption of larks or linnets, that had unhappily fallen into the hands of bird-catchers; that it was also usual to run between a dog and a bull to keep them from hurting one another, or to lose the use of a limb in parting a couple of mastiffs.

There is also the tale in the *Adventurer* for Tuesday, November 21, 1752, in which a young man falls off his horse and becomes through transmigration, in succession, a dog that is beaten to death by inhuman carpenters, a bullfinch whose eyes were put out to insure a better singing voice, a cockchafer that was impaled by an unfeeling boy, a worm used for fishing, a cock, a lobster, a flea, and finally a beautiful woman! The passage on the worm's being impaled on a hook is of particular interest: "The wretched animal writhed itself on the bloody hook in torture which cannot be conceived by man, nor felt in any creature that is not vital in every part."

A scheme of things, suggested in Montaigne, in which animals and plants are of an importance comparable to that of man finds expression in the "Universal System" of Shaftesbury's *Characteristics:* "All things in this world are *united.* . . . Thus contemplating all on Earth, we must of necessity view *All in One,* as holding to one common stock. Thus too in the System of the bigger World. See there the mutual Dependency of Things! . . . from the minutest Ranks and Orders of Beings to the remotest Spheres."[11] Having built his philosophy on the theory that man is inherently virtuous, Shaftesbury quite logically insists that cruelty and barbarity are unnatural, and that inhumanity in any form is the result of ill-breeding. His philosophy, therefore, leads to much more than the mere recognition of the "mutual dependency of things." He plainly states that man's social affections must include lower animals:

Without demurring on the profound modern hypothesis of animal sensibility, we are to believe strongly and resolutely "that other creatures have their sense and feeling, their mere passions, and affections, as well as ourselves." And in this manner we proceed accordingly . . . to inquire what is natural to each creature, and whether that which is natural to each, and is its perfection, be not withal its happiness or good.

Shaftesbury's brief attack on bearbaiting illustrates his strong feelings on the subject of cruelty to animals:

... to delight in torture and pain of other creatures indifferently, natives or foreigners, of our own or of another species, kindred or no kindred, known or unknown; to feed as it were on death, and to be entertained with dying agonies; this has nothing in it accountable in the way of self-interest or private good ... but is wholly and absolutely unnatural, as it is horrid and miserable.[12]

It is true that what Shaftesbury says specifically about the matter of benevolence toward animal life would not fill many pages. The philosopher does not pause even in his miscellaneous ramblings to write any sort of disquisition on the subject. But his insistence upon the divine harmony of nature and upon man's development of his social affections perhaps makes such a disquisition superfluous. No one who accepted Shaftesbury's philosophy could very easily slight the importance of animal life or condone any form of cruelty to animals.

Classical authority for expressions of tenderness for animal life was easy for the eighteenth-century poet to find. Montaigne, although he took no great stock in metempsychosis, pointed the way back to Pythagoras, to whom some of Shaftesbury's ideas have been traced by way of the Cambridge Platonists. The great French essayist also cited numerous other classical sources for his humanitarian ideas. The Greek Anthology contains a number of poems expressing sympathy for animal life. In spite of the delight of the Romans in such a brutal sport as the combat of wild beasts, Roman poets and philosophers frequently manifest a high degree of sensitivity to animal suffering.[13] One has only to mention the tender interest in animal life of Virgil, Ovid, Lucretius, and Catullus. Plutarch was an ardent champion of kindness to animals. In the *Guardian* essay Pope cites Latin and Greek authorities, most of which were suggested

by Montaigne. The tenderness for animal life achieved by
one who drank almost exclusively from the classical stream
is illustrated by Vincent Bourne—Cowper's beloved master
"Vinny" of Westminster. Cowper shows his consciousness
of classical authority when he writes on the occasion of the
death of Mrs. Throckmorton's bullfinch: "Did ever fair lady
from Lesbia or Catullus to the present day lose her bird
and find no poet to commemorate the loss?"[14]

It would perhaps be unwise to say just at what point in
the century animal life came to be regarded as of poetic
interest in other respects than that of *mise en scène*. However, by the time that we reach John Philips's *Cyder* of 1708
we find something that definitely approaches a genuine interest in animals, especially birds. At least one humanitarian sentiment in the poem seems to have been borrowed
by Pope. Of the sad plight of birds beset by fowlers, Philips
writes:

> sulphureous death
> Checks their mid flight, and heedless while they strain
> Their tuneful throats, the towering, heavy lead,
> O'ertakes their speed; they leave their little lives
> Above the clouds, precipitant to earth.[15]

Lady Winchilsea was among the first in the century to
use animals extensively as poetic material. Although she
expresses no very important humanitarian ideas, she does
suggest that but for the tyranny of man animals would not
suffer.

Pope's *Windsor Forest*—published in 1713, but in part
written somewhat earlier—stands with *Cyder* among the
first poems of the century to voice a protest against hunting. The pheasant passage is one of the best-known passages in the poem. Only a few months after *Windsor
Forest* was published Pope wrote his *Guardian* essay on
cruelty to animals.

The *Guardian* essay is as important for what it sums up as for what it foreshadows. It begins with a comment on Montaigne's observation that "few people delight in see-ing beasts caress or play together" and the observation that cruelty toward animals is developed in childhood. Later Pope paraphrases Montaigne's description of the death of the stag, "a helpless, trembling, and weeping creature." As classical sources of humanitarian sentiment he cites Plutarch, Cato the Censor, and Ovid, all of whom seem to have been suggested by Montaigne. He then cites the authority of the Bible and ends with the story of the traveler and the adder from the Persian fables of Pilpay. He also cites "an Arabian author." Here, therefore, we may see already at work some of the most important influences on literary expression of eighteenth-century sentiment for kindness to animals: Mon-taigne, the classics, Oriental literature, and the Bible—the last of which does not seem to have been invoked often for such humanitarian sentiments before Wesley, Christopher Smart, and Cowper. Although there is a hint of the "all preserving Soul," the benevolent philosophy that Shaftes-bury had already begun to make popular seems to have little place in the essay.

Pope exalts the intelligence of lower animal life, vigor-ously condemns bearbaiting, cockfighting, and hunting, and attacks the luxury that condones the practice of roasting animals alive, whipping pigs to death, and sewing up fowls. It is remarkable that twenty years later when Pope was writing the third epistle of the *Essay on Man,* he found occa-sion to use much of the same material, remoulded but slightly to fit into the system of benevolence championed by Shaftesbury and Bolingbroke. A close study of the *Guardian* paper and the epistle will reveal a considerable dependence of the later work upon the earlier. It will also reveal the remarkable amount of space given to the subject of cruelty to animals in an epistle ostensibly designed to

discuss "the nature and state of man in respect to Society."
Like Shaftesbury, Pope is not content with a mere statement
of the "mutual dependency of things." He dwells with
emphasis on man's duty to help "another creature's wants
and woes." Among the ideas that he repeats from the
Guardian essay is that of the right of animal intelligence
to challenge comparison with human intelligence. He also
concerns himself again with the proper way to care for
and kill an animal designed for food.[16] After describing a
Golden Age in which men and beasts lived in perfect harmony, he exclaims, almost paraphrasing the prose essay:

> Ah! how unlike the man of times to come!
> Of half the butcher and of half the tomb;
> Who, foe to Nature, hears the gen'ral groan,
> Murders their species, and betrays his own.
> But just disease to luxury succeeds,
> And every death its own avenger breeds;
> The Fury-passions from that blood began,
> And turned on Man a fiercer savage, Man.[17]

At least two poets, Henry Baker and James Thomson,
preceded Pope's *Essay on Man* in giving poetic expression
to the fashionable optimistic philosophy of the age. Baker
made in *The Universe* (1727) a rather complete statement
of the place of animal life in the eternal chain of being and
protested against the "murder" of dumb brutes.

Thomson's treatment of animal life is of first importance.
He accepts the "mighty chain of being" as sufficient to assure
the brute creation a right to happiness. His treatment of
bird life is one of the remarkable features of *The Seasons*.
His plea to men not to catch birds and put them in cages
is too well known to require quotation. The picture of the
mother bird returning home to find an empty nest is one
of the most touching bits of eighteenth-century sentiment.
The robbing of the bees provides material for an exclama-

tion on the tyranny of man and the groans of prostrated
Nature.[18]

Throughout *The Seasons* much is said on the inhumanity
of hunting.[19] So far as eating flesh is concerned, the very
idea that man could stoop to the bestial level and "dip his
tongue in gore" is abhorrent to the poet.[20] In *Autumn* he
inveighs against bird hunting:

> Oh! let not, aimed from some inhuman eye,
> The gun the music of the coming year
> Destroy; and harmless, unsuspecting harm,
> Lay the weak tribes a miserable prey,
> In mingled murder, fluttering on the ground.
>   [Ll. 983-87.]

There is also in *Autumn* the same kind of picture of the
stag at bay that Montaigne and Pope had already given in
prose:

> The big round tears run down his dappled face;
> He groans in anguish; while the growling pack,
> Blood-happy, hang at his fair jutting chest
> And mark his beauteous chequered sides with gore.
>   [Ll. 454-57.]

In the passage following, the poet begs sportsmen to hunt
destructive animals if they must hunt—not hares and deer.
He then pours out another bitter denunciation of "the falsely
cheerful, barbarous game of death":

> Upbraid, ye ravening tribes, our wanton rage,
> For hunger kindles you, and lawless want;
> But lavish fed, in Nature's bounty rolled,
> To joy at anguish and delight in blood,
> Is what your horrid bosoms never knew.

After *The Seasons* the rights of animals became a somewhat popular subject with the poets. Such poems as John
Gilbert Cooper's *The Power of Harmony* (1745), James

Harris's *Concord* (1751), and Browne's *De Animi Immor-*
talitate (translated by Soame Jenyns in 1754) expressed a
cognizance of the "sacred sympathy" of all nature and insisted that man's benevolence should descend to the meanest
animals. Dyer's insistence in *The Fleece* (1757) upon a
shepherd's tender care of his lambs may hardly seem to be
humanitarian when we consider that the poem is on sheep-
raising; but the fact that the second book opens with a
"recommendation of mercifulness to all animals" should
convince any sceptic of Dyer's sympathy for animal life:

> gluttons ever murder when they kill.
> Ev'n to the reptile every cruel deed
> Is high impiety.[21]

William Hamilton of Bangour's "Doves" and "On a Dog,"
Richard Jago's three "elegies" on birds, John Langhorne's
"Monody" and "To a Redbreast," and Joseph Warton's
"Ode on Shooting" all attest the growing interest in animals as material for poetry. Although James Beattie does
not protest directly against hunting in *The Minstrel* (1771-
1774), he views as ideal the primeval groves where

> Nature supply'd the wish she taught to crave.
> None prowl'd for prey, none watched to circumvent.

There is, however, a spirited protest in *The Hares:*

> Our harmless race shall every savage
> Both quadruped and biped ravage?
> Shall horses, hounds, and hunters still
> Unite their wits to work us ill?

Shenstone attacked huntsmen in "Rural Elegance."
     Few things in the century are more widely known than
the kind of sentimentality that Sterne lavished on the fly,
the ass, and the caged bird. To this kind of sensibility
Mackenzie's *The Man of Feeling* (1771) and Henry
Brooke's *The Fool of Quality* (1766-1770) fell heir. With

the popularity of the "man of feeling" at the end of the century we are not surprised to find that such a character as M. de St. Aubert of Mrs. Radcliffe's *The Mysteries of Udolpho* or Fleetwood of Godwin's novel objects to hunting and fishing. Harry Sandford, the "child of nature" in Thomas Day's *Sandford and Merton* (1783-1789), refuses to steal bird eggs, gives up his own food to the redbreasts, steps aside to avoid worms (thus making himself eligible to Cowper's friendship), and treats spiders and toads with proper deference![22]

By this time we are able to see some of the most important commonplaces of sentiment regarding animal life before Cowper. The following ideas seem most firmly established: that all things are bound up in some scheme of mutual dependency; that animals have some sort of divine guidance; that all animals, no matter how insignificant, have an equal right with man to a happy existence; that it is man's duty to make the life of other creatures happy; that the intelligence of animals is worthy of challenging comparison with that of man (this respect for animal intelligence often follows upon a theory of divine guidance, but not always is this true); that the only excuse for eating flesh is dire necessity (this is, of course, most probably "poetic vegetarianism" rather than an actual rule for living); that the Golden Age ended when man became carnivorous; that animal suffering is comparable to human suffering, and, therefore, that hunting and all other forms of cruelty to animals are barbarous. The "timorous hare" and the "stricken deer" were well established as objects of sympathy; and not a few writers before Cowper knew that the ultimate achievement of humanitarian sensibility was sympathy for the lowly worm, exuding its life on the garden path beneath a heedless foot, or writhing in untold agony on the hook of a cruel fisherman.

§ 2

The finding of a place for animals in the ethics of the Christian church is a modern development. Sir Henry Salt, the distinguished champion of animal's rights, has argued that the primitive Christian in laying emphasis on future life in contra-distinction to this life and in placing animals outside the pale of hope laid the foundation for the utter disregard of animal life. Thus the indifference of the medieval Catholic Church to animal life he sees unbroken save by St. Francis of Assisi.[23] Lecky has observed that although animal rights found no place in the ethics of the Church, there was some indirect inculcation of a feeling of sympathy for animal life in medieval hagiology.[24] It was quite natural that the life of the hermit should lead him into contact with animals and it was equally natural that popular imagination should develop picturesque and sometimes touching legends from these contacts. Then, too, such incidents were not without parallel in Old Testament story. Thus we find St. Theon, St. Jerome, St. John the Silent, St. Guthlac, and St. Simeon, among many others, figuring in legends of comradeship and mutual helpfulness between human and animal life. The hermit who closed his heart to the interests of the world is depicted as opening it freely when confronted with suffering animal life. The fact remains, however, that the Church took no direct cognizance of animal rights.

In the eighteenth century the discussion of the immortality of animals began as a philosophical rather than as a religious problem. It is significant that before the end of the century immortality of animals had been admitted as a logical probability by the most important figure in the Evangelical revival.

In his *Essays on Human Knowledge* Lord Bolingbroke had pointed out the close relationship between men and animals:

As these animal systems come to be more and more sensible to us, and as our means and opportunities of observing them increase, we discover in them . . . the same appearances, that denote a power of thinking in us. . . . . I think it indisputable that the distance between the intellectual faculties of different men is greater than that between the same faculties in some men and some other animals. . . . There is in the whole animal kingdom one intellectual spring common to every species, but vastly distinguished in its effects . . . though it seems to be the same spring in all, yet it seems to be differently tempered, and to have more elasticity and force in some and less in others.[25]

In *Observations on Man* David Hartley observed similarities between the intellect, memory, and passions of man and beast.[26] Soame Jenyns championed the immortality of animals in his *Free Inquiry into the Nature and Origin of Evil*,[27] and in "the Swan of Lichfield" Miss Anna Seward introduced the subject into her poetry.[28]

John Wesley was able to postulate animal immortality not on a basis of similarity between man and beast but on the divine plan, as he saw it worked out. It is interesting that on this point Toplady, Wesley's bitterest opponent, agreed, finding no argument against the immortality of brutes that would not work equally well in an argument against the immortality of man.[29] Wesley's sermon on "The General Deliverance" opens with a moving humanitarian sentiment: "Nothing is more sure, than that as 'the Lord is loving to every man,' so 'his mercy is over all his works'; all that have sense, all that are capable of pleasure or pain, of happiness or misery . . . he directs us to be tender of even the meaner creatures; to show mercy to these also."[30] Beasts, according to the great preacher, lived in Paradise in a state of happiness, enjoying liberty and will. "And they too were immortal," he continues, "for 'God made not death; neither hath he pleasure in the death of any living.' " (Coleridge, who annotated Southey's biography of Wesley, remarked that Wesley meant *imperishable* rather than *immortal,* and looked upon the passage as proof that Wesley's intellect never rose above logic.)[31] Wesley felt that in Paradise animals had a highly developed understanding through which their lives were regulated. In this state the blessings of God flowed through man to them as inferior creatures. When these blessings were lost to man, they were naturally lost to animals. Animals lost greatly in understanding and in liberty. After the Fall, beasts fled man, defied him, fought among themselves, and were subject to torment at the hands of their former benefactors. "But will . . . the brute creation always remain in this deplorable condition?" Perish the thought! "While the whole creation groaneth together, whether man attend or not, their groans are not dispersed in the idle air, but enter into the ears of Him who made them." Wesley felt that the whole brute creation would undoubtedly be restored to what it had lost, with a large increase of faculties. The creator might indeed raise dumb creatures higher in the scale of beings. If he makes men equal to angels, suggests the founder of Methodism, he may make animals "what we are now, creatures capable of God, capable of knowing and loving, and enjoying the author of their being." In the religion of Wesley men and animals were no longer isolated.

The Reverend James Hervey, a disciple of Wesley who gave a factitious elegance to ideas of Methodism in his euphuistic *Meditations and Contemplations* and in *Theron and Aspasio,* did not neglect animal life. In the *Meditations* (1746-1747), which was one of the most popular books of the century and which Cowper read with some admiration, Hervey looks in ecstasy upon the "immense chain . . . this universal scale of existence" with the realization that from the "loftiest seraph to the lowest reptile" all things are works of God's hands.[32] Even the microscope of Leeuwenhoek is invoked by the euphuist to bring into focus the minutiae over which God exercises parental care.[33] If this should seem to be largely a matter of pursuing religious ecstasy to an *O Altitudo!* there are passages in "A Descant Upon Creation" that show a sympathy for bees approaching Thomson's.[34]

Since the Calvinistic doctrine of "election" did not even admit all humanity to the possibility of eternal blessing, it is not surprising that John Newton does not conceive so generously as Wesley of the future life of animals. His respect for the brute creation is, however, very solidly founded on a recognition of God's guardianship over animal life and on the belief that animal wisdom has its source in the Divine Mind.[35]

The effect of the religious awakening on poetic appeals for kindness to animals is to be seen in Christopher Smart, who in several respects anticipates Cowper. In "The Goodness of the Supreme Being" Smart writes of the fatherly function of the Divine Being in regard to animal life. In *A Song to David* he does not forget to plead for humane treatment of domestic animals, invoking Jewish law as Cowper was later to do:

> Be good to him that pulls thy plow;
> Due food and care, due rest, allow,
>   For her that yields thee milk.[36]

The "Ode on an Eagle Confined in a College Court" is a protest against caging birds. The height of Smart's tenderness is to be found in his *Hymns for the Amusement of Children,*[37] written perhaps in the closing years of his life. "Good-Nature to Animals" possesses the very essence of Christian humanitarianism. After instructing children to be kind to horses and dogs and to give crumbs to the wren and redbreast "when frosty winter comes," the poet writes:

Tho' these some spirits think but light,
And deem indifferent things;
Yet they are serious in the sight
Of CHRIST, the King of Kings.

"For Saturday" offers the following naïvely beautiful argument against robbing the lark's nest:

your play-mate begs
You'd spare herself and speckled eggs;
Soon she shall ascend and sing
Your praises to the Eternal King.

§ 3

It is not necessary to demonstrate further that Blake, Burns, and Cowper were inheritors of a substantial tradition of kindness to animals. The three poets who heralded the changes in poetry at the beginning of the new century each made a distinctive treatment of the subject. Blake represents the mystic's conception of a scheme of love including all sentient beings. We know little or nothing about his actual contacts with animal life. Burns, the poet who served his apprenticeship at the plow, achieved a feeling of comradeship with animal life and of brotherhood in adversity that is unlike anything to be found in Cowper and Blake. Cowper succeeds Christopher Smart in expressing his humanitarianism in terms of Evangelicalism. He was not drawn as Wesley was into the dangerous and difficult consideration of the immortality of the brute creation. He is free of Blake's complicated metaphysics. He is, in the main, content with no more intricate doctrine than the commonplace extension of God's personal superintendence over human life to the realm of nature. Whereas Burns's feeling toward animal life is one of brotherhood, Cowper feels a parental relationship. To his animal poetry Cowper gave a charm that has rarely been excelled; and to poetic appeals for kindness to animal life he gave a new dignity and beauty.

Although we are principally concerned here with the theme of kindness to animals as a literary phenomenon, we may with advantage examine some of the aspects of Cowper's actual contacts with animal life in order to understand his humanitarian sentiments. There is no scarcity of evidence to prove Cowper's keen delight in animal life. In fact, we might almost rewrite his biography in terms of his pets, whose activities are charmingly chronicled in his letters and in his verse. The habit of keeping pets was developed early. Cowper tells an amusing story of a rat that he kept when he was a student at Westminster. When it produced a litter of six, he was delighted; but he was later horrified to discover that the mother rat had eaten her young![38] A cat was one of the few things that he was concerned about when he left his lodgings in the Temple to go to St. Albans. In September, 1795, after he had left his beloved Weston forever, he wrote pathetically from Norfolk to the Reverend John Buchanan: "Tell me if my poor birds are living? I never see the herbs I used to give them without a recollection of them, and sometimes am ready to gather them, forgetting that I am not at home."[39]

Orchard Side, the Olney residence, must have been almost a menagerie. Lady Hesketh records of Cowper "that he had at one time five rabbits, three hares, two guinea pigs, a magpie, a jay, and a starling; besides two goldfinches, two canary birds, and two dogs. It is amazing how the three hares can find room to gambol and frolic (as they certainly do) in his small parlour; and," she adds, "I forgot to enumerate a squirrel which he had at the same time, and which used to play with one of the hares continually."[40] The three hares were Puss, Tiney, and Bess, who, as Cowper tells us, were all males in spite of their names, and who were immortalized in the delightful essay published in the *Gentleman's Magazine* in June, 1784. Since the hall door at Orchard Side opened into the street, callers were often

sent to the back, lest the opening of the door should allow
the hares to escape. Even a parliamentary candidate might
have to use the kitchen entrance. When Puss did escape,
the whole of Olney was stirred to give chase. The "Run-
away Hare" letter is the charming record of this momentous
event. Tiney's bad disposition is delightfully commem-
orated in verse.

Puss expired at the venerable age of eleven years, eleven
months. A succession of three dogs now claimed the poet's
affection—Mungo, the Marquis, and Beau. The gallantry
of the last of these gives him an important place with Her-
rick's Tracy and Pope's Bounce in the galaxy of literature's
famous dogs. Beau enters charmingly into both the verse
and the letters of his master.[41] But Cowper's love for dogs
did not extend to Mr. Pearson's "great mastiff" which on one
occasion attacked the poet. He promptly wrote the owner
that unless the dog were tied up he would "send him a worse
thing, commonly called . . . by the name of an attorney.
When I go forth to ramble in the fields," he continued, "I
do not sally like Don Quixote, with a purpose of encountering monsters . . . but am a peaceable poor gentleman, and a
poet, who means nobody any harm. . . ."[42] Many other
delightful animal stories appear in the letters and in the
poetry: Mungo's barking at the thunder; the sad tale of
"Bully," Mrs. Throckmorton's bullfinch, who was eaten by
a rat; the narrow escape of three kittens from a snake; the
cat that "retired" in a chest of drawers; the goldfinch that
nobly refused to leave its mate. In the last decade of his
life Cowper turned to writing animal epitaphs: on Mrs.
Throckmorton's "Fop," on a pointer of Sir John Throckmorton, and on a "Free But Tame Redbird." Surely, nobody ever wrote of animals with more grace.

There are several ways of viewing Cowper's great affection for animal life. In the first place, animals provided
for him a means of escape from the broodings of his tor-

tured mind. Newton records that the breaking of the cloud
of the second derangement came in May, 1774, while the
poet was feeding his chickens. He then smiled for the first
time in sixteen months.[43] He himself confesses in his
epitaph on Tiney, the surly old hare:

> I kept him for his humour' sake,
>   For he would oft beguile
> My heart of thoughts that made it ache,
>   And force me to a smile.

The cast of the contemplative mind, like that of Montaigne,
not infrequently inclines it to delight in the observation of
animal life even when its desire of escape from a world of
men is not a primary motive. But Cowper's feeling toward
animal life lies even deeper in the nature of the man.

Cowper perhaps nowhere approaches the ascetic temperament more closely than he does in his interest in animal
life. In commenting on the frequent occurrence of stories
concerning tenderness to animal life in medieval saints'
legends, Lecky remarks, "A refined and subtle sympathy
with animal feeling is indeed rarely found among those
who are engaged very actively in the affairs of life, and it
is not without a meaning or a reason that Shakespeare
placed that exquisitely pathetic analysis of the sufferings of
the wounded stag, which is perhaps its most perfect poetical
expression, in the midst of the morbid dreamings of the
diseased and melancholy Jacques."[44] An eighteenth-century
ascetic whose case is in point is William Law, who had a
passionate desire to free caged birds and whose life with
his two old ladies at King's Cliffe parallels Cowper's later
years in many ways. Jeremy Bentham, who considered
himself a recluse (though of quite a different sort), was ex-
ceedingly fond of animals, once remarking, "I love everything that has four legs." He petted the mice that played

in his workshop, and his devotion to his cat, Sir John Langborn (in his last years Reverend Dr. Langborn), is famous.

The only study of Cowper's mental derangement from
the standpoint of modern psychiatry makes no attempt to
show the relationship of animal life to Cowper's mind,
either as an aspect of its abnormality or as a healing function.[45] But even one who is not a trained psychologist may
see many evidences of the fact that Cowper's interest in
animals is to a large extent a modification of his parental
desire. In the *Olney Hymns* we may find that one of Cowper's most successful approaches to the idea of God is
through the idea of mother love, and that he shows some
fondness for the biblical figure of the mother hen and her
brood.[46] Cowper's own desire to "mother" the brute creation is to be found in a letter to Hurdis, written on June 13,
1791:

I am glad to find that your amusements have been so similar
to mine; for in this instance too I seemed to have need of some-
body to keep me in countenance, especially in my attention and
attachment to animals. All the notice that we lords of creation
vouchsafe to bestow on the creatures, is generally to abuse them;
it is well therefore that here and there a man should be found a
little womanish, or perhaps a little childish in this matter who
will make some amends, by kissing, and coaxing, and laying
them in one's bosom. You remember the little ewe lamb, mentioned by the prophet Nathan; the prophet perhaps invented the
tale for the sake of its application to David's conscience; but it is
more probable that God inspired him with it for that purpose.
If he did, it amounts to a proof that He does not overlook, but
on the contrary much notices such little partialities and kindness
to His *dumb* creatures, as we, because we articulate, are pleased
to call them.[47]

The step from the "motherhood" of God to man to the
"motherhood" of man to animals is not a difficult one for a
sensitive poet.

On April 15, 1792, Cowper records for Hayley a some-what amazing dream: "I dreamed last night that a beau-tiful red-breast, while I sat in the open-air, flew to me and perched on my knee. There it stood quietly awhile to be stroked, and then crept into my bosom. I never in my wak-ing hours felt a tenderer love for anything than I felt for the little animal in my sleep. . . ."[48] This is no mere senti-mental effusion. Whereas we do not here have to trouble about the unhealthiness that a Freudian would perhaps see in it, we can hardly fail to view it as evidence that Cow-per's emotional repression sought compensation in affection lavished on animal life.

Cowper's animal poetry, then, is not merely an expres-sion of the fashionable sensibility of his age. It is an integral part of his emotional pattern. This fact has much to do with giving it freshness and intensity, and with giving it the impression of being Cowper's own complete creation rather than a sort of capstone of a cumulative tradition.

The logic by which Cowper justifies his respect for an-imal life is not very different from that of Wesley, Hervey, and Newton. In *Retirement* the poet asserts that even the most minute design of nature shows the imprint of divine power. He marvels at the intricacies of insect life:

> The shapely limb and lubricated joint,
> Within the small dimension of a point,
> Muscle and nerve miraculously spun. [Ll. 57-59.]

He continues by musing on the way insects might "mock the majesty of man's high birth" if they were enlarged several hundred times. But the ability to find manifesta-tions of the divine in the smallest things of nature is no deistic leaning. Cowper is careful to add that although all nature is the work of God, nature itself is not sufficient to reveal God. The surest guidance is to be found in God's words, which reveal him more clearly than works. The

adoration of nature alone is not the adoration of God. But
we may rise from inferior things up to the Divine; it is to
this end that the things of earth are formed for us. Earth
is made for man, and man is made for God. The Platonic
thought is scarcely less commonplace than the conception
of the passage of God's goodness through man to animal
life. Cowper is careful to stress the responsibility of man
to created things. The earth is not designed to bring about
man's own gratification or exaltation but to provide a "scale
by which the soul ascends."

In Book VI of *The Task* the poet offers the Christian
substitute for pantheism: not God is everything and everything is God, but—

> there lives and works
> A soul in all things, and that soul is God.   [Ll. 184-85.]

To Cowper God actively controls the universe, and all life
and beauty are his. The poet undertakes to refute the
philosophers who postulate a clockwork universe set in
motion by the hand of God but not actually guided by it,
and asserts with marked nobility of verse that

> The Lord of all, himself through all diffus'd,
> Sustains, and is the life of all that lives.
> Nature is but a name for an effect,
> Whose cause is God.   [Ll. 221-24.]

Having identified Christ as the ruler of the universal nature,
the poet maintains that he who walks with nature walks
with Him.

§ 4

Cowper's earliest models for animal poetry were the
Latin poems of Vincent Bourne[49] and the fables of John
Gay. "Vinny" Bourne was one of Cowper's most pleasant
memories of his Westminster days; and the pupil has re-
warded the master with the most reliable immortality that

he now has—some delightful translations of his poems and a few vividly descriptive strokes in the letters. Cowper did not consider Bourne a great success as a teacher: he was indolent and he was a poor disciplinarian. His slovenliness of dress was notorious, and his idleness was contagious. Cowper evidently got a great deal of pleasure out of telling how the rascally young Duke of Richmond set fire to Bourne's greasy locks and boxed the master's ears to extinguish the blaze. As a poet, Bourne was extravagantly praised by his erstwhile pupil. Cowper declared that he was superior to Propertius, Tibullus, and Ausonius, and not inferior even to Ovid. Needless to say, posterity has not sustained the judgment. Charles Lamb, who shared many of Cowper's sympathies, also considered Bourne delightful. He was so pleased with Bourne's treatment of "this human and quadrupedal alliance, this dog and man friendship" in *Epitaphium in Canem* that he included the poem, together with a translation, in one of his essays.[50]   It is easy to understand how Bourne's simple pathos, his warmth of sympathy for human life, and particularly his tenderness for animals appealed to Cowper.

Cowper seems to have begun translating Bourne's poems about 1780. Eight poems, including the "Invitation to the Redbreast," were translated as late as 1799. It is worthy of notice that of the twenty-three translations in all, thirteen are animal poems. These concern the glowworm whose little light is shed on the garden path, the jackdaw that looks down upon the vanities of men, the cricket that chirps joyfully on the kitchen hearth, the parrot that is well matched with her mistress, the sparrows that beg their daily fare at Trinity College, Cambridge, the tabby that jokingly scratches her mistress, the silkworm whose usefulness excels that of many human beings, the snail that carries his house on his back, not to mention the redbreast and Strada's nightingale. In addition to these poems there are "Reciprocal

Kindness the Primary Law of Nature," a retelling of the story of Androcles and the lion, and "The Cantab," whose secondary moral has to do with cruelty to horses.

Although Cowper modestly tells of the difficulties he has encountered in giving the poems the proper "turn," they are for the greatest part delightfully translated. In spite of the translator's evident desire to preserve the spirit of the original, he can hardly keep from making the poems peculiarly his own. Such a simple touch as the rendering of *felis* in *"Nulli te facias nimis sodalem"* as "youthful tabby" in "Familiarity Dangerous" makes the English version even more charmingly intimate than the original. The translation of *"Cicindela"* ("The Glow-Worm"), perhaps done early in 1780, is definitely colored by Cowper's own religious and humanitarian thinking. The poem of Bourne is a pagan little piece with the naïve theme that even the most insignificant thing in nature has its splendor. Such a theme is to be found in Cowper's translation; but Cowper has given to the poem a significance not to be found in Bourne —a significance that makes it fit in beautifully with his own thinking in regard to animals. He deftly writes his theory of the divine guardianship of the universe into the poem. Whatever may be the cause of the glowworm's light, or the reason for it—we read in the translation—there is certainty that it is a part of the divine scheme of things. Whereas Bourne has

> Nam superas stellas quae nox accendit, et illi
> Parcam eadem lucem dat, moduloque parem,

Cowper writes

> But this is sure—the hand of might
>   That kindles up the skies,
> Gives *him* a modicum of light
>   Proportion'd to his size.

Thus pagan *nox* becomes "the hand of might," with Christian connotation enough. Again, where Bourne has

> Sive usum hunc natura parens, seu maluit illum,
> Haud frustra accensa est lux, radiique dati,

Cowper translates

> What e'er she meant, this truth divine
> Is legible and plain,
> 'Tis pow'r almighty bids him shine,
> Nor bids him shine in vain.

Thus "natura parens" becomes "pow'r almighty," and "truth divine" is thrown in for good measure.

This particular translation is definitely related to one of Cowper's first animal fables, "The Nightingale and Glow-Worm,"[51] written in February, 1780. The nightingale of the poem, thinking that he will make supper of the glow-worm, is reminded by the lowly animal that

> 'twas the self-same pow'r divine
> Taught you to sing, and me to shine.

The moral concerns the Christian's duty to promote peace and understanding among all things. "The Nightingale and Glow-Worm" is, moreover, illustrative of the way in which Cowper gave a religious turn to the animal fable, made popular by John Gay and widely imitated during the century. The Philosopher of the "Introduction" to Gay's *Fables* explains:

> The daily labours of the bee
> Awake my soul to industry:
> Who can observe the careful ant,
> And not provide for future want?
> My dog (the trustiest of his kind)
> With gratitude inflames my mind:
> I mark his true, his faithful way,

And in my service copy Tray.
In constancy and nuptial love,
I learn my duty from the dove.
The hen, who from the chilly air,
With pious wing, protects her care,
And every fowl that flies at large,
Instructs me in a parent's charge.

It is noteworthy that this quotation sums up many of Cowper's incidental animal poems.[52] Of the seven animal poems written in 1779 and 1780, however, only two—"The Bee and the Pine-Apple" and "The Pine-Apple and the Bee"— bear a close resemblance to the form and spirit of the Gay fable, embodying the kind of wise comment on the ways of the world that Gay might have written for the young Duke of Cumberland. "The Nightingale and Glow-Worm" and "A Fable" are religious in purpose. "A Fable" teaches the Calvinistic lesson of the overruling of Providence. There is a lyric strain in "The Doves," one of the several poems written by Cowper in protest against his cousin Madan's notorious *Thelyphthora.* The use of doves as symbols of domestic blessedness is, of course, commonplace; and the appeal to the superiority of the animal's instinct over that of man is scarcely less conventional. "A Tale Founded on a Fact," the earliest of these poems in point of composition, makes no pretense to the fable form. Although it has to do with cockfighting, the purpose is not so much to protest against the important gambling game as to relate a typical Evangelical "conversion" story; hence, the poem is much more distinctly religious than humanitarian. As a matter of fact, Cowper's poetry shows no real sympathy for animal suffering until he wrote "On a Goldfinch Starved to Death in his Cage" in the summer of 1780. In spite of its sentimentality, this little poem has a ring of true feeling.
    In the didactic poems Cowper has less to say about kind-

ness to animals than one might expect. It is true that in *The Progress of Error* and *Conversation* he satirizes the "reeking, roaring hero of the chase," but his satire is moral rather than humanitarian in its purpose. Cowper looks upon hunting as one of the vanities of society's upper crust, and hence it is to him despicable in much the same way that card-playing and duelling are. The story of the hunter who is killed in taking a jump and who is brought home like a slain dog in a tumbrel—"unmiss'd but by his dogs and by his groom"—is inserted to prove that

> pleasure brings as surely in her train
> Remorse, and sorrow, and vindictive pain.
>
> [*Progress of Error*, ll. 43-44.]

The fox-follower of *Conversation* is a social parasite. The "cassock'd huntsman" in *The Progress of Error* can find a prototype at least as early as Chaucer's "out-rydere, that lovede venerye."

The humanitarian feeling in these selections from the satires must be sought in the indirect condemnation of hunting through the poet's low conception of the huntsman. Of the fox hunter Cowper always managed to conceive most ignobly. He is always dissolute and worthless. Drunkenness is a sure concomitant of the sport. The huntsman of *Conversation* is so degraded that only "beasts acknowledge him a man." Riders coming with savage whoops over the hills could suggest to the poet little more than abject barbarism.

Cowper's own experience with hunting was doubtless limited to some bird hunting in his youth and, later, to having his walks around Olney disturbed by the occasional halloo of a hunting pack. As a youth of twenty-three he wrote the following letter, probably to Clotworthy Rowley, a fellow Templar—a letter filled with a spirit notably different from that of the later poet:

Dear Toby,—I am in such a hurry, I hardly know how to set one leg before t'other to get to the end of my letter, and God knows if I shall be able to do it to-night. Dancing all last night, in bed one half of the day, and shooting all the other half, and am now going to—what? to kill a boding screech owl perched upon a tree just by my window. Have at you, old Wise Acre. What an Irishman am I! I went to destroy one of Dame Pallas' poultry, and she to defend her songster cast a cloud before my eyes, and behold, I could not see to the end of my gun. I have had no time, Toby, to versify for you except what I stole under a hedge to-day, while I was shooting, so there I sat me down with my pencil in my hand and my gun by my side *in utrumque paratus*.[53]

In "The Symptoms of Love," probably written some two years earlier than the letter, Cowper had also written of bird hunting:

> Let her guess what I muse on, when rambling alone
> I stride o'er the stubble each day with my gun,
> Never ready to shoot till the covey is flown.

This may have been before Cowper read Thomson's impassioned pleas for the "feathered tribe." But throughout his poetry the plea for the preservation of bird life is somewhat neglected. He shows little feeling toward bird hunting comparable to that of Thomson and Jago. Even in his youth he probably never rode to the hounds. It was not until a day in March, 1788, while he and Mrs. Unwin were walking in the Throckmorton estate that he saw the end of a fox hunt. He describes the brutal spectacle with remarkable equanimity.[54] The explanation may be that some of Cowper's beloved "Frogs" (Throckmortons) themselves were participants in the chase. We have seen Cowper's tendency to look more leniently upon the vices of his friends than upon the vices of the world at large.

Cowper's first important attack on hunting from the standpoint of a humanitarian comes in Book III of *The*

Task. The poet is discussing the true value of rural life. There are few, he concludes, who seek in the country what it is best prepared to give—meditative peace and tranquillity:

> They love the country, and none else, who seek
> For their own sake its silence and its shade. [Ll. 320-21.]

But man, like his first progenitor, is ever prone to forsake substantial happiness for transient joy. Many people take supreme delight in filling the quiet scenes of the countryside with the noise of the chase and with the blood of slaughtered animals. If there were no game to be shot and no fish to be caught, few would find delight in rural life. The poet now speaks out more boldly:

> Detested sport,
> That owes its pleasures to another's pain;
> That feeds upon the sobs and dying shrieks
> Of harmless nature, dumb, but yet endu'd
> With eloquence, that agonies inspire,
> Of silent tears and heart-distending sighs!
>
> [Ll. 326-31.]

Thomson, Beattie, Shenstone, and Jago had protested against the hunting of the timorous hare. This is the "detested sport" against which Cowper now chiefly directs his attack. He is thankful that one hare will never be the object of a chase. Puss has enjoyed sheltered existence as an "innocent partner" of the poet's peaceful home and has become "happier in human society than when shut up with his natural companions." The basis of the poet's protest is further explained in his essay on the pet hare in the *Gentleman's Magazine:*

It is no wonder that my intimate acquaintance with these specimens has taught me to hold the sportsman's amusement in abhorrence; he little knows what amiable creatures he persecutes, of what gratitude they are capable, how cheerful they are in their spirits, what enjoyment they have of life, and that impressed as they seem with a peculiar dread of man, it is only because man gives them peculiar cause for it.[55]

Between 1781 and the publication of Cowper's essay on the hares there had been a number of articles and poems on hunting in the *Gentleman's Magazine*. Not all of these were condemnatory. There were, for example, excerpts from "Essays on Hunting," an anonymous pamphlet which attempted to vindicate "such country diversions from the contempt generally thrown upon them by the literary and speculative part of mankind."[56] This indicates that the "literary and speculative" people were at least not winning their argument by forfeit. "Partridge Shooting," a poem with all the apparatus of the conventional pastoral, is humanitarian only in urging the huntsman not to shoot more than his quota of birds—"nor merciless the total race extirpate."[57] The writer of the "Ode to a Goldfinch" warns the bird:

> Go not near the wicked man,
> He will kill thee if he can.[58]

The issue of February, 1781, carried a protest against the "custom of throwing at cocks." There is a long quotation from a pamphlet of a minister who was crusading against the barbarous sport and who descanted on the Christian way of caring for all domestic animals.[59]

Cowper manages to insert a plea for domestic animals into Book IV of *The Task*. The exhortation to the waggoner is unfortunately marred by an execrable metaphor:

> The waggon is thy wife; and the poor beasts,
> That drag the dull companion to and fro,
> Thine helpless charge, dependent on thy care.
> Ah, treat them kindly! rude as thou appear'st,
> Yet show that thou hast mercy!   [Ll. 367-71.]

In Book V the poet's heart is touched with compassion for birds in winter. Shut off from sustenance by snow and frozen ground, they are forced to seek an "unmolested end" in chinks and holes "as instinct prompts" (ll. 80 ff.).

In the final book of *The Task* Cowper comes nearer than anybody else in the century to writing a poetic counterpart of Wesley's humanitarian appeal in the sermon on "The General Deliverance." The resemblance of the long blank verse passage to a sermon is suggested chiefly by its constant reliance upon biblical authority and by its use of an exemplum. Before the "sermon" on kindness to animals begins, Cowper has discussed the immediacy of God's influence in the universe. From a discussion of his delight in his familiarity with the hare, the stock-dove, and the frisking squirrel, the poet comes to the conclusion that the heart unpleased by "sight of animals enjoying life" is hard, indeed (ll. 324-25). In *Charity* he had insisted upon the right of animal life to freedom:

> Nature imprints upon whate'er we see
> That has a heart and life in it—Be free! [Ll. 169-70.]

Here he exults in the freedom of the bounding fawn and the ramping horse in the meadow. This, he muses, is nature's design. How flagrantly man has defeated it!

So much for the exordium. The "sermon" proper begins, as Wesley's does, with a consideration of the state of animals in Eden. It is only natural that Cowper's Golden Age should be the biblical one. To man God gave dominion over all animal life—

> Vast was his empire, absolute his pow'r,
> Or bounded only by a law, whose force
> 'Twas his sublimest privilege to feel
> And own—the law of universal love.
>   [*Task*, VI, ll. 357-60.][60]

Eden was the scene of harmless sport, and there was tran-
quil confidence among all forms of animal life. "But sin
marr'd all." The revolt of man from God was followed
by a revolt of animals from man. Each animal was filled
with jealousy and instinctive fear, and either fled the abode
of man or growled at him in defiance. Thus the family
accord between man and beast was broken. In the hour
of the Fall were sown the seeds of cruelty, and animals
were thereafter destined to suffer at the hands of man—
either to make sport for him, to furnish an outlet for his
wrath, or to satisfy his gluttony. Although Cowper does
not dwell as Wesley does on the warfare of animals among
themselves, he writes of the groans of earth "beneath the
burden of a war wag'd with defenseless innocence." Man's
consummate cruelty is seen in the fact that he causes needless pain, "and first torments ere he devours." One is here
reminded of Pope's vigorous protest against cruelty to animals used for food, and his suggestions about the proper
method for killing animals. Animals, Cowper continues,
are now happiest when they are farthest from the abode
of man. Those that have remained in man's protection have
paid dearly. Witness the spaniel beaten to death for some
"venial fault," the ox goaded to madness on its way to
slaughter, the horse driven to death by a ruthless rider who
in his cups will boast of the deed at the inn.

Does modern law, "so jealous in the cause of man," pro-
nounce no judgment on those who are brutal to animals?
Cowper can answer his own question with some authority:
None. As a former student of law the poet was doubtless
cognizant of laws protecting animals as private property.
There seem, however, to have been no laws designed specifically to protect animals from cruelty. Humane laws did
not begin to get into the statute books until the third decade
of the next century.[61] But if English law fails to protect

animals, the law of God as made manifest to the Jews definitely holds man responsible for the care of his property. From Exodus 23:5 the poet cites the law that a man shall help even the beast of his enemy if it has fallen under its burden. From Deuteronomy 22:6-7 he cites the law forbidding the "bush-exploring boy" to take away the parent bird. This is proof enough that even his meaner works did not escape the Divine Law-Maker. Cowper then examines that charter that God gave to Noah, "by which we hold the flesh of animals in fee" (Genesis 9:2-5), and finds no warrant for tyrannous control of animal life. We may feed on animals: we have become carnivorous through the Fall. But, insists the poet, we should "spare the living brute."

Not only are there laws of God to protect the brute, but there are also records of God's punishment of offenders against these laws. The often-repeated story of Balaam's ass is cited as evidence that even a prophet might not abuse an animal without reproach. The poet is willing to believe that God even inspires dumb animals with

> such sagacity to take revenge,
> That oft the beast has seem'd to judge the man.
> [*Task*, VI, ll. 477-78.]

At this point is inserted the exemplum—the preposterous story of Misagathus and Evander. Misagathus, "manmonster" and "scorner of God and goodness," meets on a journey the pious Evander, who plies his ears with Christian truth. Misagathus, to show his contempt for what he considers superstition and to show his scorn of the fear of death, madly rides his horse up to a precipice. When the horse refuses to jump, Misagathus in anger, "with sounding whip, and rowels dyed in blood," makes another attempt and is equally unsuccessful:

> The Providence, that meant
> A longer date to the far nobler beast,
> Spar'd yet th' ignobler, for his sake.   [Ll. 528-30.]

(The Calvinism is apparent.) Proud that he has defied death,
Misagathus allows his rage to cool, and he rides on with
Evander. Suddenly, the abused horse without warning
dashes his inhumane rider to a cliff and catapults him over:

> So God wrought double justice; made the fool
> The victim of his own tremendous choice,
> And taught a brute the way to safe revenge.   [Ll. 557-59.]

Thus, we are led to believe, may atheistic and inhumane
horsemen meet their end—and all as Providence overrules!

The end of the exemplum makes way for perhaps the
best known of all Cowper's humanitarian utterances:

> I would not enter on my list of friends
> (Tho' grac'd with polish'd manners and fine sense,
> Yet wanting sensibility) the man
> Who needlessly sets foot upon a worm.   [Ll. 560-63.]

Both Thomson and Gay had felt compassion for the tor-
tured worm on the fish-hook, although neither had very
much sympathy for the fish. Canto I of Gay's *Rural Sports*
ends with the poet's plea for the "feather'd hook":

> Around the steel no tortur'd worm shall twine,
> No blood of living insect stain my line.

Out of their context Cowper's verses appear more sentimental than they actually are. His respect for living things is
not without reservations. Vermin, he agrees (having doubtless had some experience with them at Orchard Side), may
die, for they invade the habitation of mankind with filth
and their death becomes a necessity. But the animals that
"range the air, or take their pastime in the spacious field"
are in their own domain; and the huntsman who kills one
of these disturbs the economy of nature. The poet sums
up his position with the terseness and clarity of one who is
rounding out a logical argument rather than one who is
indulging his sensibility:

> If man's convenience, health,
> Or safety, interfere, his rights and claims
> Are paramount, and must extinguish their's.
> Else they are all—the meanest things that are—
> As free to live, and to enjoy that life,
> As God was free to form them at the first,
> Who, in his sov'reign wisdom, made them all.
>
> [Ll. 581-87.]

Like Montaigne, Pope, and Addison, Cowper insists that the cruelty inherent in human nature is likely to crop out in children. He, therefore, warns parents to check cruelty in youth lest, unrestrained, it should attain "luxuriant growth."

Wesley does not admit that human beings are to be distinguished from animals on the basis of reason. Cowper accepts reason as a basis of distinction. Neither troubles very much about a definition of the term. Since we are distinguished from animals by reason and by a capacity for divine grace, the poet argues, God holds us responsible especially for the welfare of those animals that serve us. Cowper is willing to admit that our superiority to animals is not without its limits. Animals are not more dependent upon man than man is upon them. Brutes, moreover, are capable of attainments in their own sphere that put to shame the attainments of men. Cowper can hardly avoid an expression of an idea that Pope, Gay, and others had made an eighteenth-century commonplace—that animals are capable of teaching man many lessons, the most important of which is that of fidelity,

> that neither bribe nor threat
> Can move or warp; and gratitude for small
> And trivial favours, lasting as the life,
> And glist'ning even in the dying eye.   [Ll. 628-31.]

Ardor for the cause of kindness to animals rises to a climax in the poet's reinterpretation of his poetic mission.

No longer, as in the didactic poems, is he contented with a "monitor's praise." He now sees in his poetry some definite humanitarian purpose. "Man praises man," he writes. But—

> I, contented with an humble theme,
> Have pour'd my stream of panegyric down
> The vale of nature, where it creeps, and winds
> Among her lovely works with a secure
> And unambitious course, reflecting clear,
> If not the virtues, yet the worth of brutes.
> And I am recompens'd, and deem the toils
> Of poetry not lost, if verse of mine
> May stand between an animal and woe,
> And teach one tyrant pity for his drudge.   [Ll. 719-28.]

The "sermon" on kindness to animals fittingly ends with the restatement of the biblical prophecy of the blessed state of the New Jerusalem, in which the groans of nature will have an end and the original accord of harmony of nature will return as before the Fall.[62] Unlike Wesley, Cowper does not bother about postulating an increase in animal understanding, or their rise in the scale of beings. He is content to rhapsodize, not without an unfortunate Herveyesque touch, on the family accord of nature in the earth's new state:

> the mother sees,
> And smiles to see, her infant's playful hand
> Stretch'd forth to dally with the crested worm,
> To stroke his azure neck, or to receive
> The lambent homage of his arrowy tongue.
> All creatures worship man, and all mankind
> One Lord, one Father.   [Ll. 778-84.]

Incidental animal poems like the poems about Beau, "The Faithful Friend," "The Colubriad," "On the Death of Mrs. Throckmorton's Bullfinch," "The Retired Cat," and "To a Nightingale" are charmingly humorous and tender expressions of the poet's interest in animal life, but they add no new humanitarian sentiments. "The Cock-Fighter's Garland," inspired by an account in the *Gentleman's Magazine* for April, 1789, is a protest against cockfighting, which, like the story of Misagathus and Evander, is in bad taste on account of its Calvinism rather than on account of excessive sentimentalism. The villain of the piece is a man who is blessed with wealth and good birth but who is "cruel as hell." He has a favorite cock that turns coward in the fight. In rage the owner picks up the luckless animal and rushes off to wreak on it a horrible vengeance. But in his anger he drops dead. Thus was the judgment of the sky brought about.

Accepting more calmly than Pope and Thomson the fact that we are "carnivorous through sin," Cowper makes no pretense to vegetarianism. His humanitarianism did not impair his taste for pheasants or venison. To thank John Johnson ("Johnny of Norfolk") and "his kind friend Mr. Copeman" for some pheasants, Cowper wrote on January 31, 1793:

> In Copeman's ear this truth let Echo tell,—
> "Immortal bards like mortal pheasants well:"
> And when his clerkship's out, I wish him herds
> Of golden clients for his golden birds.[63]

Furthermore, Cowper boasted of being "the most ichthyophagous of all Protestants."

§ 5

The course of literary sentiment in regard to animal life in the century is reasonably clear. The poet of the Augustan Age might have found authority for the theme of respect for animal life in classical literature and philosophy, in Montaigne, and in the Oriental romance, even if the great popularity of a benevolent philosophy eager to include all forms of life in its golden chain had not made the subject inevitable. In general, literary expression of regard for the brute creation might take two forms: a carefully reasoned treatment of the ethical relationship of man to animals as in the *Essay on Man* and Baker's *The Universe,* or a more sentimental protest against man's cruelty as in Thomson. The ultimate in pure sentimentalism is, of course, to be found in Sterne, where the feeling is entirely detached from any philosophy of the universe or any reasoned defense of animal rights.

If interest in animal life during the century is at least partially traceable to the tendency to rationalize religion and to the consequent denial to man of any special claim on divine favor, the great spiritual revival, far from relegating animal existence to a negligible position in a scheme in which man's salvation is of supreme importance, seems to have accepted the dignity of animal life and even to have added weight to the plea for kindness to animals. If to the benevolists animals were worthy of respect because they were links in a perfect chain of being, to the Evangelicals they were worthy of kindness because they were creatures of a God whose immediacy in the universe was everywhere apparent. The parental guardianship of God included all creatures, and man's responsibility to preserve family accord was not to be evaded. The subject was not unknown to the pulpit and to the devotional literature of the Evangelical movement.

Cowper stood in a position to fall heir to the sentiment toward animal life that had developed steadily since the opening years of the century. He naturally assumes the Evangelical position, being careful, as usual, to meet the rationalists on their own ground and to substitute his own reasoned scheme of benevolence for theirs. We know from the facts of his life that he possessed an ideal humanitarian temperament, and that he had an irrepressible love for pets and an instinctive desire to exercise parental care over defenseless creatures. Tenderness for animal life he always has, but it is rarely extravagant. His sense of humor enables him to avoid in his verse absurdities of sentiment into which his sensibility might have led him. We may see, indeed, that he makes surprisingly small appeal to sentimentalism when he argues against cruelty to animals. In the didactic poems the passages dealing with hunting seem to be in the category of the Puritan's desire to suppress bearbaiting—not because of the pain to the animals but because of the pleasure to the participants. Cowper's significant plea for the protection of dumb brutes is carefully reasoned and is well buttressed with biblical authority.

Whereas he does accept some of the sentimental conventions of the century, he does not do so in excess. The deer, long established as an object of sympathy, gets no special plea in his poetry. (The famous "stricken deer" passage is not humanitarian in its implications.) In spite of his admiration for bird life and his tenderness to his bird-pets, nowhere in his poetry does he approach the fervor of Thomson. He does not become a poetic champion of vegetarianism. He is wise enough to ignore the matter of animal immortality. Whatever may be said about his sensibility as the motivating force of his benevolence, it rarely obscures the need for practical remedial efforts. Although in the closing decades of the century Granville Sharp attacked cruelty to animals in his tract "On the Injustice of Slavery" and although Jeremy Bentham insisted that cruelty to animals should be a crime cognizable by law, legislative action for protection of animals was still far off. It should be remembered that Cowper pointed out the need for legal protection of domestic animals almost forty years before Richard Martin, fighting against such powerful opponents as Canning and Peel, succeeded in carrying into law an act "to prevent the cruel and improper treatment of cattle." Again, Cowper fought in the vanguard.

Chapter IX

A GREAT COADJUTOR

§ 1

MARIANNE DASHWOOD of *Sense and Sensibility* used a bit of Cowper's verse to test the sensibility of her sister's lover; and Mr. Augustine Birrell liked to remember Cowper as the charming wag who said, "Miss Catlett, shall I give you a piece of cutlet?"[1] With the exception of a few people like Sir Leslie Stephen and Stopford Brooke, most critics have for one reason or another chosen to overlook the essential seriousness of his poetic purpose. Very little is left to be said about his "domestic poetry" and his nature poetry. The perennial controversy about the relation of his religion and his insanity goes on without clearing up the very real Cowper enigma. There is still need to argue that Cowper does not have to be patronized. If his message was more for his age than for all time, it is nevertheless an important message.

In *Table Talk,* the initial poem of the 1782 volume, Cowper sets up his poetic ideal, the Miltonic ideal of poet-prophet. His modesty causes him to disclaim immediately any similarity; but anyone who has attempted to follow his serious thought will be convinced that he aimed at the qualifications of his true poet: a sensibility to human woe, the fire of indignation and the lash of scorn for ignoble deeds and ideals, and a "terrible sagacity" informing the poet's heart. Although he promises different methods and a different emphasis, he plainly sets out to scourge folly in the succession of the century's great satirists. It is true that his aspirations are toward religious poetry—religious poetry, of course, far different from that of Donne, Crashaw, and

Herbert. But if he did not feel worthy of being considered a poet-prophet in any sense, he was at least eager for a "monitor's praise." Though this may not be a lofty poetic ideal, we at least owe Cowper the compliment of taking him at his own word.

Cowper admits that the basis of his humanitarian sympathy is his own suffering; but his suffering has been sentimentalized much more than he sentimentalized the woe of others. The very force that for a long time was pointed out as the cause of his insanity seems to be the stabilizing influence in his sentimentalism—Evangelicalism itself. In spite of the emotional excesses unfortunately attendant upon the revival, the great religious movement proved highly practical in the direction of social reforms. There is infinitely more hard common sense than fanaticism in Wesley's famous *Appeals*. There can be little doubt that sentimentalism flourishes best with a conception of the natural goodness of man and with the idea of his perfectibility. A great amount of such sentimentalism was fostered by the optimistic philosophy of the first of the century and by the Rousseauism of the last. This kind of sentimentalism, writes Professor Bernbaum,

... has encouraged religious sects that deny the reality of sin. It has led us to entrust the slave with freedom, and to bestow upon the average man unprecedented political responsibilities. It has revolutionized education by insisting that the child, whose instincts it regards reverently, shall not be hampered by discipline. It remains the animating impulse of our most conspicuous movements toward social reform. It asserts that the poor are not responsible for their poverty, nor the criminals for their offenses. It supports the socialist and the pacifist in their hope that the world order they desire will survive the test of actual practice.[2]

This is patently not Cowper's kind of humanitarian thought. Starting as all Evangelicals did with the assumption of man's depravity and his need for moral and spiritual regeneration, Cowper arrives at conclusions vastly different from those at which we might expect a sentimentalist to arrive. He did not succumb to the Noble Savage cult. Although he could admire with Cook some of the aspects of life on the South Sea Islands, he was under no delusions about the "natural" state. Crantz had no trouble in convincing him that the Greenlander in his natural state lived anything but a beautifully idyllic life. He was under no delusions about the poor. He knew that they were often slothful, and that they got drunk and robbed chicken coops. He held them largely responsible for their own condition and envied their state only in so far as it kept them from the temptations of the rich.[3] He could praise efforts of prison reform and condemn the illogic of the law without treating the criminal with sentimentality. He did not sentimentalize the child in the educational process. He could accept some Rousseauistic educational principles and at the same time maintain a rather rigid adherence to discipline as an educational ideal. In the matter of pacifism he indulged in no impractical idealism. He expected wars to continue until man's nature was definitely changed. He was a staunch exponent of freedom, but his ideal of freedom was a conservative one. He argued for the abolition of slaves because he saw no logic that could deny them the freedom that Englishmen enjoyed. He did not sympathize with the American Revolution, as many of his distinguished contemporaries did, because he saw in it not a fight for freedom but a vicious attempt to undermine the British Empire. Even in his plea for kindness to animals, one finds Cowper's sentimentalism far less obvious than that of such poets as Thomson and Jago. This, of course, does not mean that Cowper's sympathy was not very real or that his heart never got the better of his head. It is true that he often condemned in general what he could not condemn in the individual and that he had a tendency to defend the underdog in the fight. But this last tendency was not always uncritical.

The late Mr. Paul Elmer More attacked Christian humanitarianism—"that evergrowing belief in the equality and brotherhood of man"—as a "vague sentimentality of a mind that refuses to distinguish between the golden rule and the precept of Apollo."[4] His contention is that modern religion, no longer so much concerned with the salvation of individual souls as with the regeneration of society, has tended to confuse the laws under which society and the spirit function. Such a confusion the humanitarianism of Cowper does not present. The obvious reason is that Evangelicalism was supremely concerned with the individual, in his regard to his responsibility both for salvation and for social well being. Wesley could advocate a return to the communism of primitive Christian society without invalidating the money-making process. Cowper champions the civil virtues of justice, mercy, and charity, without once confusing them with the ideal non-resistance and poverty of the strict Christian interpretation. Although Cowper could talk about the brotherhood of man, he was very little of a leveller. Like those of Wilberforce and even those of the famous "Christian socialist" of the nineteenth century, Charles Kingsley, his humanitarian principles were guided by aristocratic instincts. His conception of a great spiritual kingdom in which all men are equal before God did not cause him to renounce inequality among men. Obviously, he does not have a far-reaching concept of society as a whole. He is not very close to Christian socialism. His dream of a Utopia was more like the millennium of the orthodox than any of the idealistic schemes of the very unorthodox dreamers of the new generation. He is far removed from the kind of political theorizing that led to the "pantisocratic" project of Southey and Coleridge. But if his passion for liberty is

very unlike that of Shelley and Byron, he does not champion
freedom with the sublime disregard of the masses that Milton seemed to have.

Cowper definitely prepared the way for Wordsworth in
giving dignity and worth to humble life. In actuality he
was doubtless a good deal closer to the poor than Wordsworth was. Whereas Wordsworth's chief interest in the
poor is in "their passions and their feelings . . . essential and
eternal in the heart," Cowper is interested in their suffering
and in the social problems they present.

Most of Cowper's humanitarian ideals are perfectly practical. He preaches a doctrine of work as the best method
of eradicating poverty and maintaining the dignity of the
poor. "Earn if you want; if you abound impart" is the text
of his whole philosophy of practical charity. He deprecates
poorly directed and spasmodic philanthropic efforts. He
urges the relaxation of laws that make poverty a crime and
fill debtors' prisons. He points out the corruptions of England's educational system and champions a restoration of
religious training and discipline. He depicts slavery as a
foul blot in the history of English freedom and insists upon
its abolition. He urges freedom for India. He sees the necessity of sending Christianity to the heathen. He is among
the first to suggest the need of legal protection for dumb
animals. He reveals the true causes of conflict and shows
the devastating effect of warfare on private and public
morals. For war he wisely offers no panacea.

To Evangelicalism should go the credit of first developing in the century the power of social salvation inherent
in religion. Social criticism is one of the main functions of
Augustan literature, but the things that critics attacked were
usually the trivialities of urban society. A genius like Swift
could see the lack of real social ideals and could recognize
in the poor a natural and inevitable tragedy; but Swift
offers little constructive criticism. He fails completely to

recognize the possibility of religion as a social force.[5] Cowper, standing in the mid-region between the social satirist of the eighteenth century and the social philosopher of the nineteenth, presents religion as a liberating force and as an instrumentality for social and moral regeneration. He saw nothing of the cramping influence of religion that Shelley was to throw himself madly against. At least as Cowper presents it in his poetry, religion is a powerful inner force capable of achieving a freedom of mind far superior to physical freedom. That it did not work thus in the poet's own mind is his great tragedy.

Cowper's religion itself is, then, in essence humanitarian. But when Evangelicalism and the poet's humanitarianism chance to disagree, Cowper frequently allows his humanitarianism to temper the severity of his religious beliefs. He refuses to postulate damnation for the heathen who have not had a chance to accept or reject Christianity. He refuses to accept the idea of submission to Providence when injustice is involved. He repeats the Evangelical commonplace of condemning charity not motivated by Grace, but in practice he is more likely to condemn philanthropy because it is superficial and trivial than because it is not Christian.

§ 2

Cowper's humanitarian poetry reflects the change that had come about in philanthropy during the century. At the beginning there was a vigorous philosophic interest in benevolence that found expression in poetry and doubtless had some influence on actual philanthropic effort. In the last half of the century the philosophic interest in benevolence was steadily supplemented and, in a sense, superseded by interest in practical humanitarian efforts. Not only had philanthropy widened its scope under the impetus of the religious revival, but its methods were undergoing drastic change. For the largest part of the century a need for charitable aid led to the organization of a society or the raising of a subscription. Efforts were made chiefly to alleviate distress rather than to correct social evils. At the end of the century humanitarianism had increasingly become a matter of social reform, looking toward legislative action for the accomplishment of its objectives. Its two basic processes involved, first, an investigation of the evil to determine what was to be done, and, second, an attempt to convince the community that the duty should be discharged.[6] John Howard became an earnest student of jails, and Thomas Clarkson gathered material on the slave trade with the methods of a scholar. Cowper, of course, had no part in the first process. But the second naturally placed great emphasis on the propagandist. It was here that Cowper performed his most valuable humanitarian function. Although he had official connection as a propagandist with only the abolitionist cause, he performed a valuable service in calling the attention of his large audience to other humanitarian projects already afoot and even in anticipating actual humanitarian effort. No poet before him had touched such a wide range of benevolent activities. Of all the major humanitarian efforts of the closing years of the century, Catholic emancipation is the only one conspicuously absent from his verse. If Cowper had met the Catholic Throckmortons and their amiable "padre" Gregson sooner, even that might have been included.

Cowper's effectiveness as a propagandist is convincingly attested by Clarkson, and by the anonymous critic of *The Pamphleteer,* who complains of the widespread influence of the poet's educational ideas. There are two interesting evidences of respect for his influence in the last decade of his life. In June, 1793, Richard Phillips (afterwards Sir Richard), bookseller and editor of the Leicester *Herald* who had been jailed for selling Thomas Paine's *Rights of Man,* sought Cowper's aid, requesting a poem or song in his behalf. After some hesitation Cowper actually wrote a sonnet on the case, but he yielded to advice not to publish it.[7] If in 1793 he thus narrowly escaped being branded a Jacobin, five years later the *Anti-Jacobin: or Weekly Examiner,* in calling upon English poets to come to the defense of their country, seemed to make a direct appeal for the services of the recluse of Olney—

> Now, far aloof retiring from the strife
> Of busy talents, and of active life,
> As from the loop-holes of retreat he views
> Our Stage, Verse, Pamphlets, Politics, and News.[8]

This can leave little doubt of the regard in which his influence was held.

A study of the influences on Cowper's own thought will convince one that his isolation, of which much has been made, is more apparent than real. In the last half of the century Olney was almost ideally located for stimulation to religious and humanitarian thought. Aside from the fact that it claimed Newton and Scott, it was also the home of Sutcliff, the Baptist divine whose spiritual stimulation laid the groundwork for the great Baptist missionary project. John Howard began his work in neighboring Bedfordshire. At Hackleton, a few miles away on the highroad from Olney to Northampton, lived William Carey, the shoemaker who became a great religious and humanitarian hero. Through the connection of John Thornton and Newton, Henry Thornton, Wilberforce, and other members of the "Clapham Sect" must have seemed to move on the fringe of Olney life. Cowper, who had helped dispense the bounty of the elder Thornton, could hardly have remained cold to the more important philanthropic efforts of his son.

One should not neglect Cowper's relation to the "Clapham Sect," one of the most interesting phenomena of the Evangelical revival. The group of wealthy, aristocratic young men meeting at Clapham in a great oval-shaped library designed by no less a personage than Chatham constituted a remarkably powerful force for religious and humanitarian endeavor.[9] Besides Wilberforce and Thornton, it included John Shore (Lord Teignmouth), James Stephen, Edward Eliot, John Vann, and Zachary Macaulay —all Clapham residents—as well as Babington, Clarkson, young Bowdler, Milner, and Gisborne, who did not live at Clapham but who were constantly guests there. Hardly a significant humanitarian project escaped the attention of these saintly and energetic men. To these philanthropists and reformers of religion and morals, Cowper seems to have been a significant force. Thomas Gisborne modeled his poetry on Cowper;[10] and a volume of Cowper was for Wilberforce an almost inseparable companion.[11] The respect of Clarkson needs no further emphasis. If we accept Sir James Stephen's estimate of their humanitarianism and their religion, we may see plainly how Cowper anticipated them:

> Their philanthropy did not languish without the stimulant of satire; nor did it degenerate into a mere ballet of tender attitudes and sentimental pirouettes. Their philosophy was something better than a collection of hard words. Their religion was something more than a collection of impalpable essences; too fine for analysis, and too delicate for use. It was a hardy, serviceable, fruitbearing, and patrimonial religion.[12]

One can scarcely conceive of a more remarkable fulfillment of the humanitarian and religious ideals that had animated Cowper's verse.

A few years after the opening of the new century the literary reputation of Cowper apparently wanes. The references to Cowper in the correspondence and journals of the "Lakists" are not indicative of his importance as a literary ancestor. Even Wordsworth's expressions of admiration are meager in comparison with the importance of the older poet's influence. Southey, it is true, was later to become Cowper's first great editor and one of his sanest critics. Byron held Cowper in contempt as a poet, although he several times quoted the Olney versifier's neat turn of phrase. We are not surprised that Cowper's religious views and his conservative ideal of freedom had no appeal for such a flaming evangel of a new social order as Shelley. If Lamb's own suffering engendered in him a warm sympathy for Cowper, Hazlitt saw chiefly his effeminacy. But the real index of his reputation and influence is not here. It should be remembered that a large part of Cowper's audience consisted of people of middle-class taste who were slow to accept the revolutionary changes in poetry. However sharp may seem to be the decline in Cowper's reputation, the scores of editions and biographical studies issued between 1800 and the publication of Southey's edition of the *Works* in 1835 argue that Cowper was still a very popular poet while new and greater poets were struggling for recognition. The number of editions in America steadily increased. The Bible and Cowper seem to be the most constant elements in the reading of the New England poets. The real extent of Cowper's influence on their humanitarian and nature poetry has yet to be determined, but it was undoubtedly of importance. We do know that in the American abolitionist fight Cowper's anti-slavery poetry was found to be useful as propaganda.

One would not want to displace the figure of the charmingly whimsical and pathetic person who pottered about among his cucumbers and amused himself with pet hares. But in justice to the man and to his achievement, one must place beside this figure the figure of a staunch friend of truth and a fearless foe of oppression—a quiet man of Olney who became "a great coadjutor" to outstanding leaders in the cause of humanity.

NOTES

Quotations from Cowper's letters are throughout from *Correspondence*, edited by Thomas Wright, London, 1904. All verse quotations unless otherwise indicated are from *The Poetical Works*, edited by H. S. Milford, London, 1926.

Chapter I

1. Sir Henry Salt, "Humanitarianism," *Encyclopaedia of Religion and Ethics*, New York, 1914.

2. *Ibid.*

3. Crane Brinton, "Humanitarianism," *Encyclopaedia of the Social Sciences*, New York, 1932.

4. John Brown, *Estimate of the Principles and Manners of the Times*, London, II (1758), 40.

5. Sir Leslie Stephen, *A History of English Thought in the Eighteenth Century*, New York, 1927, II, 437.

6. Anthony Ashley Cooper, Lord Shaftesbury, *Characteristics*, ed. by J. M. Robertson, London, 1900, I, 251-266, 285-293.

7. Stephen, *op. cit.*, II, 6.

8. Henry St. John, Lord Bolingbroke, *Works*, Dublin, 1793, V, 95.

9. Lois Whitney, *Primitivism and the Idea of Progress*, Baltimore, 1934, p. 23.

10. C. A. Moore, "Shaftesbury and the Ethical Poets in England," *PMLA*, XXXI (1916), 300-308.

11. Daniel Defoe, *A Tour Thro' the Whole Island of Great Britain, etc.*, II, 121. Quoted by J. B. Botsford, *English Society in the Eighteenth Century*, New York, 1924, p. 290.

12. H. R. Fox Bourne, *English Merchants*, London, 1886, pp. 244, 340.

13. R. K. Gray, *A History of English Philanthropy*, London, 1905, pp. 126-127.

14. For this discussion I am chiefly indebted to W. J. Courthope, *A History of English Poetry*, London, 1925, V, 20 ff., and to Professor C. A. Moore's valuable supplementary article, "Whig Panegyric Verse, 1700-1760; A Phase of Sentimentalism," *PMLA*, XLI (1926), 362-401.

15. Later in the century Henry Brooke takes substantially the same position in *The Fool of Quality*.

16. W. E. H. Lecky, *History of England in the Eighteenth Century*, New York, 1891, V, 274.

17. J. H. Overton, *The Evangelical Revival*, London, 1886, pp. 2-3.

18. Stephen, *op. cit.*, II, 336.

19. Hannah More, "An Estimate of the Religion of the Fashionable World," *Works*, Philadelphia, 1830, I, 312-313. Quoted by Lecky, *op. cit.*, V, 274 n.

20. See W. J. Warner, *The Wesleyan Movement in the Industrial Revolution*, New York, 1930, *passim*.

21. John Wesley, *Works*, London, 1829, V, 385.

22. *Ibid.*, VI, 139 ("The Good Steward").

23. Warner, *op. cit.*, p. 154.   See Wesley, *op. cit.*, VI, 137.

24. Sir Leslie Stephen, *English Literature in the Eighteenth Century*, New York, 1904, p. 204.

25. Warner, *op. cit.*, pp. 162-163.

26. Sir Leslie Stephen, "Cowper and Rousseau," *Hours in a Library*, New York and London, 1894, II, 231-232.

27. Warner, *op. cit.*, p. 163.

28. Wesley, *op. cit.*, VIII, 352.

Chapter II

1. Oliver Elton, *A Survey of English Literature, 1780-1830*, London, 1912, I, 80.

2. William Cowper, *The Didactic Poems of 1782*, ed. by H. T. Griffith, London, 1874, p. ix.   Hereafter cited as Griffith.

3. William Cowper, *Poems*, ed. by J. C. Bailey, London, 1905, p. ix.   Hereafter cited as Bailey.   The tradition is continued *ad nauseam* in Mr. Chard Power Smith's *Annals of the Poets*, New York, 1935.

4. See "Power and Gentleness," *TLS*, No. 1555 (Nov. 19, 1931), pp. 901-902.

5. Overton, *op. cit.*, p. 134.

6. C. J. Fox, *Speeches in the House of Commons*, London, 1815, IV, 427; see also Cowper, *Works*, ed. by T. S. Grimshaw, London, 1835-36, V, 380.

7. *The Flapper*, Dublin, Feb. 2, 1795-Feb. 4, 1796.   Nos. 30, 34, 38, and 41 are essays on Cowper.

8. *Edinburgh Review*, II (1803), 69-86.

9. Thomas Clarkson, *The History of the Abolition of the Slave Trade*, London, 1808, I, 108.

10. An enlightening discussion of this period is to be found in Dr. N. C. Hannay's *The Religious Elements in the Life and Character of William Cowper* (Harvard University dissertation), 1919.   (Unpublished.)

11. *Correspondence*, I, 103.

12. Lord David Cecil, *The Stricken Deer*, New York, 1929, p. 174.

13. Charles Augustin Sainte-Beuve, *Causeries du Lundi*, Paris, n. d. (Édition Garnier Frères), XI, 181.

14. Salt, *loc. cit.*

15. George Saintsbury, *The Peace of the Augustans*, London, 1916, p. 217.

16. See Hannay, *op. cit.*, for a sane appraisal of Newton's influence.

17. *Correspondence*, II, 7.

18. The italics are mine.

19. Henry Brooke, *The Fool of Quality*, New York, 1860, II, 244.

20. Cowper, *Works*, ed. by Robert Southey, London, 1835-37, VII, 273. Hereafter cited as Southey.

21. Arthur Redford, *The Economic History of England (1760-1860)*, London, 1931, pp. 58-59.

22. *Correspondence*, III, 99.

23. F. M. Eden, *The State of the Poor*, London, 1797, I, 350 ff.; T. W. Fowles, *The Poor Law*, London, 1898, pp. 65-70.

24. Redford *op. cit.*, pp. 102-104.

25. C. G. Robertson, *England Under the Hanoverians*, London, 1930, p. 536.

26. Bailey (p. 693) says that the reference is to Thornton, but see *Correspondence*, II, 252 and n.

27. Richard Cecil, *Memoir of the Reverend John Newton*, New York, 1809, pp. 108-109.

28. Hugh I'A. Fausset, *William Cowper*, New York, 1928, pp. 180-181.

29. See "Lace" in the *Encyclopaedia Britannica;* also C. C. Channer and M. E. Roberts, *Lace Making in the Midlands, Past and Present*, London, 1900, *passim.*

30. *Correspondence*, I, 210.

31. *Ibid.*, II, 26.

32. See "Debate on the Budget" of March 15, 1780, *Parliamentary History*, XXI, 168-170. Lord North's proposal for a tax on salt touched rich and poor alike. Cowper was likely to object strenuously to any taxation that would affect the poor. In 1784 he voiced his disapproval of Pitt's duty on candles. See *Correspondence*, II, 224, 334.

33. *Correspondence*, I, 209-210.

34. *Ibid.*, p. 265. The italics are mine.

35. *Ibid.*, II, 422. The italics are mine.

36. Lady Harriet Hesketh, *Letters to the Reverend John Johnson*, ed. by Catharine Bodham Johnson, London [1901], pp. 25-26.

37. *Ibid.*, p. 63.

CHAPTER III

1. F. J. Klingberg, *The Anti-Slavery Movement in England: A Study in English Humanitarianism*, New Haven, 1926, p. 15; also Lois Whitney, "English Primitive Theories of Epic Origin," *Mod. Phil.*, Vol. XXI (1924), *passim.*

2. H. N. Fairchild, *The Noble Savage*, New York, 1928, pp. 10-11.

3. Klingberg, *op. cit.*, p. 10; G. L. Craik, *The History of British Commerce*, London, 1844, III, 112-113.

4. J. R. Spears, *The American Slave Trade*, New York, 1910, p. 150.

5. L. Tyerman, *The Life of the Reverend George Whitefield*, New York, 1877, II, 205-206.

6. See John Locke, *Works*, London, 1812, V, 212; also Stephen, *A History of English Thought*, II, 139.

7. Clarkson, *op. cit.*, I, 143; Hannah More, *Works*, I, 30.

8. Moore, *PMLA*, XLI, 391 ff.

9. Clarkson (*op. cit.*, I, 58-59), nevertheless, listed the poem as effective anti-slavery poetry. See *The Fleece*, Bk. IV, in John Dyer, *Works*, London, 1761.

10. *The Works of the English Poets from Chaucer to Cowper*, ed. by A. Chalmers *(CEP)*, London, 1810, XI, 325-327.

11. *CEP*, XIII, 277.

12. See Steele's highly sentimental tale of Inkle and Yarico in *Spectator* No. 11. This story contributes less to anti-slavery sentiment than Clarkson intimates.

13. Charles Churchill, *Poems*, London, 1766, II, 98.

14. See Prince Hoare, *Memoirs of Granville Sharp*, London, 1820, pp. 69 ff.

15. There is, of course, a great deal of anti-slavery sentiment in *Sandford and Merton*. See the "Socratic" dialogue between Mr. Barlow and Tommy Merton, whose father is a Jamaica planter. (Day, *Sandford and Merton*, London, 1855, pp. 33-35.)

16. See Fairchild, *op. cit.*, p. 46.

17. Boswell, *Life of Johnson*, ed. by G. B. Hill, New York, 1891, II, 549-551. Quoted by Klingberg, pp. 41-43.

18. *Gentleman's Magazine*, LXI (1771), 357-358.

19. Warner, *op. cit.*, pp. 239 ff.

20. *Arminian Magazine*, XIII (1790), 502. Quoted by Warner, p. 244.

21. Abbé Guillaume Raynal, *A Philosophical and Political History of the Settlements and Trade of the Europeans in the East and West Indies*, trans. by J. O. Justamond, London, 1798, IV, 122-124.

22. *Ibid.*, p. 121.

23. Jean-Jacques Rousseau, *Oeuvres Complètes*, Paris, 1823, I, 269.

24. Jean-Jacques Rousseau, *Du Contrat Social*, Livre 1, Ch. IV.

25. William Massey, *A History of England During the Reign of George III*, London, 1860, III, 345-346.

26. See "The Clapham Sect" in Sir James Stephen's *Essays in Ecclesiastical Biography*, London, 1860, pp. 521-582.

27. Klingberg, *op. cit.*, p. 75. I have followed Dr. Klingberg's excellent account of the anti-slavery movement in Parliament.

28. *Parliamentary History*, XXVIII, 41 ff.; also R. Coupland, *Wilberforce: A Narrative*, Oxford, 1923, pp. 119-130.

29. William Law, *A Serious Call to Holy and Devout Living*, London, 1802, p. 62.

30. It should be observed that the undisputed evidence for Cowper's reading in Rousseau is restricted to *Émile*. (See *Correspondence*, I, 53, 161.) But if it is not possible to prove conclusively further reading in the French philosopher, it seems equally impossible to disprove it. See Sir Leslie Stephen, "Cowper and Rousseau," *loc. cit.*

31. Stopford Brooke, *Theology in the English Poets*, London, 1896, p. 54.

32. Brown, *op. cit.*, II, 35.

33. The italics are mine.

34. For the historical inaccuracy of this passage see Bailey, p. 682. Raynal's *History* has many stories of Spanish atrocities.

35. Brown, *op. cit.*, I, 152-153; see also Raynal, *op. cit.*, VI, 347, 388 ff. Henry Brooke (*op. cit.*, I, 92) dilates at length on the function of the merchant in bringing about the brotherhood of man.

36. *Correspondence* II, 235.

37. Fairchild, *op. cit.*, pp. 104 ff., *q. v.*

38. *Correspondence*, II, 258-259.

39. See James Cook, *A Voyage to the Pacific Ocean*, London, 1784, II, 157 ff.

40. Fairchild, *op. cit.*, pp. 71 ff.; also Chauncey B. Tinker, *Nature's Simple Plan*, Princeton, 1922, pp. 75 ff.

41. Cowper had written to Newton on October 16, 1783 (*Correspondence*, II, 109): "We brought away an Indian, and having debauched him, we sent him home again to communicate the infection to his country; fine sport to be sure, but such as will not defray the cost. Nations that live upon bread-fruit, and have no mines to make them worthy of our acquaintance, will be but little visited for the future. So much the better for them! their poverty is indeed their mercy."

42. Clarkson, *op. cit.*, I, 571.

43. More, *op. cit.*, I, 28-31.

44. Cf. *Truth*, ll. 515 ff.

45. *Correspondence*, III, 226-227; also Southey, II, 314.

46. *Correspondence*, III, 230.

47. Milton Perceval, *Political Ballads Illustrating the Administration of Sir Robert Walpole*, Oxford, 1916, pp. xxxiv ff.

48. Milford, *op. cit.*, pp. 371-376.

49. *Correspondence*, III, 243-245.

50. *Ibid.*, p. 248.

51. *Ibid.*, pp. 245-246.

52. See *ibid.*, pp. 249, 250-254, 257.

53. Several months later Cowper (*Correspondence*, III, 281) wrote to Bagot that he had sent "The Morning Dream" because it was the best of the lot.

54. Clarkson, *op. cit.*, II, 190-191.

55. *Gentleman's Magazine*, LXII (1793), 1133, and LVIII (1788), 1008-1009.

56. *Correspondence*, III, 281-282.

57. *Ibid.*, p. 294.

58. Cf. *Task*, II, 75 ff., where Cowper treats the Sicilian earthquake as a visitation of God's wrath.

59. *Correspondence*, IV, 72 (May 27, 1791).

60. *Ibid.*, pp. 187-188. The insets are Wright's.

61. *Ibid.*, pp. 189-190.

62. Coupland, *op. cit.*, 155-156.

63. Clarkson, *op. cit.*, II, 348.

64. Teedon's diary for March 8 runs as follows: "The petition against the Slave Trade was brought by Bean, Sutcliffe, and Hillyard to be signed" (i. e., by the vicar, and Baptist and Congregational ministers). See Wright's note, *Correspondence*, IV, 190.

65. Milford does not date the poem. In placing it along with the ballads, he says (p. 657): "Probably . . . in strict chronology, this is here out of order; but its subject makes this position, immediately after the other poems about slavery, suitable enough." But is it suitable enough? Since the "Epigram" deals with the ban on sugar and since it was published on the heels of Cowper's being accused of pro-slavery sentiments for not sanctioning the ban, it should plainly be grouped with the sonnet to Wilberforce as a defense of the poet's position. It seems to have been written at the end of April or in the first weeks of May, 1792. The shorter anti-slavery poems should, therefore, be dated as follows:

"The Negro's Complaint," March 12-17, 1788.

"The Morning Dream," March 17-19, 1788.

"Sweet Meat," March 17-19, 1788.

"Pity for Poor Africans," July-August, 1788.

"Sonnet to William Wilberforce," April, 1792.

"Epigram," April-May, 1792.

CHAPTER IV

1. See discussion of Cowper's theological independence in Griffith, p. xxi.

2. Robert Barclay, *An Apology for the True Christian Divinity* [London?], 1678, p. 259; see also C. J. Abbey and J. H. Overton, *A History of the English Church in the Eighteenth Century*, London, 1878, I, 561.

3. Thomas Scott, *Theological Works*, Philadelphia, 1810, III, 147-190.

4. Williston Walker, *A History of the Christian Church*, New York, 1918, pp. 429-430; also the article on missions in *Encyclopaedia Britannica*.

5. First charter of Virginia in William Macdonald, *Documentary Source Book of American History, 1606-1926*, New York, 1926, p. 2.

6. George Smith, *Short History of Missions*, Edinburgh, 1894, pp. 157-159.

7. David Crantz, *The History of Greenland containing a Description of the Country and its Inhabitants: and Particularly, a Relation of the Mission, carried on for above these Thirty Years by the Unitas Fratrum at New Herrnhuth and Lichtenfels, in that Country*, 2 vols., London, 1767; see also J. E. Hutton, *A History of Moravian Missions*, London [1922?], *passim*.

8. See Jonathan Edwards, *An Humble Attempt, etc.*, ed. by John Sutcliff, Northampton, 1789, *passim*.

9. Eustace Carey, *Memoir of William Carey*, Boston, 1836, pp. 29 ff. See also J. C. Marshman, *Life and Times of Carey, Marshman, and Ward*, London, 1859, I, pp. 15 ff., and *The Victoria History of the County of Northampton*, ed. by R. M. Serjeantson and W. D. R. Atkins, London, 1906, I, 73-74.

10. John Newton, *Works*, New York, 1810, I, 84.

11. Scott, *op. cit.*, III, 223.

12. Carey, *op. cit.*, pp. 26-29; also T. Wright, *The Town of Cowper*, London, 1892, p. 164.

13. *Periodical Accounts Relative to the Baptist Missionary Society*, Clipstone, I (1800), 1-6.

14. Carey, *op. cit.*, p. 73.

15. Louis F. Benson, *The English Hymn*, New York, 1915, p. 324.

16. Churchill, *op. cit.*, II, 100.

17. See James Montgomery, "Greenland" (1819), *Poetical Works*, Boston, 1879, III, 5 ff.

18. Crantz, *op. cit.*, I, 189.

19. *Ibid.*, p. 198.

20. *Ibid.*, p. 145.

21. *Ibid.*, p. 176.

22. *Ibid.*, II, 444.

CHAPTER V

1. *Correspondence*, IV, 376 (March 4, 1793). See discussion of Cowper's patriotism and politics in Griffith, pp. xlvii ff.

2. *Correspondence*, I, 455. Also Griffith, *loc. cit.*

3. Written in February, 1780. Cowper repented of the attack on Burke after Burke's speech on economical reform. See Bailey, p. 678 n.

4. *Correspondence*, II, 39-40. The italics are mine.

5. *Ibid.*, I, 142.

6. See J. A. Williamson, *A Short History of British Expansion*, London, 1927, p. 408; also Lecky, *op. cit.*, IV, 362.

7. *Cambridge History of India (CHI)*, ed. by H. H. Dodwell, Cambridge, 1929, V, 186.

8. *Ibid.*, pp. 205 ff.

9. Lecky, *op. cit.*, V, 233.

10. *CHI*, V, 181.

11. Churchill, *op. cit.*, II, 101-102.

12. See, for example, the long attack on British rule in India by Harley, the hero of Henry Mackenzie's *The Man of Feeling* (1771).

13. Horace Walpole, *Letters*, ed. by Mrs. Paget Toynbee, London, 1903, VIII, 149.

14. *Annual Register*, 1772, p. 102.

15. *CHI*, V, 187.

16. Sophia Weitzman, *Warren Hastings and Philip Francis*, Manchester, 1929, p. 13 and Appendix I, No. 1.

17. Wesley, *op. cit.*, XI, 125-126.

18. *Monthly Review*, LXIV (1781), 153.

19. Edmund Burke, *Works*, London, 1803, III, 39-40.

20. *Correspondence*, II, 135-136. Mongolfier was a French balloonist.

21. *Ibid.*, pp. 141-142 (Jan. 3, 1784).

22. *Ibid.*, pp. 153-154.

23. *Ibid.*, pp. 163-164.

24. *Ibid.*, p. 174.

25. Bailey, p. 683.

26. Thomas Babington Macaulay, *Critical and Historical Essays*, Boston and New York, 1899, III, 117-118.

27. Madame d'Arblay, *Diary and Letters*, ed. by Charlotte Barrett, London, 1905, III, 424.

28. Sir Alfred Lyall, *Warren Hastings*, London, 1908, pp. 180 ff.

29. *European Magazine*, XIII (1788), 130-131.

30. *Correspondence*, III, 227-228. The second man was Hornby, the President of the Bombay Council.

31. Lyall, *op. cit.*, p. 206.

32. *Correspondence*, IV, 200.

33. *Ibid.*, II, 16.

34. *Observations on a late Publication, entitled 'Thoughts on Executive Justice,'* London, 1786. See also Lecky, *op. cit.*, VII, 316.

35. 2 George II, 1729. *Parliamentary History*, VIII, 707-755. See also Verner W. Crane, "The Philanthropists and the Genesis of Georgia," *American Historical Review*, XXVII (1921), 63-69.

36. B. M. Jones, *Henry Fielding, Novelist and Magistrate*, London, 1913, *passim*.

37. *Correspondence*, I, 172.

38. Burke, *op. cit.*, II, 376-381. See *Gentleman's Magazine*, L (1780), 618-619.

39. John Aiken, *A View of the Life, Travels, and Philanthropic Labours of the Late John Howard, Esq.*, Boston, 1744, *passim*; see also article on Howard in *DNB*.

40. John Howard, *An Account of the Principal Lazarettos in Europe*, Warrington, 1789.

41. *The Life of Sir Samuel Romilly*, written by himself, ed. by his sons, London, 1842, I, 125.

42. Hayley's ode is reviewed and quoted in the *Monthly Review* for February, 1781 (LXIV, 103-105). The portion of Burke's speech in praise of Howard is also quoted. Cowper may have read the review; however, his tribute to Howard shows no influence of Hayley's poem.

43. W. L. M. Lee, *History of Police in England*, London, 1901, p. 70.

CHAPTER VI

1. A. C. F. Beales, *The History of Peace,* New York, 1931, pp. 33-36.

2. Jean-Jacques Rousseau, *L'État de Guerre,* ed. by S. G. Patterson, New York and London, 1920, p. 4; also *Contrat Social,* Livre 1, Ch. IV.

3. Hugo Grotius, *De Jure Belli ac Pacis,* selections translated by W. S. M. Knight, London, 1922, p. 55.

4. Jeremy Bentham, *Works,* ed. by John Bowring, Edinburgh, 1843, II, 548.

5. Beales, *op. cit.,* p. 33.

6. See Moore, *PMLA,* XLI, 368.

7. Wesley, *op. cit.,* IX, 221 ff.

8. Newton, *op. cit.,* IV, 423.

9. Sir G. O. Trevelyan, *George the Third and Charles Fox,* New York and London, 1927, II, 77.

10. Wesley had attacked the indolence and inefficiency of British generals in America. See his *Account of the Conduct of the War* (1780).

11. *Correspondence,* I, 410.

12. *Ibid.,* II, 41-42 (Feb. 2, 1783).

13. *Ibid.,* p. 43.

14. *Ibid.,* I, 333-334 (July 29, 1781).

15. Cf. Rousseau, *Oeuvres Complètes,* I, 271-272.

16. Cowper's strictures on the flagrant eighteenth-century evil of duelling— "private war"—are very much like those of Addison, "Estimate" Brown, and many others. They are a part of his attack on the superficiality and godlessness of London society rather than an important element of his humanitarian philosophy. Cf. *Conversation,* ll. 163-202 and Brown, *op. cit.,* II, 153-154.

CHAPTER VII

1. See Lecky, *op. cit.,* VII, 355.

2. Hermann Hartmann, *"Über William Cowpers Tirocinium,"* Festschrift zum Siebzigsten Geburtstage Oskar Schades, Königsberg, 1896, pp. 375-397. It is easily apparent that this study is based on few authorities and that the author has no wide understanding of educational theory and practice in eighteenth-century England. The influences on Cowper's educational thought are not considered.

3. Cowper, *Poems,* ed. by H. I'A. Fausset (Everyman edition), London, 1931, p. viii.

4. See *The Pamphleteer,* IV (August, 1814), 104-130.

5. See Willy Hoffmann, *William Cowpers Belesenheit und Literarische Kritik,* Berlin, 1908 (Inaugural-Dissertation, Friedrich-Wilhelms-Universität zu Berlin), p. 47. See also the derogatory reference to Wesley in Cowper's discussion of "Arminian errors."—*Correspondence,* I, 416.

6. See John W. Prince, *Wesley on Religious Education,* New York and Cincinnati, 1926, *passim.*

7. *Correspondence,* I, 137.

8. Saintsbury, *op. cit.,* p. 249 n.

9. See "Some Thoughts Concerning Education," *The Educational Writings of John Locke,* ed. by J. W. Adamson, New York, 1912.

10. *Correspondence,* I, 237-239.

11. Paul Monroe, *A Text-Book in the History of Education,* New York, 1918, p. 542.

12. *Ibid.*, p. 546.

13. *The Letters of the Earl of Chesterfield to His Son*, ed. by Charles Strachey and Annette Calthrop, New York and London, 1927, I, lxxv.

14. *Ibid.*, p. 183.

15. *Ibid.*, pp. lxv ff.

16. Wesley, *op. cit.*, IX, 193.

17. Law, *op. cit.*, p. 298.

18. Wesley, *op. cit.*, VII, 90. ("On the Education of Children.")

19. *Ibid.*, XIII, 436-437. ("A Thought on the Manner of Educating Children," printed 1783.)

20. Cf. Alexander Pope, *Dunciad*, IV, 453 ff.

21. Prince, *op. cit.*, p. 5; also Wesley, *op. cit.*, VII, 90.

22. Wesley, *op. cit.*, VII, 76 ff. ("On Family Religion.")

23. *Ibid.*, pp. 92-93.

24. Brown, *op. cit.*, I, 34.

25. Adam Smith, *The Wealth of Nations*, London, 1843, p. 129.

26. Chesterfield, *Letters*, I, 153 n.

27. *Ibid.*, p. 163.

28. *Ibid.*, p. 169.

29. *Ibid.*, p. 170.

30. Jonathan Swift, *Works*, ed. by Temple Scott, London, 1907, II, 55.

31. Boswell, *op. cit.*, I, 59.

32. Smith, *The Wealth of Nations*, p. 112.

33. Brown, *op. cit.*, II, 65.

34. As quoted by Coupland, *op. cit.*, pp. 5-6.

35. Southey, I, 237. The italics are mine.

36. Goldwin Smith, *Cowper*, New York, 1880, p. 50.

37. *Correspondence*, I, 348. Even when *Tirocinium* was completed William, junior, was not old enough to begin his education. For Cowper's delightful comment on the anticipatory nature of the dedication, see *Correspondence*, II, 277.

38. *Ibid.*, I, 362.

39. *Ibid.*, p. 376.

40. *Ibid.*, p. 395. The italics are mine.

41. *Ibid.*, II, 253-254.

42. *Ibid.*, p. 269.

43. Smith, *The Wealth of Nations*, p. 117.

44. Chesterfield, *Letters*, I, 400.

45. *Ibid.*, II, 23.

46. Wesley, *op. cit.*, VII, 83.

47. *Ibid.*, XIII, 255-267.

48. Southey, I, 8.

49. *Loc. cit.*

50. *Correspondence*, III, 80.

51. Cowper, *The Poetical Works*, ed. by W. Benham, London, 1889, p. xxiv.

52. Gilbert Thomas, *William Cowper and the Eighteenth Century*, London, 1935, p. 72.

53. Southey, I, 11.

54. *Correspondence*, II, 264.

55. Cowper is eager not to have the reference to "mythologic stuff" misunderstood. He writes in a footnote that he "does not mean to censure the pains that are taken to instruct a schoolboy in the religion of the heathen, but merely that neglect of Christian culture which leaves him shamefully ignorant of his own."

56. Samuel Foote, *Works*, London, 1799, I, 142-143.

57. Day, *op. cit.*, pp. 257-258.

58. The italics are mine.

59. The italics are mine.

60. Jean-Jacques Rousseau, *Émile, ou de l'Éducation*, Paris, n.d. (Edition Lutetia), I, 47-48.

61. Locke, *op. cit.*, p. 71.

62. John Milton, *Tractate of Education*, ed. by E. E. Morris, London, 1918, pp. 7-8.

63. Southey, I, 12-13.

64. *The Pamphleteer*, IV, 113. See also Hartmann, *op. cit.*, p. 388.

65. Hartmann, *op. cit.*, p. 392.

66. *The Pamphleteer*, IV, 113-114.

67. Hartmann, *op. cit.*, p. 396.

68. Thomas, *op. cit.*, p. 68.

69. Warner, *op. cit.*, p. 234.

70. F. P. Graves, *A Student's History of Education*, New York, 1917, p. 237.

71. Lord David Cecil, *op. cit.*, p. 164.

72. *Correspondence*, II, 358-359.

73. Goldwin Smith, *op. cit.*, p. 57.

Chapter VIII

1. An exhaustive study of this phase of humanitarianism has been made by Dr. Dix Harwood in *Love for Animals and How It Developed in Great Britain*, New York, 1928. For the greatest part, the material for my chapter was obtained independently of Dr. Harwood's commendable work. I have been able to supplement his eighteenth-century material at several points and to make reinterpretations at others. My occasional indebtedness will be apparent. I am also indebted to R. D. Havens, "Romantic Aspects of the Age of Pope," *PMLA*, XXVI (1912), 297 ff.; Myra Reynolds, *The Treatment of Nature Poetry Between Pope and Wordsworth*, Chicago, 1896, *passim*; C. E. DeHaas, *Nature and the Country in English Poetry of the First Half of the Eighteenth Century*, Amsterdam, 1928, *passim*; C. A. Moore, "The Return to Nature in English Poetry," *Studies in Philology*, XIV (1917), 243-291.

2. *Measure for Measure*, III, i, 78. Dr. Harwood (*op. cit.*, p. 65) traces attacks on hunting in England at least as far back as *De Nugis Curialium*.

3. See Lecky, *op. cit.*, II, 194 and n. Pope and Dr. Johnson were among those who protested.

4. *Spectator*, No. 141; *Tatler*, No. 134; *World*, No. 190; also Pope's *Guardian* essay, No. 61, for which see below.

5. Michel de Montaigne, *The Essayes*, trans. by John Florio, London, 1886, p. 42.

6. *Ibid.*, p. 215.

7. Miss Martha Conant unfortunately has nothing to say about the influence of the Oriental romance on the humanitarian literature of the century. See *The Oriental Tale in England*, New York, 1908.

8. First English version between 1704 and 1712.

9. G. P. Marana, *The Eight Volumes of Letters Writ by a Turkish Spy*, London, 1753, Vol. IV, Bk. I, Letter V. Evidence that Cowper had read the work is found in *Correspondence*, I, 23.

10. Pope, *Essay on Man*, III, 265 ff.

11. Shaftesbury, *op. cit.*, p. 287.

12. *Ibid.*, pp. 314-316.

13. W. E. H. Lecky, *History of European Morals*, New York, 1880, II, 161 ff.

14. *Correspondence*, III, 328.

15. *Cyder*, Bk. II in *The Works of the British Poets (ABP)*, ed. by Robert Anderson, London, 1795, VI, 554. Cf. *Windsor Forest*, ll. 133-134.

16. Pope, *Essay on Man*, III, 63-68.

17. *Ibid.*, ll. 162-169. Cf. James Thomson's *Autumn*, ll. 1349-1351.

18. *Autumn*, ll. 1172 ff.

19. There were, of course, a number of poems in praise of hunting; *e. g.*, Somerville's *The Chase*, Gay's *Rural Sports*, and Parnell's *Health: an Eclogue*.

20. Thomson, *Spring*, ll. 350 ff.

21. *ABP*, IX, 560.

22. Day, *op. cit.*, p. 3.

23. *Loc. cit.*

24. Lecky, *History of European Morals*, II, 168, *quod vide*.

25. Bolingbroke, *Works*, London, 1809, V, 340. The matter of animal immortality is treated at some length in Harwood, *op. cit.*, pp. 143-153.

26. David Hartley, *Observations on Man*, London, 1834, pp. 253-260.

27. Soame Jenyns, *Free Inquiry, etc.*, Dublin, 1758, p. 57. Jenyns's essay "On Cruelty to Inferior Animals" in *Disquisitions on Several Subjects*, London, 1772, pp. 21 ff., provides an excellent compendium of most of the commonplaces of sentiment toward animals from Pope to Cowper.

28. Harwood, *loc. cit.*

29. Robert Southey, *The Life of Wesley*, London, 1925, II, 386.

30. Wesley, *op. cit*, VI, 241.

31. Southey, *Wesley*, II, 75 n. Another divine who wrote on the future life of brutes was Richard Dean, Curate of Middleton (*An Essay on the Future Life of Brutes*, Manchester, 1767). This gentleman met his match in Dr. Johnson (Boswell, *op. cit.*, II, 54 and n.), as did Soame Jenyns.

32. James Hervey, "Contemplations on the Starry Heavens," *The Whole Works*, Philadelphia, 1810, I, 345.

33. *Ibid.*, p. 356 and n.

34. *Ibid.*, p. 196.

35. Newton, *op. cit.*, IV, 403.

36. Christopher Smart, *A Song to David*, London, 1763, ll. 250-252.

37. I have used Dr. Robert Brittain's transcript of the unique copy of the 1791 American edition in the Library of the American Antiquarian Society at Worcester, Mass. See Brittain, *The Religious Poetry of Christopher Smart, 1722-1771*, Princeton, 1934 (Unpublished Dissertation), p. 193 and n.

38. *Correspondence*, II, 448-449.

39. *Ibid.*, IV, 491-492.

40. As quoted by Thomas Wright, *The Life of William Cowper*, London, 1921, p. 121.

41. See *Correspondence,* III, 194, "The Dog and the Water Lily. No Fable,'' "On a Spaniel Called Beau," and "Beau's Reply."

42. *Correspondence,* III, 457.

43. Wright, *The Life of William Cowper,* p. 118.

44. Lecky, *History of European Morals,* II, 168.

45. James H. Lloyd, "The Case of William Cowper, the English Poet," *Archives of Neurology and Psychiatry,* Vol. XXIV, No. 4 (October, 1930), pp. 682-689. An unilluminating study based on Hayley's unreliable life of Cowper as the chief biographical source.

46. See *Olney Hymns,* Bk. I, pp. cxvii, lxxii; Bk. II, p. xii.

47. *Correspondence,* IV, 74-75.

48. *Ibid.,* p. 185.

49. Vincent Bourne, *Poematia Latine Partim Reddita Partim Scripta,* ed. by the Rev. John Mitford, London, 1840. The first edition was published in 1734, and there were eight editions before Mitford's. A copy of the third edition (1743) was in Cowper's library.

50. Charles Lamb, "A Complaint of the Decay of Beggars," *Essays of Elia,* London, 1929, pp. 159-160.

51. Inspired, according to Cowper, by a philosophical tract in the *Annual Register.*

52. Cowper did not make his Latin translations of two of Gay's fables and a fragment of another until January, 1800.

53. *Correspondence,* I, 8-9.

54. See *ibid.,* III, 240-241.

55. See *Gentleman's Magazine,* LIV (June, 1784), 412-414.

56. *Ibid.,* LII (April, 1782), 179.

57. *Ibid.* (Oct., 1782), p. 493.

58. *Ibid.* (Sept., 1782), p. 447.

59. *Ibid.,* LI (Feb., 1781), 72.

60. Pope is more terse. Cf. *Essay on Man,* III, 159-160.

61. "Martin's Act" for animal protection was passed in 1822. Richard Martin, the father of the bill, formed the Royal Society for the Prevention of Cruelty to Animals in 1824. See E. G. Fairholme and Wellesley Pain, *A Century of Work for Animals: the History of the R. S. P. C. A., 1824-1924,* London, 1924.

62. See Isaiah 64: 17 ff.

63. *Correspondence,* IV, 364.

CHAPTER IX

1. Augustine Birrell, *Res Judicatae,* New York and Boston, 1892, p. 114.

2. Ernest Bernbaum, *The Drama of Sensibility,* Boston and New York, 1915, pp. 2-3.

3. Sir Leslie Stephen, "Cowper and Rousseau," *loc. cit.,* II, 231-232.

4. P. E. More, "The Religious Ground of Humanitarianism," *Shelburne Essays, First Series,* New York and London, 1905, pp. 225-253.

5. Vida D. Scudder, *Social Ideals in English Letters,* Boston and New York, 1923, p. 98.

6. Gray, *op. cit.,* p. 171.

7. At first Cowper refused the request, saying that although he could see the evils of the existing administration he was not ready to quarrel with the govern-

ment for the suppression of seditious literature. (*Correspondence*, IV, 413—June 14, 1793.) On June 18, 1793, however, he wrote to Samuel Rose that he had been touched by the case and had written a sonnet which he was withholding from publication until he had the advice of "some wiser man than myself." (*Unpublished and Uncollected Letters*, ed. by T. Wright, London, 1925, pp. 75-77.) Rose seems to have advised immediately against publication. (See *Correspondence*, IV, 417-418.) The poem turned up at a manuscript sale in 1923. Milford's date "about the year 1793" (p. 668) may be amended to June 14-18, 1793.

8. *The Anti-Jacobin: or Weekly Examiner*, London, 1799, II, 623 ff. The poem, "New Morality," was published in No. 36, June 9, 1798. The part including the quoted lines is ascribed to Frere. (J. H. Frere, *Works*, ed. by W. F. and Sir Bartle Frere, London, 1872, I, 139.) See also Hesketh, *op. cit.*, p. 64. The quoted lines paraphrase *Task*, IV, 88 ff.

9. Sir James Stephen, "The Clapham Sect," *loc. cit.*, pp. 521-582; Coupland, *op. cit.*, pp. 248 ff.

10. Coupland, *op. cit.*, p. 533.

11. *Ibid.*, p. 524. See also the tribute to Cowper in William Wilberforce, *A Practical View of the Prevailing Religious System*, Philadelphia, 1798, p. 228 n.

12. Sir James Stephen, *op. cit.*, p. 536.

INDEX